P9-DEU-613

BLACK, JEWISH, AND INTERRACIAL

BLACK,

JEWISH,

AND INTERRACIAL

It's Not the Color of Your Skin,

but the Race of Your Kin,

Other Myths of Identity

Katya Gibel Azoulay

Duke University Press   Durham and London

1997

© 1997 Duke University Press All rights reserved

Printed in the United States of America on acid-free paper ∞

Typeset in Sabon 3 with Antique Olive bold display by Keystone Typesetting, Inc.

Library of Congress Cataloging-in-Publication Data appear on the

last printed page of this book.

For my grandparents,
Dora Aberbach Lederer, Robert Fleishman Lederer, and
Wilhemina Goffe Gibel
and my children, Gaby-Tzvi, Ron Marcus,
and Dorit-Chen

Power doesn't back up in the face of a smile, or in the face of

a threat, or in the face of some kind of nonviolent loving action.

It's not the nature of power to back up in the face of

anything but some more power.

MALCOLM X

I myself feel more of the "ebiger Jude" than ever before.

EMMA GOLDMAN

We Jews should trust no one but ourselves. The emancipation of

the Jewish people can be gained only by our own efforts.

DOV BER BOROCHOV

Black is a shade of brown. So is white, if you look.

JOHN UPDIKE

CONTENTS

ACKNOWLEDGMENTS

This book would not have been possible without the willingness of strangers to respond positively and enthusiastically to my request for an interview. I hope I have lived up to their expectations and done justice to their narratives.

The year during which this research endeavor was undertaken and completed was a period of transition that tested my fortitude and resilience. There are several people without whom I would not have survived, and to them I owe special thanks: Denise Eileen McCoskey, whose steadfast loyalty never waivered and whose friendship has been an immeasurable source of inspiration; Shireen K. Lewis who transmitted a steady supply of encouragement and support via AT&T; Andre Alexis Robinson, who promoted me without my knowledge and prohibited any negative comments; Pegge J. Abrams, whose patience and presence were an anchor; and Maude Elizabeth Hines, who gave me the title for this book and always kept a sense of proportion.

Many thanks to Eli Azoulay, the father of my children.

My family is special: thanks to my parents — (Inge) Miriam A. Lederer, my best friend, my role model, and the personification of integrity, who has nurtured my identity as a Jew and as a Black woman and instilled a commitment to social justice without regard for the politics of the day; and Ronald L. X. Gibel, who listens to my dreams and disappointments, lets me learn from my mistakes, and, most of all, believes in me. Without my parents, this book — as idea and event — would not have been conceived. Thanks to my children, Gabriel-Tzvi, Ron Marcus, and Dorit-Chen, each of whom represents a victory against Hitler and a triumphant strike against racists and anti-Semites alike.

Special thanks to Officers Evon Williams and Willie Hocaday, Duke University Public Safety, for helping to alleviate the stress of finding a place to park at each of my "this is the last time" runnings to the library.

My deep appreciation to Raymond Gavins, who provided encouragement starting from an early stage, advising me how to navigate southern waters; to D. Soyini Madison, whose friendship and invaluable assistance intervened just when writer's block interfered; and to

Michael Eric Dyson, who encouraged my work and whose moral integrity gave me strength when I needed it most. My immeasurable gratitude to the dean of graduate students at Duke University, Leigh De Neef, and to his wonderful assistant, Susie Waller. Professor De Neef's generosity of spirit and, more significant, professional integrity can rarely be matched. Along the route of this project, a number of people offered critical suggestions, references, and constructive feedback: many thanks to Anne Allison, David Bell, Tim Boyd, Reginald Daniels, Sophie Glazer, Sander Gilman, Lawrence Grossberg, Thomas Lahusen, Roger Loyd, Deborah Johnson, V. Y. Mudimbe, Sydney Nathans, Beverly Richardson, Ari Senghor Rosner, Karen Brodkin Sacks, Jon Michael Spencer, Orin Starn, Ken Surin, Naomi Zacks, and, in particular, Homer D. Hill.

My gratitude to two of my Grinnellian students, Kara Roberts Murphy and Shaka Paul McGlotten (class of 1997), who shared the agonizing process of compiling and collating the index with grace and good humor, and my sincere appreciation to Grinnell College for providing the financial support to complete this last stage of the project.

Finally, my special thanks to Sharon Elaine Parks and Reynolds Smith at Duke University Press. During the process of turning my manuscript into a book, their enthusiasm and encouragement were wonderfully empowering.

PRELUDE:

IDENTITIES AND THE LOGIC OF COUPLING

In 1994, the historian John Hope Franklin reminded those who might have forgotten that as we approach the end of the twentieth century, the color line remains a central issue in the United States. In respect to that issue, the interrelationship of race, culture, and identity has profound implications for those of us in the middle of the intersection — those who can claim descent across racial and ethnic lines. The idea for this research project originates with my personal background as the daughter of an interracial couple who insisted on the compatibility of raising me with a sense of a dual heritage, Jewish and Black. Their approach eliminated in our home the alternative of accepting or conveying the idea of half-white and half-black that permeates the public and scientific discourse about racial identities of interracial children.

This book explores the significance of Jewishness, Blackness, and "race" in a context whose focal point is identity. It aims to add to a growing body of literature written by people who embody "microdiversity" and who draw on this resource to challenge deeply ingrained monocultural presuppositions that regulate and discipline thinking about identity/ies (Zack 1995). Readers who are neither Black, Jewish, nor interracial but are intrigued by the themes of diversity and identities — the primary motif of discussions and debates over "multiculturalism" — are invited to consider and engage with the ideas offered. Those with limited patience for theory may wish to skim ahead at times and even postpone reading the first half of chapter 2. Readers should feel free to read the coda at any time: it is the section that will bring the book to a close, but it does not represent a closure.

One of this book's underlying themes is that politics of very personal intersubjective relations foreground and fashion the debates and dilemmas surrounding racial and ethnic identities in the public sphere. It will be argued that claiming particularistic identities and grounding them in historical landmarks leads to neither exclusivity nor the incapacity to celebrate others. As expressed by Stuart Hall, "the logic of coupling, rather than the logic of a binary opposition" expands, rather than exhausts, one's multiple identities (1992, 29). My interest in the manner in which and the conditions under which individuals think about their identities in relation to their racial, religious, and ethnic backgrounds, given the nature of the United States as a race-conscious society, is both personal and intellectual — indeed, the line dividing the two areas is artificial.

The issue of personal identification, as Naomi Zack points out, "is now required in public from people who want to be heard on matters of class, race and gender" (1993, 52). According to Zack, the reference point from which people project this personal identification is located in family history. Given the political importance attributed to a link between personal identity and those with whom one aligns oneself in the public sphere, biological genealogy has everything to do with a sense of identity. Zack proposes, and I am sympathetic to her argument, that in a race-conscious society, a person of interracial background is challenged by social constraints that insist on a coherence between self-identification (a public presentation) and self-identity (how one conceptualizes oneself) vis-à-vis the race of one's parents.

If, as historian Michael Goldfield maintains, the "defining, paradigmatic, idiographic characteristic" (1991) of American politics and culture has been the persistence and importance of white supremacy, then identifying *racially* with a white parent has political implications inextricably linked to the history of racial relations in the United States (Rosin 1994). Although the legal imposition of ascriptive racial classifications has been undermined, though not delegitimized,[1] the social custom of applying the "one-drop rule" has endured in the public imagination — among both *american* Blacks[2] and whites (F. Davis 1991;

1. By dismissing an appeal against Louisiana racial classification in 1987, the Supreme Court implicitly upheld the principle that having ancestors of African descent marked one legally Black regardless of skin color. Thus *Plessy v. Ferguson* (1896) remains unchallenged *despite* the fact that judicially sanctioned segregation has been abolished.

2. I have adopted, and will employ here, Nikki Giovanni's use of *american* as the adjective and *Black* as the noun, thus supporting the concept's introduction into academic writing as legitimate, rather than marginalized as polemical (1994). See Houk (1993) for one discussion on terminological shifts.

Fredrickson 1988, 1972; Kovel 1970). A person with a Black ancestor is considered Black. The option of passing and "becoming white" has been viable only to fair-skinned individuals, which in itself has involved a conscious decision to conceal or entirely suppress an identity that in-cludes Blackness. At the same time, the tenacity of American dis-ease over racial classifications has been commented on in personal accounts from phenotypically white African Americans who have encountered racial biases when an observer finds out about their Black background and experiences a rupture in his/her social order (Derricote 1993; Piper 1992).

Whiteness as a point of identity, according to the logic of Goldfield, includes accepting, indeed perpetuating, a racial polarity that made the initial opposition thinkable. Corollary and essentialist notions of Black-ness accumulate meaning and acquire legitimacy only in juxtaposition to this amorphous white identity.[3] In both cases, the validity and the viability of using race as a foundation for identity or a mobilizing strategy evidences a biologization of ideology. One may argue per-suasively against the "bogus basis for solidarity," which is projected and propelled by "illusions of race" (Appiah 1992),[4] but race, as an ab-stract, nonscientific construct has become so embedded in social rela-tions, political interactions, and economic structures that the idea of implicitly advocating racial ambiguity is politically charged (Wright 1994).

In sum, identity for interracial children, insofar as self-identification is considered separately from self-identity, has been and continues to be a contentious and public issue. It is also somewhat circular: one begins with the notion that race only exists in the public imagination, and one returns to the arbitrary nature of race as a salient feature of American culture. Arbitrary, invented, or constructed, the metaphors provide no escape from the demand for—and vocalization of—a racial identity grounded in a history of family and community. And this identity is reduced to, and insists on, a negotiation between whiteness and Black-

3. The term "amorphous" is culled from reading Frantz Fanon's powerful *Black Skin, White Masks* (1967).

4. This position is eloquently argued by Kwame Anthony Appiah (1985; 1992) and as astutely disputed by his colleague, philosopher Lucius Outlaw (1990; 1992).

ness as social facts. It is not really the color of one's skin that matters, but the "race" of one's kin.

Although issues of interethnic identities include any combination, the Black/white theme has a dominance that eclipses other racial combinations.[5] Reginald Daniels, a sociologist teaching in the field of multiracialism in California, where the combined Chicano and Asian population is larger than the american Black presence (and often in political and economic competition with them), noted that his class on multiracial identities is annually the site for heated discussion, as Black students insist on focusing on the specificity of the African American experience with interracial liaisons.[6] They articulate their resistance to the inclusion of other racial combinations through the argument that this negates the profound implications of the history of biracial (Black/white) sexual relations in the United States.

If the discourse of race in America is founded on the dichotomy of Black and white, historically, the reaction of the Black community to "passing" as white has ranged from limited sympathy to hostility. Likewise, varying degrees of resentment have characterized attitudes toward interracial marriage. Marrying across the color line has raised questions about group loyalty and where families will position themselves in the larger society, where informal racial divisions operate. To a large extent, then, where families will live, with whom they will associate, and how their children will be socialized are directly linked to ideas about the significance of maintaining raced-based communities of meaning.

Studies of interracial marriage and children of parents from different racial backgrounds presuppose and identify interracial liaisons in the

5. Regional differences in the demographic contour of the United States make it appear as if the Black/white binary has been disrupted. For a discussion of this, see the Roundtable Symposium on race ("Race and Racism" 1995; Robinson 1994).

6. Conversation with Professor Daniels. Under the clever headline "Hilary's Nightmare," columnist Jennifer Bradley writes about Wendy Lee Gramm, a fifty-year-old right-wing economist married to Senator Phil Gramm, whose absolute professional independence is a political asset for her husband because she can attract the vote of independent Republican women. Gramm is Korean American, and Bradley astutely points out, "Were Phil Gramm married to a black or Hispanic woman, even an impeccably conservative one, he'd probably risk some white votes. But white Americans think of Asians and Asian Americans as the 'model minority'" (Bradley 1995).

private sphere as problematic in the public domain (Motoyoshi 1990; Root 1992; Zack 1995). In 1994, much media attention was drawn to the topic of "biraciality," and books by people of interracial backgrounds began to enter the market with titles such as *Miscegenation Blues, Race and Mixed Race,* and *Black, White, Other.* I have been intrigued by the predisposition of some of my own generation of rainbow children to project themselves as if they occupied an ambiguous status, particularly with the revival of the metaphors of "mixed-race" and "hybrid." Addition of the label "other" — often to ridicule official forms with their assumptions of ethnic, racial, and religious homogeneity — does not seem to negate this dis-ease, for the concept of "other" itself is not unambiguous. Rather it attracts attention to a philosophical conversation in which Self and Other are constituted as an existential problem involving notions of conflict, responsibility, and intersubjectivity, a theme explored in chapter 1. Indeed, discomfort with the label "other" is evidenced by a countermove to insert the rather elusive category "multiracial" in the next U.S. Census. In this context, recent appeals for new classifications such as "multiracial" do not undermine race thinking; they can, however, obscure the history of racial and sexual violence for those whose multiracial genealogy was involuntary. In addition, instituting "multiracial" as an alternative to unscientific homogenous race categories or hyphenated pseudoethnic classifications threatens to resurrect the ghosts of color-based divisions within the Black community, never entirely erased even during the era of Black Power and Black Consciousness (Russell, Wilson, and Hall, 1992).

In contrast to advocates for identifying oneself as "biracial" and "multiracial," other children of interracial background emphasize that one does not negate a white parent by self-identifying as Black. Instead, as Carol Camper — editor of *Miscegenation Blues* — writes in her introduction, they refuse to adopt the assimilationist disposition that threatens to annihilate existing racial groups, their histories and cultures "as if they were obsolete" (1994, xxiii). This should be viewed very specifically as a political position in which race may indeed be theorized as a social construct but is *also* an experienced thing, which philosopher and artist Adrian Piper describes as a cognitive feel (1992).

Naming and redefining categories of identity is not a new issue in the Black community. The major shift that took place in the 1960s, with the diffusion of Black consciousness that included such phrases as "Black is beautiful," rekindled debates on the meaning and significance of using the concept of race to mediate between language, attitudes, and behavior. "Black" was persuasively defined as "a state of mind," not a biological trait. Too often, however, this state of mind is burdened by stereotypes linking Blackness to socioeconomic class behaviors.

From ghetto studies of the 1960s to analyses of gangsta rap in the '90s, the american Black underclass has been marketed as representative of the authentic Black experience. In the 1960s, social scientists in general and anthropologists (following the sociologists) in particular, targeted Black communities without problematizing and defining their criteria for privileging racial over class boundaries. Specifying class divisions would have furthered an interracial and intraracial dimension.[7] In retrospect, sociologist Franklin Frazier's (1957) objections to anthropologist Herskovits were not without merit. As Randall Kennedy points out, undisciplined generalization in social science literature inscribes Black as a signifier for poor, culturally deviant/deficient, and criminal even where the intent has been to refute pathological depictions. Too often the literature has ignored the diversity of Black experiences, including regional, ethnic, class, and gender differences. Kennedy (1989, 1817n.304) notes that one of the hallmarks of the social science literature is that "black traits are superior to white traits or are functionally valuable to blacks given the social context in which they live." In the 1990s, this separation of traits by "race" is evident in remarkable resistance to viewing gangsta rap as "an embodiment of the norm of (American) mainstream culture" (hooks 1994).

In the last decade, a major theme in the exposition and exchange of ideas among american Blacks has been to articulate a more inclusive definition of Blackness that can account for the diversity of the Black experience in the United States. This discussion gained momentum at the same time that the issue of pedagogical principles and curriculum revisions provoked a larger national debate on American iden-

7. For examples of this practice see Kochman (1981) and Grimshaw (1990a). See Wilson, with attention to the appendix, "Urban Poverty: A State of the Art Review of the Literature" (1987, 165–87) and Sowell (1981). For an earlier essay that indirectly, but significantly, addresses these issues, see Huggins (1971).

tity, which in turn regenerated debates over the meaning of pluralism (McLaren 1994; Mohanty 1994). And the redefinition of pluralism, with the intent to demonstrate that it is different from assimilation, renews an old argument over public and private identities (Shumsky 1975; Walzer 1990; Zangwill 1909).

The politics of race continue to include competition over definitions. In this context, the assertion and affirmation of one identity from a range of possibilities is always contingent on the context. Hence the practice of naming also reflects struggles over identity, which, in turn, are efforts at gaining recognition by others. Consequently, names and labels have associations, and the manner in which they are employed confers or withdraws legitimacy. It is for this reason that critics of the latest efforts to change the census categories and include the category "multiracial" argue that such a change may not be as provocative a challenge to narrow race-thinking as it first appears. Thus the political implications of racial ambiguity, encouraged by "multiracial" categories, threaten to resurrect invisibility and passing as tolerable. Indeed, cultural critic and theomusicologist Jon Michael Spencer contends that adopting ambiguity may reinsert "Black" as a negative idea — indeed as a lack.[8]

The debate on how to redefine categories of people with parents of different racial backgrounds is contentious and originates from the public domain but resonates sharply within private, personal arenas. At the same time, the semantics of racial identifiers — Negro, Colored, Black, African American — are prescribed and circumscribed by politics in inescapable ways. Thus, to institute an identity is to assign a social essence (whether a title or a stigma), to impose a name and to impose a right to be as well as an obligation to be so. As French sociologist Pierre Bourdieu underscores: "The institution of an identity . . . is to *signify* to someone what he is and how he should conduct himself as a consequence. . . . To institute, to give a social definition, an identity, is also to impose *boundaries*" (1991, 120).

A name — Jew or Black, human or American — is "a *distinctive mark* which takes its *value* from its position in a hierarchically organized system of titles" (Bourdieu 1991, 240). The significance — politically

---

8. Conversation with Jon Spencer. On the issue of lack as negation, see chapter 1.

and personally — of how one is labeled and how one labels oneself received critical comment in an infrequently cited passage from Frantz Fanon. In this case, he refers to being labeled human:

> Since I was not satisfied to be racialized, by a lucky turn of fate I was humanized. I joined the Jew, my brother in misery.
> An outrage!
> At first thought it may seem strange that the anti-Semite's outlook should be related to that of the Negrophobe. It was my philosophy professor, a native of the Antilles, who recalled the fact to me one day: "Whenever you hear anyone abuse the Jews, pay attention, because he is talking about you." And I found that he was universally right — by which I meant that I was answerable in my body and in my heart for what was done to my brother. Later I realized that he meant, quite simply, an anti-Semite is inevitably an anti-Negro. (1967, 122)

I do not think one can overstate that how one identifies and how one *is identified by others* have a mutual impact on the range of identities from which one chooses a position. The question of physical appearance — phenotype — in the United States has had a significant impact on how people identify and are identified, as evidenced by the laws, social practices, and attitudes affecting people who in the past were involuntarily but officially categorized as "Negro" or "Colored."[9] Those who were visibly white could "pass," that is disappear into a white community provided their family history remained a secret.[10] Some African Americans who look visibly white, however, have insisted on making their racial identity explicit (Sandler 1992; Walker 1984, n.303).

---

9. The inherent tension between observation and ideas of knowledge is linked to and intensified by physical encounters where identities are forged, negotiated, and contested. Thus, the mode of thinking "difference," through the spatial references of Greek geographers, was radically altered when physical attributes such as skin color ceased to be merely a curiosity and an observation, to become a phenomenon explained through biology, and in turn facilitated the biologization of racist ideology (Arendt 1958; Hodgen 1964; Mudimbe 1993). For a discussion of how race operates as a metonym of culture at the price of ideology, see Kwame Anthony Appiah (1992), especially chapter 2, "Illusions of Race."

10. The issue of Jewish assimilation is similar but I will attend to it in more detail in chapter 1. For two salient discussions on light skin and the temptation of and distaste for passing in southern Black communities, see Mamie Fields (1983) and Paul Murray (1984); for a contemporary personal autobiography, see George Howard Williams (1995).

In my own research, one of the themes that surfaced in both the literature and interviews, indicates that — in the United States — "looking Black" precluded the possibility that an interviewee would be mistaken for Jewish; therefore a Black identity was reinforced where a Jewish one did not exist. In part, this situation is linked to the issue of recognition, which will be taken up in later chapters. Interestingly, Sander Gilman's detailed research on anti-Semitic rhetoric about the Jewish mind and body demonstrates the intimate association of images of Blackness with Jewishness (Gilman 1985; 1991). What happens, however, if one moves away from the narrow confines of thinking in terms of the biracial categories imposed by American law and custom that provoke questions of loyalty and betrayal (Rosin 1994; Wright 1994)?

In the general field of interracial relations, the subtopic of Blacks and Jews has received an inordinate amount of attention. The significant body of literature on the interaction between and comparison of Jews and Blacks (Bracey and Meier 1993) in the United States focuses attention on either alliances or conflicts between the two groups.[11] As a result, the dimension of personal relationships that crossed these boundaries has been obscured.[12] One result from this proliferation of writing is that the issue of unique histories — of oppression and discrimination — converges and conflicts in the public mind. Within both the Jewish and Black diaspora, the issues of slavery and freedom and the existential issues of historical memory, continuity, and group consciousness have helped to fashion individual and group attitudes toward assimilation, nationalism, and cultural identities (Cleage 1968; Gilroy 1993; St. Claire Drake 1984).

For instance, it was culturally graspable and seemingly natural when Texas State Representative Al Edwards sponsored the bill to celebrate Junteenth (an Afro American freedom-day celebration)[13] and chose to remind his constituents, "the Jews say, if they ever forget their history,

11. For some examples see Baldwin 1970, 1988; Branch 1989; Carson 1984; Kaufman 1988; Melnick 1993; W. M. Phillips 1991; Singer 1978; Spaights 1983; Weisbord and Stein 1970; and Weisbord and Kazarian 1985.

12. A reading of the following texts illustrates this observation: COI 1964; Cruse 1967; Gordon 1964; Lester 1988b; Levine 1993; Melnick 1993; Podhoretz 1966; Turner 1963; Washington 1970.

13. See Berlin 1994.

may their tongues cleave to the roof of their mouths . . . let the same thing happen to us" (quoted in L. Jones 1994, 192). Although the promotion of parallels between Jews and Blacks is particularly evident at the level of political discourse, it has also been a theme within academic research. In both media and scholarly writing that have (re)presented parallels, analogies, and interaction between Jews and Blacks the languages have utilized tropes of lynching and pogroms; freedom and liberation; exile and diaspora; honeymoon, marriage, and divorce.[14] In this context, the question of how the discourse on Blacks and Jews funnels itself into a discourse on Black Jewish identity that invites a closer examination.

In the United States, where most Jews are white-skinned and of European origin, a person who is marked as different by skin color will be perceived as visibly different in the company of a group of Jews. S/he will arouse curiosity. Equally, a Black person who puts on a Star of David or a yalmulka to mark his/her Jewishness will also invite interest. Having a Jewish last name may, in some circumstances, also prompt questioning. In some ways, one might speculate whether, given the stereotypes about Jews and Blacks, it is easier for a brown-skinned person to pass as *not* Jewish than for a Jew to pass as *merely* white.

Approaching this from a different perspective, where Jewishness becomes associated with whiteness as a racially significant mark, an even greater effort has to be made to insist on the distinction between one's race as it is understood in America and one's reference group orientation. Thus a Black person who is Jewish may find him/herself emphasizing different aspects of his/her identity among Jews or among Blacks. As a Jew, s/he may insist on the absence of any relation between Jewishness and race. As a Black person, the insistence might be on a distinction between American notions of race, which promote the illusion of community by fetishizing race, in contrast to Judaism as a religious and cultural entity that bonds its adherents on the basis of shared beliefs and

14. A brief search in the Nexis database displays many examples including "A Perfect Combination of Chutzpah and Soul" (Waldman 1991), "Truce Ends: Troubled Marriage" (presented in a 1989 MacNeil/Lehrer news hour), "Blacks and Jews: Like Partners in a Troubled Marriage" (a 1988 *Chicago Tribune* article), "Cokley Furor Ends the Honeymoon between Chicago's Blacks and Jews" (*Chicago Tribune*, 1988).

rituals, an ancient language, historical continuity, and a geographical center (Israel). The dispersion of Jews across the globe produced a diaspora of people whose skin color ranges from the dark African and Asian to the pale northern European Jews. Why, then, are those who are identifiably Black seen as "different" or "unique" when they present themselves as Jewish? The issue of (re)presenting one's self as both Black and Jewish, however, introduces the question of the meaning of being Jewish in a secular context, which (arguably) is parallel to the issue of (re)presenting *Blackness* in a race-neutral environment.

This book initiates, and thus paves the way for, explorations of how people with a similar background to my own consider and articulate a sense of personal identity and group identity. The objective here is to highlight the personal domain and meaning of "biracialism" in general, and the significance of being both Black and Jewish in particular. Specifically, I am interested in how adult children of interracial parents, where one parent was Jewish and one was Black, think about their personal identity/ies and relationship to these two communities and to the worlds in which they move. The investigation thus centers around whether, how, and why Americans of both African American and Jewish heritage identify themselves as members of, or in relation to, groups whose histories include a legacy of legal and political discrimination based on their being racial Others (slavery and the Holocaust). Although this study area has specific relevance to the persistent public discussion of Jewish-Black relations, it deliberately moves beyond traditional foci on organized interest groups (while laying a foundation for rethinking their roles).

A general incentive for pursuing a personal topic was my dissatisfaction with discussions about multiculturalism. More significant, my decision to pursue the topic felt more urgent after I read a number of books on mixed-race people that had no material on the intersection of american Black and Jewish identities. The neglect of critical analysis of the extent to which anti-Semitism among Blacks and racism among Jews have fostered or inhibited the formation of a dual identity also seemed curious (Bracey and Meier 1993; Cruse 1967; Kaufman 1992; Labovitz 1987; Lerner and West 1996; Tsukashima 1978; Washington 1984; West 1993b). Although there is an extensive literature on Black anti-Semitism, which occasionally addresses how some aspects of Christianity have informed Black attitudes toward Jews as an ethnic group (Bond 1965; Locke 1994; Washington 1994), the question of the extent to which among Jewish Americans "whiteness" has been an ambiguous and ambivalent racial and social identity has been neglected in academic studies (Aronowitz 1992; Dolgin 1977; Frankenberg 1993; Lincoln 1970; Marshall 1993; Messer 1986).[15]

In terms of a discussion of interracial relations within interracial families and among interracial children, when the Jewish partner is of European background it is simply taken for granted, rather than questioned, that s/he is merely "white." As Ari Senghor Rosner, one of the people who graciously provided me with initial assistance in networking, stated, "it is curious how 'Jewish' blends into an amorphous sense of 'white' in people's minds."[16]

At both the intellectual and political levels, however, this presupposition contradicts my own socialization. The racially coded language, consisting of labels such as "biracial" and "mixed-race," confers legitimacy to the concept "interracial" and thus imposes artificial limitations on how to identify the children of Jewish and Black parents. I felt that if I used my own background as a starting point, there was an alternative to acquiescing to the dichotomy of biracialism that is embedded in American ways of thinking about race.[17]

15. Anthropologist Karen Brodkin Sacks, who asks "How Did Jews Become White Folks?" is an exception in this regard (1992; 1994). There seems to have been more questioning among radical Jewish activists who were aligned with the political objectives of the New Left and the Black Power movement, but alienated from the anti-Semitic trend articulated with greater intensity and frequency after 1967. For an excellent collection of essays, see the anthology edited by Porter and Drier (1973) with particular attention to Zuckoff (1973). Innumerable articles on Negro-Jewish and later Black-Jewish relations, in Jewish journals such as *Judaism, Commentary,* and *Moment,* frequently include reference to the fact that Judaism is color-blind.

16. Telephone conversation with Rosner. See also Jane Lazarre's personal account, *Beyond the Whiteness of Whiteness: Memoir of a White Mother of Black Sons* (1996), in which the slippage between "being white" and "being Jewish" is not fully interrogated in an otherwise sensitive introspection.

17. The attitude regarding experience as a legitimate resource in scholarship has been adopted by numerous "mixed-race" people, and it is also a stance that has been adopted by many scholars from other marginalized groups and is specifically linked to debates over experience and voice. For example, see Zack (1995).

How are Jews as an *ethnic* minority thought of in relation to "whites"? If Jews are not a *racial* category, then how do we find a language to describe the identities of children of Jewish and Black parents. Is being Jewish a *cultural* identity? A *political* identity? How does this cohere with the idea of Blackness as a cultural and political identity? In other words, can we transcend the racial codes imposed on the language of racial identities? Do we disrupt naturalized ways of thinking about Jews and Blacks when we insist on a coupling that does not exist in, and possibly negates, the current discourse on bifurcated racial identities that is grounded in the terms "interracial" and "mixed-race"?

The reactions I have received to the idea of writing about children of interracial parents and narrowing the field to include only those who are Black and Jewish have been interesting. White Christian colleagues have looked dismayed and wondered whether I was fabricating a notion of Jewishness that was divorced from whiteness. Often they have been visibly agitated by the attention to anti-Semitism as a product of white (European) Christianity in which theology cultivated and nurtured political racism. Black Christians have displayed moderate interest, but have asked whether for an African American one should distinguish between Jewishness on the one hand, and Jews as part of white America on the other hand. The relevance of Jewishness for a Black person surfaces in the context of a *religious*, not cultural or ethnic, affiliation.

The reaction of a number of Jews was more ambivalent. Some were enthusiastic about the necessity for moving away from discussions of Black Jewish relations; others felt that the research would inevitably highlight more about the contradictions among American Jewish attitudes toward African Americans than the reverse (which indeed is what occurred, as will be seen in later chapters). This latter concern highlighted the extent to which research is never purely an intellectual exercise but rather returns one to the public arena of politics. If my research indicated a pattern of racial prejudice among Jewish families, might this provide further fodder for anti-Semites among the Black community? Alternatively, if I discovered that Jewish parents themselves laid little emphasis on any Jewish identity, would that reinforce arguments about the dangers of marriage outside one's own group—

regardless of the "race" of the non-Jewish partner — and thus augment fears of the assimilation and disappearance of the Jewish community in America?[18] Were these not individual, personal choices that had nothing to do with the way Americans think about race? This question led me to consider whether I was taking the issue of Blackness for granted and assuming that Jewish identity was something one worked at and consciously subscribed to.[19]

Yet overriding these questions is one potentially more explosive. Those who have profited as "stars" from the various "dialogues" between Blacks and Jews have been secure in their positions as mediators, particularly at times of controversy. If people who are *both* Black and Jewish, and interracial as well,[20] should begin to be heard from the

18. In August 1995, the United Jewish Appeal (UJA) brought the first mission of intermarried couples to Israel as a tactic for dealing with what has been called "one of the most contentious issues in American Jewish life." Initiated by the UJA Federation of Westport, Connecticut, with the support of the national organization, the local executive director, Robert Wexler, argued that a main objective was "to encourage participation in the Jewish community and improve the odds for a Jewish future for the children of intermarried couples." The mission, however, has been criticized for lending tacit support to intermarriage, which reportedly has risen to 52 percent in the United States (Henry 1995, 12).

19. There is no mysterious answer left to the conclusion: *both* parental racial prejudice *and* lack of commitment to Jewishness contribute to countless passive Jewish identities among interfaith marriages in general and interracial ones in particular. *To be* Jewish one has simply to be born to a Jewish mother (or to convert, which is a separate discussion). But *being* and *doing* are not the same thing, an issue that will be taken up in chapter 1. On the other hand, *to be* Black one must be visibly marked by color or socially defined as Black and it is less a matter of *doing* than of *being done to* — even if only implicitly or potentially. In America, one need not work at *being* Black to be reminded of it, and there is no better example than the clichéd anecdote of Black professionals finding a taxi in downtown New York City.

20. This should not be misinterpreted: there is no intent here to disparage american Blacks who have converted to Judaism, particularly under the auspices of Orthodox rabbinical authorities, but rather to underscore Jewishness under the matrilineal law of descent. Of course, the situation changes with the second generation of children whose american Black mothers and fathers are Jewish — that is, the children of Jewish women of European origin (for instance, the orientation of the issues discussed in this book would not have the same relevance for the child from the marriage of Lisa Bonet, whose mother is Jewish, and Lenny Kravitz, whose father is Jewish).

sidelines, the authority of those occupying mediating and leadership positions might be challenged. In pondering this question, it began to seem increasingly odd to me that although Jewish organizations consistently argued that Jews come in all shades and that spokespersons in the Black community persistently claimed that expressions of animosity toward Jews were misinterpreted as anti-Semitic, rather than as antagonism toward white arrogance, at times of crisis neither group sought out representatives who could speak as members of *both* communities — from the standpoint of being Jewish, Black, and interracial (Gilman 1994; A. L. Goldman 1992; Miron 1994; Wolfson 1995). Or was it simply that like myself, others who are Black and Jewish are simply reluctant to participate in either the politics of dissension or to assume the public role of being a token, a symbol of unity or a mascot for bridging communication gaps.

Here the background of Lani Guinier was of personal as much as public interest. I first heard that she was Jewish from an attorney-friend, Shireen Lewis, who lives near Washington, D.C. Shireen had heard this biographical detail through the local grapevine of Black lawyers. When this information later appeared in the press, I thought that both Jewish and Black organizations would capitalize on the information. I was therefore surprised and quite dismayed that no Jewish organization formally took a position against President Bill Clinton's failure to support her nomination to head the Civil Rights Division of the administration. In fact, I called one organization and was told that no position had been taken because by the time it might have come up on the agenda, her name had already been withdrawn. The problem, perhaps, was twofold: on the individual level, Professor Guinier herself did not dwell on the issue of being Jewish and it was unclear if she identified herself with the Jewish community. This might have been a criterion for partisan lobbying on her behalf. On the general national level, the issue of affirmative action remained a sensitive and contentious point of disagreement between the Jewish and Black communities (Lerner and West 1996, 166–79).

Of more relevance to the lack of a joint Black-Jewish lobby on behalf of Guinier's nomination is a letter from Corey Gordon to the *Star Tribune* (accessed through Nexis) that criticizes inclusion of Guinier's mother's religion in an article about the Clinton decision: "I find the

reference to the mother's religious heritage racist and deeply offensive."
The *Tribune* response is pertinent, especially in the context of the disappearance of this matter from the public agenda in general and the
silence in the Jewish press in particular,[21]

The word "Jewish" was inserted by Carl Sims, an editor on the national desk,
he said, "so that the reader would understand that Guinier has some knowledge
firsthand of what it is like to be treated as a different person in U.S. society."
Sims said, " 'Jewish' to me says a whole bunch of people got wiped out in World
War II and have been dumped on for centuries. Guinier is a product of that
background and, therefore, has a heightened sense of what it is to be different in
U.S. society." (Gelfand 1993, 21)

As I tentatively sent out letters of inquiry, I began to have my own
doubts about the feasibility of a project on "invisible communities"
(Rosaldo 1989, 29), where I would find people to interview, how contacts might be established, and whether my own notion about the compatibility of Jewish and Black as particularistic identities that could be
articulated without negotiating the more vacuous terrain of thinking in
terms of "mixed-race" was peculiarly unique. From the viewpoint of
traditional anthropology, I had set up a problem that could not be
located in a particular fieldwork setting (Clifford and Marcus 1986).
However, the very notion of a field, as Arjun Appadurai demonstrates,
seems to have lost its usefulness: "The landscapes of group identity —
the ethnoscapes — around the world are no longer familiar anthropological objects, insofar as groups are no longer tightly territorialized,
spatially bounded, historically unselfconscious, or culturally homogeneous" (1991). This idea of global ethnoscapes insists on their porousness. I decided that although the research project focuses on a small
percentage of the population, who do not live within the boundaries of
a cohesive, small-knit community, the role of an investigator empowers
one to define and highlight a field of research that has been neglected,
overlooked, or ignored.

Considering the meaning, significance, and relevance of being Jewish and Black does move away from traditional anthropology's notion

21. This conclusion is based on a fruitless search through library computer data-
bases to find some reference from specifically Jewish institutions or spokespersons
who would echo the comments of the *Tribune* editor.

of distinct cultural units. Yet it has opened up the door to exploring *something* (which remains to be defined) recognizable and thereby *culturally* graspable, exemplified by material of rap singer Justin E. Warfield (Warfield 1993; Bourdieu 1984). With the introduction of Renato Rosaldo's notion of "invisible communities," one anthropological hypothesis that serves as a departure point is that both an abstract and a concrete sense of community does exist for people who can claim membership in two reference groups.[22] My brother and I were witness to the existence of this sense of community.

This personal knowledge does not resolve the issue of objectivity and participant observation, which continues to distress anthropologists. How can one observe "identity" outside some sort of institutional structure, however informal? How can a member of a group maintain enough distance to objectively represent or comment on the group? A general consensus seems to have worked itself out among social science practitioners that the issue of objectivity can never be conclusively resolved.[23] One is always positioned, and how one observes and interprets is always already transfigured through the lens of personal experiences and training.

Anthropologists institutionalized a discipline with the invention of natives, bounded cultures, and neutral observers (Kuper 1988; Said 1979; Trouillot 1991a). If the mystique of fieldwork, as theory and technique, is disintegrating, and the concept of "native" has become more ambiguous, one may suggest that an existential commitment to a group provides *the cognitive feel* (Piper 1992), which refutes the inauthenticity of neutrality (Rigby 1991). Thus although in theory I concede that "the best translation is always a reflection, or more specifically, a metaphoric construct" (Mudimbe 1991, 171),[24] I subscribe to the

22. The availability and awareness of choice — options — is the relevant point and *not* their actualization, which can always be undertaken.

23. Allan Megill has compiled an excellent collection of reflections on objectivity/objectivities from contributors who come from a range of disciplines (1994). See also Bourdieu's discussion of the manipulation of language and the pretense of scientificity (1991, 137–59).

24. Mudimbe's allowance seems to absolve the impatience of Lévi-Strauss's (1991) position on ethnographic authority, about which the latter states: "Of course one must remain aware that while transcribing an observation, whatever it is, one is

possibility that a *native* representation may instance a more perceptive transformation of the cultural place into a discursive invented space (De Saradan 1992; A. E. Goldman 1993; Wagner 1981; Wiredu 1993).

In recent years anthropologists, spurred on by the intervention of literary critics and the institutionalization of cultural studies, have debated methodological and epistemological issues of fieldwork and ethnography and the politics of representation (Alcoff 1991/2; Clifford 1983, 1986; Dominguez 1989; Geertz 1973, 1983; Gluck and Patai 1991; A. E. Goldman 1993; hooks 1990; Kuper 1988; Min-ha 1989; D. Scott 1992; Sangren 1988). At the same time, people with "multicultural" backgrounds, both within and outside the academy, have become more numerous and outspoken about the absence of literature that accurately reflects their own and their families' backgrounds. They are producing a new literature that documents, interprets, and rethinks issues of identity, spatiality, temporality, and historical memory while avoiding notions of biological essentialism or reactionary particularism (Apparduai 1991; Abu-Lughod 1991; Alcoff 1988, 1995; Fields 1983; Rigby 1992; Rodriguez 1989; Squire-Hakey 1995; Trouillot 1991b). My position in relation to the selection and interpretation of this topic thus warrants attention.

I was born and raised in the United States and am of Jewish and West Indian descent. As a child, my mother escaped Nazi Austria, where Jews were listed as a *racial* category.[25] My father emigrated to the

---

not preserving the facts in their original authenticity; they are being translated into another language, and something is lost in the process. But what can we conclude from it? That one can neither translate nor observe?" (155).

25. Sander Gilman interrogates the conceptual confusion of religion and race that marks nineteenth-century scientific theories of difference and disease applied to Jews. For instance, one Viennese proverb encapsulates contemporary European views that it is not "religion but race that defines the Jews: '*Was der Jude glaubt ist einerlei / in der Rasse liegt der Schweinerei!*' (The Jew's belief is nothing / it's race that makes him swinnish!)." Gilman points to Hitler, who rephrased this popular comment in *Mein Kampf* (1925) " 'the whole existence (of the Jews) is based on one single great lie, to wit, that they are a religious community while actually they are a race — and what a race!' Thus the double bind of fin-de-siècle Jewry is the desire 'to go beyond Judaism' paired with the impossibility of this undertaking once 'Judaism' is defined racially. And it is in the science of the time that the debate about the racial identity of the Jews was joined" (Gilman 1993, 12).

United States as a young boy. His ancestral genealogy includes ancestors from Cuba and Scotland and relatives, by marriage, of Chinese descent. My 1952 New York City birth certificate classified my father's "Race" as "Negro" and my mother as "White," thus designating me a Negro — by law. I lived in Israel for twenty-one years, and my Israeli identity card registers only my "Nationality," as Jewish.[26] This background informs my perspective, influences my opinions, and shapes the manner in which I have engaged with the people I have interviewed. Indeed, it provided the opening for soliciting both their time and their candid responses.

The problem of where and how to find interviewees quickly resolved itself. In the first place, I decided that each individual and family present a unique history, so my efforts were not going to be invested in attempting broad generalizations. Instead, I would focus on ten to fifteen individuals as a first step toward expanding the conversation of multiculturalism as well as broadening the discourse of Black identities.[27]

The people I decided to speak with are all adults whose thinking has been shaped or affected by periods when a great deal of attention was given to group consciousness (1960s), Afrocentricity and Jewish nationalism (1970s), and multiculturalism (1980s and '90s). One of the first people I contacted in June 1994, Naomi Zack, had recently published a book on the subject of interracial people and how mixed race has been conceptualized in the United States. In her introduction she briefly wrote of her own Jewish and Black background. My introductory letter received an immediate answer, and shortly thereafter we had a lengthy telephone conversation in which she expressed her willing-

26. In America the pivotal classification is race, whereas in Israel nationality and religion are the primary official categories of identification. An interesting aside on the association of Jewish with "Nationality" is remarked on by *The Jerusalem Report* journalist Micha Odenheimer, who covered events in Somalia in 1992. Odenheimer writes, "I came to Somalia as a journalist but also as a Jew. Apparently, the UN official who arranged my flight to Somalia from Nairobi understood this instinctively: On the flight manifest, where the nationality of other journalists and officials had been marked "Italian" or "French," mine was marked "Jewish" — *although I was traveling on a U.S. passport*" (Odenheimer 1992, 50; italics added).

27. After conducting eight interviews, a pattern seemed to repeat itself and coincided with the findings of the North American Jewish Data Bank with regard to intermarriage (see chapter 3).

ness to participate in a telephone interview as well as provide academic support to the project. Zack recommended a number of books and gave me a list of people to contact, including the founder and president of Project Race, a grassroots organization that started in Georgia and has been campaigning for the inclusion of the category of "multiracial" on school forms and in the next census.

Susan Graham, who is (white) Jewish and married to an African American, started Project Race because of her own concerns with how her children were to identify and be identified. As Project Race is specifically organized for and around families of any mixed race combination, they do not deal with interethnic and interreligious intermarriages. Graham provided me with a number of names, one of whom was Reginald Daniels, a sociology professor whose essay I had read the previous year in a collection by people of interracial background (Root 1992).

I called Daniels, and two days later we had a long conversation on academic resistance to the subject of multiracialism as an independent course of study. We shared the view that the manner in which the American opposition of Black/White conditions the ways in which multiracialism and multiculturalism, both as concepts and as phenomena, are conceptualized and discussed is an important field of study. As with Zack, Daniels expressed his support for my project, and he gave me the name of another contact in California,[28] Ari Senghor Rosner, who was, he said, "African-American and Jewish" and had written an undergraduate honor's thesis on biracial people.

Coincidentally, the conversation with Graham occurred the same day I received a response from Deborah Johnson, a psychology professor at the University of Wisconsin, who also had a chapter in Root's edited collection and to whom I had also written. She complimented the idea "to restrict your sample to biracial individuals having one Jewish parent and one non-White, non-Jewish parent."

After these initial contacts with people in the field, one contact led to

---

28. My original plans to conduct several interviews on the West Coast had to be deferred due to financial and personal constraints. In retrospect, this proved to be less unfortunate than it first seemed because the people with whom I would have met were born and raised on the East Coast.

another, and within less than two weeks I had established a network of interviewees. Each time I called a new person, I explained that I was calling because of his or her family background and that I have a similar one. And each time the response to the project was greeted as timely and with enthusiasm. In one case, the daughter of a well-known Black actress and singer took time from a busy schedule to write me back, explaining that it was her stepfather who was Jewish; she therefore would not qualify, but she wished me luck with my project.

Although finding people to interview was relatively easy, I was turned down twice. I called the son of one of America's most prominent and controversial Black artists of the 1940s and '50s, whose wife had been the PTA President of my elementary school when I was in first and second grade. Their marriage had aroused a great deal of publicity, much of it viciously racist, which the years had eclipsed from public memory. Their children were close to my age. He had recently published a book in which he gives attention to Jews and Blacks, although he did not draw attention to his personal links to the issues. When I telephoned to inquire about interviewing his adult-children, he firmly stated that he doubted they would be interested since "it's a private matter." I pursued it, asking whether I could send them letters of inquiry and he reluctantly — but politely — gave his address. I never received a response. My efforts to establish contact with Professor Lani Guinier were unsuccessful, although her research assistant did leave a message on my machine that "Professor Guinier's schedule is full so she cannot be of assistance."

What became quickly apparent was that these interviews might also illustrate the dialogic encounter in which my role as researcher was comfortably integrated into my role as a participant. However, whether the dialogic aspect was successful seemed less important than undermining further the artificial presumption that objective distance was preferable to subjective engagement in scholarly undertakings. The issue of identity/ies in terms of having a Black parent and a Jewish parent was quite relevant to the people I called and indeed played a significant part in their thinking of what it means to describe one's racial background. Even where the immediate responses appeared to be ambivalent and vague, in seven of my eight interviews, each person had a moment in which there was a specific insistence on the fact of *being* Jewish.

Although Naomi Zack was very supportive, I decided to put the idea of conducting interviews by telephone on hold. The telephone is an extremely impersonal machine and, in general, unless there is an immediate rapport as with Zack, Rosner, and Daniels, it is difficult to establish a personal tone. But more important, I wanted to be able to see what each person actually looked like. For instance, Ari Senghor Rosner grew up in Washington, D.C., and said he looked like and was often mistaken for a Puerto Rican. How he presented himself was very much influenced by the way people perceived him and the assumptions they made about his appearance. Their misperceptions and his moods shaped the way he corrected them (Rosner 1993).

Attitudes within the Black community toward skin color and hair texture are a perennial theme, featured regularly in the Black press. The subject has been handled with sensitivity by W. E. Cross, Jr. (1991) and by Russell, Wilson, and Hall (1992) and with shrewdness by film director Spike Lee. Despite the range of colors found among and within Black families, it is almost impossible to find children's storybooks or greeting cards that reflect this diversity. Prominent figures who were, in "real life," light-skinned, have been portrayed in film by dark-skinned actors. Descriptions of what a person thinks s/he looks like are sometimes deceptive as well and have much to do with expectations. When singer Mariah Carey was first promoted by CBS/Columbia Records, she was ambiguously presented and perceived as a white artist within the white community, although many Black critics and fans were suspicious. In order to diffuse rumors that she was "passing" for white, Carey finally held a news conference in order to formally announce her "biracial" background (L. Jones 1994).

Among Jews, the question of images and physical representation has also received significant attention. Although Israel is a showcase for the rainbow of the Jewish people, even within American Jewish communities the diversity of "what a Jew looks like" is countered by stereotypes held among Jews and non-Jews alike. A person who is Jewish and looks very fair-skinned, blond, and blue-eyed—the Anglo-Saxon counterpart of the Aryan model—may also be misperceived. The classic example of such an encounter was unforgettably captured in a scene between Paul Newman, cast as an Israeli Sabra—the new Jew—and Peter Lawford as an anti-Semite, in Otto Preminger's

Exodus.[29] How one responds to such moments depends on the context and the person, but the response itself is mandatory; even allowing a misperception to stand uncorrected *is* a response.

In terms of people who are Black and Jewish, given the manner in which, in the United States, the association of Jewish blends into mental images of whiteness, it was also important for me to *see* the interviewee because self-reflexivity is always limited and the image people have of themselves does not necessarily correspond with that held by the onlooker.[30] What does it mean "to look Puerto Rican"? In a different setting, Brooklyn for instance, with its large Syrian, Lebanese, and Iraqi Jewish community, Ari might have been taken as Jewish but his African American heritage would have been vague or invisible. The Hispanic features he refers to are characteristic of the Middle East in general, where Ari could be mistaken for an Israeli, Jew, or Palestinian. Outside the United States, these physical appearances have very different meanings as are the ways of describing and attributing significance to them.

Yet I am sensitive to the fact that appearances are one of the markers by which Israeli security at airports target people for particular attention. This can be irritating and often acrimonious. Although people of color are not consistently hassled, when it happens there is a feeling that racial prejudice motivated the special treatment they were accorded. White-skinned American Jews of all ages and sizes do, periodically, have their luggage and body thoroughly searched. Not having been the target of color prejudice, however, they can usually channel any annoyance into at least nominal sympathy for Israeli concerns with international terrorism. Thus one might speak of a momentary feeling of solidarity — translated as "these are my people concerned for my safety."

Most African Americans, in contrast, have experienced at least one racial incident in their lives, whether it is being followed in a department store by an overly intrusive salesperson or being taken aback by the unexpected and insensitive racial remark. If they are also Jewish,

29. Ella Shohat (1989) gives a careful and detailed analysis of representations of Jewish Israelis as well as of ethnic and racial stereotypes of Jews and Arabs in Israeli films.

30. The topic of objectification is pursued in chapter 1.

they may arrive in Israel anticipating that the famous "in-gathering of the exiles" and the existence of dark-skinned Jews will include them as well. Israel then suggests the possibility of a place where "Jewish" is the noun and "Black" is an empty signifier.[31]

Three days after I had spoken with Daniels, he called to recommend that I get in touch with Mark Steiner. Steiner hosts his own program on Baltimore's WJHU-FM, and Daniels had participated that evening in a panel discussion that included two people, a man and a woman, who were both of African American and European Jewish background. It turned out that one of the panelists was Steiner's daughter, Chelsea Steiner. In the course of our conversation, he told me that Chelsea had visited Israel and at the departure terminal the Israeli security personnel systematically went through her luggage. Apparently her answers to their questions aroused anxiety; from my own experience, more often than not this is the primary reason the Israeli security personnel pull people aside. Nonetheless, seeing what Chelsea Steiner actually looked like, hearing her impressions of how she was treated in Israel in general and at the airport in particular, and comparing this with her experiences in America and interaction with Jews and Blacks was an important exercise for considering the interaction between impressions and public self-representation.

I have also become more sensitive to the cumulative impact of accents, physical appearance, and bodily gestures as performance — an assertion of difference that marks a person as a member of a community — as a result of watching my sons, Gabriel and Ron, acclimate to the social environment of Durham. They arrived in America from Israel at the ages of seventeen and fifteen, respectively, and went directly into the local public high school. They were immediately introduced to a clear racial division in the school as far as social networks operate, which prepared them for similar patterns in college. Although the school population is integrated, as are classes, sports teams, and after-school activities, little social interaction takes place across color lines. Within a week the two boys each arrived at the same evaluation of the school's social setting, although how they chose to accommodate themselves and (literally) to *act* was very different.

In the first place, they discovered that there were few Jewish students

---

31. The idea of Jewish as a noun is considered more fully in the coda.

and that one of the identifying traits of the Jewish students was that they were very low-key, which was a complete turnaround from the centrality of Jewishness in Israel, even for resolutely secular Jewish Israelis. In Durham the boys found that Jewishness was not something one highlighted in public. Instead, the Jewish students blended into the dominant white student body. If those students were more forthcoming around Gabriel and Ron, it had to do with the fact that the two were Israeli and therefore exotic exemplification of something other than/ more than just Jews. In the second place, Gabriel and Ron discovered that being foreign students empowered them to use their appearances and backgrounds — one is peach-colored and the other is mocha — to move between the white students and the Black students with an ease that American students lacked. For both, the element of artificiality was explicit.

Gabriel, who is more fair-skinned, resisted being identified as white yet moved into a crowd of mostly white, Christian friends. As he blandly put it one evening at dinner, "I'm not going to put up a sign that says I'm Black just to be accepted." As far as he was concerned, the idea of "learning how to act Black" was *theater of the absurd* — and he felt that outside the United States, even the language of self-description he was forced to adopt would seem ridiculous: in a class discussion, Gabriel found himself saying, "well, I may look white but I'm Black and Jewish Israeli." His experience seems to illustrate one manifestation of a deliberate distinction between self-identification in the public sphere and self-identity, which refuses to conform to reductionist and essentialist notions of either race or ethnicity.[32]

Ron, who is darker, consciously adopted the gestures, dress codes, and hairstyle that would mark him as "Black" and insisted that his Black friends respect the fact that he was Jewish and that his white friends respect his being Black. Yet both boys agreed that it was skin color that facilitated Ron's entry into the Black student camp without the subtle pressure of proving himself demanded of his older, lighter-skinned brother. As serious "play," these role performances became even more critical in their college experience at a prestigious North Carolina university.

In every respect, the experiences my sons confronted — a combina-

32. At my request, Gabriel reviewed and approved this section for accuracy.

tion of choice and imposition—with the more critical distance of children socialized abroad and peripherally exposed to the discourse of race in the United States,[33] provide insight into the public way identities are manifested and the private ways in which they are negotiated and the tension between the two. The artificiality of constructing racial identities took precedence over the philosophical and epistemological issues that engage the question of a Jewish identity in the Israeli context from which they came and the American context into which they were being incorporated. But what is particularly important for my understanding of how these two young men engaged the politics of identity is that part of the reason they were obligated to take a position at all on the issue of race had to do with *the politics of race* and, in turn, the necessity in America of publicly acknowledging and claiming their link to a history and a community.

Their experience returned me to the question of how American-born children of interracial parents internalize and articulate their public identities in a society that ambiguously positions Jews as a *white* (i.e., Caucasian) ethnic minority and explicitly defines persons with Black relatives as Black. How does this race assignment and alignment differ when one or both of the parents are immigrants to America? In my case, for instance, the fact that most of my mother's family were murdered in Nazi concentration camps and that her parents were among the relatively few to receive affidavits for entry into the United States was crucial to her political activities in the civil rights arena as well as to her insistence on raising her children consciously as both Black and Jewish. In fact, my very practical grandmother was initially concerned with why such a burden should be placed on my shoulders: "Isn't it enough that she is Black in a racist society? Why insist on her dealing with anti-Semitism as well?" My grandfather, on the other hand, took the issue of raising his grandchild Jewish for granted: I was named for his mother who was left behind in Austria because America's doors were closed. Cognizant of the profound racism in America of 1952, he

---

33. In our household, Hebrew was the only language used, although they heard English and learned it as a foreign language at school. With very few markers of "Americanness," they were, consequently, neither bicultural nor bilingual on their arrival to the States.

was anxious for the future "in a nation, indeed in a world, where her blackness might prove as dangerous as our Jewishness had already proven to us" (Gibel 1987, 154).

Other families we knew who were similar to ours deemphasized their commitment to the Jewish community precisely because the Jewish parents refused to accept the marriage. The contradiction between their parents' behavior and the liberal tenets of Jewish ethics motivated the couples to sever ties altogether rather than finding alternative contexts in which to reconcile this gap. In two cases, with the dissolution of their marriages the Jewish spouses began to tentatively reconsider their own cultural identity and attempted to encourage a sense of Jewishness in their teenage children who previously had little contact with any Jewish experience. In one case, the daughter accepted neither her father's Black nationalism nor her mother's renewed interest in Judaism. She married a practicing white Protestant much to the dismay of both parents, who had originally met in the Communist Party. In the second case, Jewishness is sort of suspended as a component of identity — the fact of being Jewish through having a Jewish mother is peripheral to her core identity yet is deliberately claimed at times in order to dislodge stereotypes either among Blacks or among Jews.

How does the environment in which one grows up — in terms of schools, regions, class — influence the manner in which the individual situates him/herself vis-à-vis the two communities? How does physical appearance influence the manner in which one is perceived and the reciprocal response this elicits for the individual? In other words, how much effort is required to gain recognition in a community and as a member of a community? One woman, with whom I spoke briefly, was raised Jewish in Brooklyn by her mother and never knew who her father was until she was a teenager. She was also very fair-skinned and did not stand out among her Jewish friends. Thirty years later, highly conscious of the meaning (or lack thereof) of the label "mixed-race," she thinks that Jews have become more inclined to categorize themselves as white than they did when she was growing up. Is this assessment due to the fact that as a child she was less conscious of race as an identity whereas as an adult, she has become more acutely self-conscious of the role appearance and perception play in mutually affecting self-identity and public self-identification?

In the multicultural and multiracial environments of New York City and Los Angeles, is the comfort level of articulating and insisting on the diversity of one's background higher than in the more racially bifurcated environment of a small town or a southern city? What institutional structures are available to reinforce a sense of identity, such as afternoon Jewish/Hebrew schools and Black student organizations? To what extent do parents instill a sense of identity in terms of linking the histories of Blacks and Jews, and how is this connection actualized in terms of formal rituals such as Passover, a holiday celebrating liberation from slavery? These are questions whose answers very much depend on individual experiences and, as will be seen, not all are addressed in this book. But they do remain significant and should be pursued in subsequent studies on this topic.

At an early stage of my research, and as a way of organizing my thoughts, I prepared an exhaustive list of the questions I wanted to consider. The detailed questionnaire was built around three major topics — personal background, Jewish identity, and Black identity — as well as the corollary subject of what it means to be "interracial." Later on, I reluctantly added the labels "biracial" and "multicultural" to the questions on self-description. During my interviews, this questionnaire was used for and useful as an informal guideline.

Three of my four interviews in New York were in restaurants. The other five interviews were in the homes of the interviewees. Only one woman was somewhat self-conscious about speaking with a tape recorder, and there were times when she asked me to turn it off while she thought about her answers. Although I kept the questions near at hand, referring back to them briefly as we moved into different topics, the interviews were relaxed and informal. At the end of each interview, I gave a copy of the questionnaire to each person. Four people took the time to read it while we were still sitting together and added a few comments to their earlier remarks. After each taped interview was transcribed and prior to any editorial changes, a copy of the transcript was sent to each interviewee. Two people did call me to correct responses that in written form appeared incoherent or, in one case, inaccurate. As will be seen, citations from all interviews were edited only for clarity; habits of speech such as "um" and the arbitrary (and not deliberately rhetorical) "you know" were deleted.

Three people asked me not to use their real names, and I have respected their request.

The remainder of this book is divided into four chapters and concludes with a coda. Chapters 1 and 2 tackle issues of identity from slightly different angles. Chapter 1 focuses on the meaning of identity as a concept and a phenomenon as it figures in philosophical and political thought. It moves from a general discussion on identity to a more specific focus on the dilemma and strategic significance of particularistic identities. Chapters 2 and 3 turn to Jewish and Black themes and introduce the idea of Jewish, Black, and interracial identities as an encompassing *identity*.

I have elected to defer a discussion of the ethnographic material (using the oral interviews/narratives) until the last chapter. The theoretical framework, mapped out in chapter 1, frames the approach to the discourses underlying the interviews in chapter 4. This last chapter incorporates the ideas of preceding chapters into a presentation and analysis of the interviews with the eight people who are Jewish, Black, and interracial.

The purpose of structuring the discussion in this manner is to accentuate the focus of attention on an *idea* of identity — being Black, Jewish, and interracial — conditioned by the specificity of the United States. Consequently, the contributions selected from the interviews should be seen as testimony on behalf of this idea and, hopefully, will be better appreciated after the theoretical context has been mapped out. Finally, this method seemed to offer the best means of using interviews as an illustration for, rather than an imposition on, the viability of my propositions.

1

PERSPECTIVES ON IDENTITY/IES

"(Identity) designates something like a person's understanding of who they are, of their fundamental defining characteristics as a human being" (Taylor 1992, 25).

This chapter represents an intellectual exercise: my intent is to deliberately trouble, in order to transcend, the divide imposed between theory and practice. There are different ways to consider what the signifier "identity" conveys, and the context is critical to such attention. My concern with "identity" here is not the word as an image of thought — a mental construct. Instead, the focus is, on the one hand, on particular people, in a specific historical moment and geographical location and, on the other hand, the actualization of the phenomenon that "identity" connotes: a continuous process of *being as becoming*. Identity, then, can also refer to a practice originating in and manifested through social interaction.[1]

Before proceeding, it cannot be overemphasized that the centrality of politics is my point of departure and return. I will argue that identity has meaning only in the context of self and other and, in the twentieth century at least, politics are inherently embedded in the encounter between the two entities. A person's self-understanding of who s/he is, is always undergoing refinement and modification. Emphasizing the theory of identity as a continuous process that transcends the dichotomous notion of public/private reveals the profound significance of *context* — separate and apart from *content*. Aspects of one's identity can be dormant, intuitively felt, explicitly articulated, or translated into action: each as a process of *being as becoming*. However, it is the context of social interaction that *may* infuse content into, but *will* always make meaningful, an understanding of self that refers to the phenomenon and practice of identity. In other words, I propose a theory of identity

1. This conceptualization is influenced by Ruth Berman (1990).

that is founded on and which makes possible those multiple standpoint positions from which an individual or a community can begin to reflect. I agree with Nancy Fraser's recommendation to move away from psychoanalytic models and toward an increased attention to identity construction in relation to public discursive arenas (1994, 97n.25).[2]

How to theorize the multiple ways in which individuals come to understand who they are as well as how they internalize and articulate this understanding integrates questions about interpretation, representation, and politics.[3] Specifically, in confronting these areas of inquiry a scholar's description can slip into prescription, producing what Pierre Bourdieu refers to as a "theory effect." His theory of practice and models of pedagogy attempt to address theorizing and the (re)production of self-evident truths. Bourdieu insists on unveiling processes that produce and naturalize predispositions. He demonstrates how, through schooling and family, one learns and internalizes a particular vision of the world, a way of seeing and thinking.

By taking into account the various ways in which public discourses on Black–Jewish relations and on procreation, marriage, and sexual relations across race lines have been constituted, one may address the effect this has on thinking about Black/Jewish identities. Bourdieu's

2. Fraser, building on Hannah Arendt's distinction between publicity and plurality, differentiates *community* as "a bounded and fairly homogenous group," which suggests consensus, from *public*, which accentuates an open-ended arena marked by diversity and plurality of perspectives (Fraser 1994, 97n.29; Arendt 1958).

3. The opinion that theory is necessarily more sophisticated than everyday language and practice has not persuaded me that the *commonsensical* definitions, reflections, and interpretations of individuals are not as tenable as theories. The theory must be subordinate to practice and as such, it is disingenuous to bracket the exceptions that do not fit into the theory. Rather, theory has to be tested against the everyday practices of concrete material beings, that is, people. It is thus prudent to be skeptical of the criteria that define expertise (De Certeau 1988). Contradictions, inconsistencies, and discrepancies in the way people internalize their experiences and then translate them into words (or acts) result from and reflect their historical, political, and social realities. Theories fail when they disregard the always present inherent possibility of incoherence between its postulates and lived experiences. Two of the most salient examples of this are the ethnicity and development paradigms of the early 1980s that were completely refuted by real events in Eastern Europe and Africa in the late 1980s.

discussion of classes thus corresponds to this comprehensive ethnographic approach:

> At the risk of unwittingly assuming responsibility for the acts of constitution of
> whose logic and necessity they are unaware, the social sciences must take as
> their object of study the social operations of naming and the rites of institution
> through which they are accomplished. But on a deeper level, they must examine
> *the part played by words in the construction of social reality and the contribu-*
> *tion which the struggle over classifications, a dimension of all class struggles,*
> *makes to the constitution of classes* — classes defined in terms of age, sex or
> social position, but also clans, tribes, ethnic groups or nations. (1991,105;
> italics added).

An "interracial" child of a Black parent and a Jewish parent can
always and often will be designated as both Black and Jewish. Membership (ascriptive or voluntary) in one or both communities manifests the
experiential dimension of race and the complexity of giving Jewishness
meaning in a secular world. Considering what happens at the intersection of these two different frames of reference as a "context of being"
brings into relief questions of alienation, subjective positions, and social experiences, as well as the place of history and memory as a cornerstone for cohesive identities (as opposed to the fragmentation suggestive of a postmodernist mood).

Identity[4] encompasses and incorporates the cognitive and experiential fact of *being and belonging* in various subject positions marked by
social boundaries. The incentive directing this text favors a focus on the
understanding individuals have of themselves as members of different
and varying sized communities. This understanding will be referred to
as *identities*. As a methodological strategy, the careful consideration
of identities as existential, ideological, and historical modes of self-
definition in relation to the world is intended to make visible and clarify
procedures and strategies employed in the assemblage and disruptions
of identities.

4. I will discuss the use of "identit*ies*" in the plural further on; however in general,
the singular, "identity," is deployed in order to accentuate the incorporation of
multiplicity without privileging either dissonance or compatibility. This concept is
analogous to the Creation in the Torah (Genesis), a multiplicity that is both complementary and complimentary; thus totalizing but not reductive.

Anthropologist Ivan Karp has prudently commented, "all attempts to understand life in its wholeness are philosophical."[5] In that context, this chapter draws on and integrates insights from philosophy that elucidate particularly compelling theoretical propositions. Specifically, the following discussion is engaged primarily, though not only, with the ideas of Hannah Arendt,[6] Jean Paul Sartre, Emmanuel Levinas, and Frantz Fanon. It seems to me that these thinkers, writing against the horror of racism and anti-Semitism, emphasize the power of the public sphere on the construction and reproduction of identities.

Chapters 2 and 3 take up more empirical discussions of interracial, Jewish, and Black identities. I will suggest that the experience and articulation of racial identities manifest an ongoing dialectical relationship between dimensions of the private self (which acquire meaning only in relation to others) and a public sphere where the variable of "race" — as *a social fact*[7] — changes the texture and contour of relations between human beings as individuals and as members of social groups

5. Cited from the book jacket of Bruce Wilshire (1982).

6. On the problematic racial attitudes of Hannah Arendt articulated in some of her writings, see Lewis R. Gordon (1995a, 88–89). Arendt's coverage of the Eichmann trial for the *New Yorker*, later published as a book, provoked a torrent of criticism against her thesis that without Jewish "complicity" less Jews would have been murdered by the Nazis. At least equally disturbing, to many of her most prominent critics, was the message contained in her choice of subtitle: *A Report on the Banality of Evil* (Podhoretz 1963; Heilbut 1983). However one feels about these and several other points in her argument, it is crucial to appreciate that the rage against Arendt *and* against her report were fueled by the timing of its publication as well as the place and audience: the *New Yorker* was famous as a magazine without a letters-to-the-editor column, that is, without any forum for response, reaction, or rebuttal. Barely a decade after the Holocaust, Arendt's reports from Jerusalem (and the ensuing book) appeared in a climate where there were no Holocaust study programs, the literature was still very limited, and the world was not yet prepared to hear the message so well known forty years later, saliently encapsulated by Lucy S. Dawidowicz's commanding title *The War against the Jews: 1933–1945*.

7. Emile Durkheim's definition of a social fact "is any way of acting, whether fixed or not, capable of exerting over the individual an external constraint; or which is general over the whole of a given society whilst having an existence of its own, independent of its individual manifestations" (Durkheim 1982, 59–60). Bourdieu refines this notion of social facts as things, to specify social facts as socially constructed objects of knowledge (Bourdieu 1991).

precisely because it is in this public space that race acquires its rhetorical, conceptual, and legal salience. This chapter, leaning toward a discussion of the public self, begins with the issue of self and identity from philosophical perspectives.

The anxiety that propels and suspends any conclusive resolution to philosophical discourse reveals the predicament of any discussion on identity. And I intentionally use the word "anxiety," for it seems to me that the philosophical quest for an understanding of the meaning of beingness arises from an original uncertainty about humankind: our relation to the external world and to each other. Existential questions that inform moral and ethical issues are fundamentally linked to the delicate problem of identity. This can be illustrated by two questions that subtly underline a reflection on identity: *who am I?* and *what am I?*

Hannah Arendt refers to Augustine, who introduced these *anthropological* questions into philosophy.[8] One poses the question to one's self and answers that *who* is a concrete material presence in the world. It expresses an assertion of particularity and uniqueness — one is a named identifiable physical presence distinguished from someone else or, as Sartre put it in *Being and Nothingness*, "The other is the one who is not me and the one I am not" (1966, 312).

The question of time and evolving identities is not always addressed by individuals. In our everyday lives, we usually do not think of ourselves as unfinished projects. In general, when faced with the question "Who are you?" one's basic tendency is to reduce and temporalize one's self with regard to others: instead of self-representation as a *being in the process of becoming*, a series of facts from the past are (re)cited. These are intended to establish the individual as different than, or set apart from, another individual.[9]

Sartre critiques this response as one governed by a process of selective information, which, in turn, evidences the failure to apprehend the self as a totality. As he demonstrates in *Being and Nothingness*, one cannot simultaneously be the subject and object of reflection. The *reflecting I* does not correspond to the *I reflected upon* and, therefore, all

8. Note that the etymological meaning of the word "anthropou-logos" is a speaking about humans (Mudimbe 1988, 1994; Arendt 1989).

9. See Lawrence Grossberg's discussion of identity and difference, which moves beyond the Cartesian problematic that privileged consciousness and which makes unity of the subject dependent on the unity of time (1993).

our efforts to present ourselves in terms of time are futile.[10] The present and past do not meet, and the complexity and unfolding dimension of selves, always in the process of creation, is occluded.

The question "*What* am I" addresses a very different inquiry. It orients both the question of one's qualities and of ontological status: What does *beingness* signify? How does *beingness* acquire meaning? However, this too is often inadequately answered by presenting a series of facts concerning one's material presence or one's socially confirmed status: I am a woman, I am an American, I am an educator, and so on. Hannah Arendt, concerned with the nature of the human condition at the level of concrete intersubjective relations, leaves the question "What am I?" to theological exegesis, in which the issue of human nature is inextricably linked to questions about the nature of God (1989, 11). She notes that

[i]n acting and speaking, men show who they are, reveal actively their unique personal identities and thus make their appearance in the human world, while their physical identities appear without any activity of their own in the unique shape of the body and sound of their voice. (1989, 179)

Similar to Sartre, Arendt contends that the projected "who" is concealed from the individual him/herself and only partially accessible to others,

The moment we want to say *who* somebody is, our very vocabulary leads us astray into saying *what* he is; we get entangled in a description of qualities he necessarily shares with others like him. (1989, 181)[11]

The specificity of an individual's uniqueness cannot be grasped in language, yet individuals are linked through action and speech. It is this *inter-est* (Arendt 1989, 182) that is subjective and intangible and which

10. Dorinne Kondo (1990) effectively discusses this in terms of the eye/I and her experience as an American anthropologist of Japanese origin conducting research in Japan, where she was often mistaken for *being* Japanese. A climax is reached when she recognizes herself as "the other" in the reflection of a mirror. From this realization, she subsequently founds her model of self as illusory.

11. In her introduction to Walter Benjamin's *Illuminations*, Arendt again points out "[t]he point is that in society everybody must answer the question of *what* he is — as distinct from the question of *who* he is — which his role is and his function, and the answer of course can never be: I am unique, not because of the implicit arrogance but because the answer would be meaningless" (1968, 3).

Arendt calls "the 'web' of human relationships, indicating by the metaphor its somewhat intangible quality" (1989, 183).[12]

It is through action and speech that individuals reveal themselves always and foremost as "subjects, as distinct and unique persons." Although the philosophical question of and approach to Being intersects uncomfortably with theology, the philosophical endeavor highlights important issues that anticipate and evidence the limitations any theory of identity can advance when the focus is on the isolated self. The "I" may be thought as analogous to a blank canvas that is filled only at death. Both Arendt and Emmanuel Levinas adopt this view of the individual as an incomplete project whose essence "can come into being only when life departs leaving behind nothing but a story" (Arendt 1989, 193).

Identity is always, and can only be, defined in front of others (regardless of their physical presence). Without falling in a mistaken diagnosis of schizophrenia, the self can be conceptualized as both stable and under continual reformulations. Or, as Levinas articulates it, "the Other as Other is not only an alter ego: the Other is what I myself am not" (1992, 48). As will be shown, Levinas is not presenting self-definition as a negation in the conflictual mode found in Cartesian perspectives, but rather self defined contextually — with others.

The Cartesian cogito reassures a sense of (inner) self through inference — thinking is a necessary but insufficient condition to bridging a distinction between one's actual presence in the world and the essence of one's being. Descartes's method of deduction, in which he can only be certain that the capacity to doubt is unequivocal evidence that one is doubting, is ultimately unsatisfying and potentially threatening for it tends toward a solipsistic perspective.[13]

The Cartesian cogito, according to Paul Ricoeur, represents a "truth as vain as it is invincible" and is also false consciousness (Ricoeur 1974, 17–18). He maintains that it is through the mediation of the exterior world that the subject of the cogito acquires significance. Existence is

12. For a variation of the metaphoric use of "webs" (webs of understanding) see Clifford Geertz (1973, 5).

13. Maurice Merleau-Ponty expands on the perspectival limitation of the Cartesian cogito, which does not account for "myself which is other" as well as "the other who is not I" (1973, 134).

translated into a sense of self that acquired meaning only through the network of relationships established within the material world and with other human beings (Ricoeur 1974, 22). Descartes's concern, in contrast, is solely with the existence of consciousness as a privileged and original point of certainty, separate from, but analogous to, the spatial world of external objects (Levinas 1992, 18).[14]

Charles Taylor, a political scientist, philosopher, and leading proponent of hermeneutics, notes that the fundamentally *dialogical* character of human life is "rendered almost invisible by the overwhelmingly monological bent of mainstream modern philosophy" (1992, 32). He centers his attention on the dialectic of identity (which is socially derived) and the modern quest for recognition. In this regard, Taylor comments on identity at two levels. He argues that in the intimate sphere, "We define our identity always in dialogue with, sometimes in struggle against, the things our significant others want to see in us" (1992, 34). In the public sphere, according to Taylor, "the modern notion of identity" has brought the politics of difference and the politics of universalism into conflict while both principles found the discourse of recognition (1992).

The roots of a political problem originate from this philosophical observation at the moment when the self is constituted as a community of selves distinct from another community.[15] In his essay "History and

14. If in the Western philosophical discourse of autonomous selves, the always already adult is, very specifically, a white, Christian, male adult, how should we respond to the *complaint* in Descartes's comment that "our predicament is that we have been children" when it is proposed for serious consideration in the late twentieth century? Thematizing from the perspective of male reason, which negates the presence of women (for there are no mothers giving birth in these meditations), male philosophers simultaneously constituted the world of females by a series of negations and thereby defined women's identity as a lack. Lack becomes that which is negative: "the lack of autonomy, the lack of independence, the lack of the phallus" (Benhabib 1992, 157). This observation leads to questioning whether profound social transformations can occur if the potentially liberating value of a philosophy is betrayed by its primary articulators.

15. Claude Lévi-Strauss articulates the consequences of this problem almost as a lamentation: "The brotherhood of man acquires a concrete meaning when it makes us see, in the poorest tribe, a confirmation of our own image and an experience, the lessons of which we can assimilate, along with so many others. . . . Being human

the Dialectic," Claude Lévi-Strauss reproaches Sartre's historical analysis of the "we" of Western culture, demonstrating that Western philosophy is a sociologization of the Cartesian cogito, which poses the consciousness of the I as the only certain mode of existence.

By recognizing the Other as merely a being *because* I can make an analogy from observation, the "we" that Sartre moves to is a sociologization — the I thus positing They as absolute Others that we imagine: I is to the Other as the We is to the They. In drawing attention to the consequences of extending this philosophical analogy to the political realm, Lévi-Strauss critiques the ethnocentricity underlying Sartre's notions of subjectivity.[16] These, he argues, negate the reality of anthropology, which undertakes to understand society on its own rationality and which should begin with a dissolution of that European category, "man" (Lévi-Strauss 1966; 1991, 117–18).[17]

A different approach to the question of self, identity, and the relation that this question has to other(s) can be elicited from the Judaic injunction, articulated by Hillel.[18] This approach also offers an excellent illustration of how to envision identity/ies in the public world: "If I am not for me, *who* will be, but if I am only for myself, *what* am I." It complements another Talmudic prescription: "it is not incumbent for

---

signifies, for each one of us, belonging to a class, a society, a country, a continent, and a civilization; and for us European earth-dwellers, the adventure played out in the heart of the New World signifies in the first place that it was not our world and that we bear responsibility for the crime of its destruction; and secondly, that there will never be another New World: since the confrontation between the Old World and the New makes us conscious of ourselves." (1973, 393).

16. This is significant particularly in the aftermath of the Holocaust and World War II. Note that Lévi-Strauss was stripped of his French citizenship because he was recognized as Jewish regardless of his personal identification.

17. For an excellent and precise discussion of the arguments of Sartre and Lévi-Strauss as well as the epistemological and political context specific to France, see Robert Young (1990).

18. Hillel (ca. 50 BCE–CE 20), one of the great Mishnaic scholars, was president of the Sanhedrin during the reign of Herod, king of Judea. Among the methods of study he formulated were the seven hermeneutic laws of exegesis. Hillel is notable for positioning himself with the lower classes. His lenient interpretations of the law characterized the legacy of the school he founded, which is associated with humility and love of humankind.

thee to complete the task, but thou must not therefore desist from it." This is the essence of a commitment to working for social justice. Both statements are political and invoke an imperative stipulation that individuals are part of a world in which there are other human beings to whom they are accountable and for whom they are responsible.

The existential predicament is not the nature of being or the certainty of consciousness but the manner in which, as human beings who are endowed with consciousness, they are to act in relationship with others. Hillel's injunction refuses solipsism, insists on the self as part of the material world in which others are always present, and thus brackets the absolute recourse to a divine revelation from which Augustine cannot escape. Finally, it does not rest on a relativism that harbors in its shadows an incipient hierarchical value system.[19]

If, as I am suggesting, reflections on identity necessarily invoke the issue of the nature of being, and if, in turn, these reflections render a sense of self that is at the foundation of identity, then it is essential to appreciate the dilemma provoked by questions of "who" and "what" one is, culminating finally in two irreconcilable positions that demand very different methodological strategies. One position, from Descartes to Sartre — despite the fact that the latter attempts to overcome the inconsistencies inherent in a self-centered theory — is anchored by a conception of a transcendental self that distinguishes subjectivity from consciousness, bracketing that which is exterior. Subjectivity and consciousness intersect at the moment when an identity is thinkable. To be the subject of one's consciousness is to project some sense of self. Thus even Sartre allows for, at least, a partial — an incomplete — definition of who one is through the encounter with others.

In other words, it is through a process of scissiparity, in which the failure to apprehend oneself as a totality but rather as a being-for-others, that one is aware of and produces a plurality of invented selves to accommodate any given or specific situation. As a being-for-others,

19. Note that the negative formulation of Hillel's admonition, "what is hateful to you, do not do unto your neighbor; this is the entire Torah, all the rest is commentary," was challenged in Christian doctrine. Inverting the negative construction of the directive (Do unto others . . .) consequently introduced the question of including or translating the other in its subjectivity, which will, ultimately, characterize Christian historiography (Jewsiewicki and Mudimbe 1993).

one has a sense of being incomplete and therefore partially out of control. We can always be terrorized by this fundamental inability to see ourselves as others perceive us.[20] Consequently, how we project ourselves is, above all, a response to what we assume are the social expectations demanded of us. And this supposition need not be conscious — quite to the contrary.

One is socialized from childhood to conform to identities consonant with social expectations. It is only when one resists and rebels — self-conscious acts — that one takes responsibility for and assumes authorship of one's identity. Yet even here, where a sense of empowerment seems most salient, the predicament of the concept of identity as an irreconcilable opposition between being the subject and object within the matrix of human relations remains striking. One acts and sets in motion a series of other actions — "reaction," as Arendt puts it, "apart

20. A personal anecdote illustrates this possibility as an always potential *disruption*. During an early revision of this chapter, I had a late-night argument with a close friend and intellectual comrade over long-distance. By the time he telephoned me, Mathieu, usually very even-tempered, was already in a bad mood because of a series of irritating events over the course of the day. A friendship of several years was irrevocably eclipsed when Mathieu injected the startling accusation: "well you wouldn't understand, you're an American!" Less than a year had passed since he had reluctantly relinquished his status as a political refugee and accepted American citizenship. When Mathieu had arrived in the United States, he had immediately entered the ranks of migrant Third World intellectuals among whom nomadism provides a stability characteristic of the national confines of the academic world in which fellow travelers sojourn with the same transient documents.

"No I am *not*," I respond with indignation. "Maybe I was born and raised here but my parents aren't American and more than half my life was spent in Israel."

The indictment was memorable, for in that instant my sense of self — in its subjective political and particularistic dimensions — was challenged abruptly and unexpectedly. In the context of a friendship between two individuals who share the experience of being multicultural, the negation of my Jamaican and Jewish ancestry, a heritage that had seemingly been taken for granted as an integral aspect of *"who* I am," was now brought into an opposition with "the *who*" Mathieu had in mind. The gap demonstrates Charles Taylor's comment, cited earlier, that "[w]e define our identity always in dialogue with, sometimes in struggle against, the things our significant others want to see in us" (Taylor 1992, 34). In an instant of momentary anger, misrecognition exemplified and accentuated the gap between being subject (a being-in-itself) and object (a being-for-others). For critical comments on Third World intellectuals who become professional migrants in the American academy, see also Aijez Ahmad (1995) and Ali Behdad (1993).

from being a response, is always a new action that strikes out on its own and affects others" (1989, 190).

The intent of this exercise is to illuminate the impotence of epistemic or foundational essentializing:[21] to think in terms of an essential human nature negates the processual attribute of *being as becoming* (West 1993a, 181). The intention here is to underline the conditions of possibility that do enable us to think of identity as both a struggle and a practical political stance. This conceptualization will lead to the suggestion — presented as a proposition in the coda — that to be Black, Jewish, and interracial is to occupy a three-tier standpoint position: it is a cognitive and physical process of *being* in the world — in, and as a result of, a race-conscious society — *to be* an interruption, *to represent* a contestation, and *to undermine* the authority of classification.

Identity is formed in the interstice between recognition and being recognized. The notion of essentialism in which there is a permanent, authentic core is invalidated with the idea of relationships as reflections of individual, but intertwined, experiences that comprise interaction and manifest varying degrees of desire for recognition (Taylor 1992). Thus the second position, that of Hillel and implicitly of Arendt and Levinas, also discerns identity as a project but is less concerned with human essence per se. They consider identity contextually within the material world. This perspective commences with a sense of self that has meaning only through immersion in a concern with the human condition. Where Hannah Arendt speaks of activity and production, the reference is not merely to labor and the production of nonperishable commodities. I suggest her focus is always, even where it is not given explicit expression in the text, on identity as a product that unfolds in the public realm and whose definition requires the presence of others.[22] It is recognition that confers legitimacy and value:

The presence of others who see and hear what we see and hear assures us of the reality of the world and ourselves, and while the intimacy of a fully developed private life . . . will always greatly intensify and enrich the whole scale of

21. Diana Fuss presents an excellent analysis of both essentialism and constructionism (1989).

22. Political theorist and feminist scholar Seyla Benhabib engages with Arendt's theory of action in order to consider judgment as a moral faculty important to public culture (Benhabib 1992; Fraser 1994).

subjective emotions and private feelings, this intensification will always come to pass at the expense of the assurance of the reality of the world and men. (Arendt 1989, 50)

The significance of Levinas lies in his empathetic representation and explication of identity of the self as being constituted in the presence of and *for* the other. In a careful reading of Levinas and his contribution to literary theory, Susan Handelman accentuates his *confirmation* of the singularity of the I in the incessant task of purging the I of its egoism and arbitrariness: "this is termed goodness." "Difference" becomes non-indifference to the other, as Levinas affirms in the following:

To utter *I* to affirm the irreducible singularity in which the apology is pursued, means to possess a privileged place with regard to responsibilities for which no one can replace me and from which no one can release me. To be unable to shirk: this is the I. (Levinas *Totality & Infinity* 245, quoted in Handelman 1991, 222)

Providing a challenging juxtaposition to Sartre, Levinas refuses a celebration of free subjectivity and instead insists on the self as linked to the other in ethics, love, and obligation. It is significant and important to present Levinas's perspective as a counter to Sartre's egoism, as expressed in *No Exit*, that "Hell is other people" (Sartre 1949). Levinas's differing view is to think of self and other, not in dialectical opposition but interconnected wherein self is both unique and particular *and* defined in relation to the other.[23] Arnold Davidson points out the contrast between Sartre's reference to the self's "power of escaping, disengaging," an autonomy that lays the groundwork for a questionable democracy, and Levinas, for whom dignity is constituted from the responsibility we have for other: "It is in calling me to other men that Transcendence concerns me" (Davidson 1990, 44).

Levinas is not advancing an abstract philosophy, divorced from the existential dilemmas of *trying* to be a good human being, and, furthermore, this effort is an intrinsic component of identity. In comparison, one might consider the abstract philosophy of *Being and Nothingness* as suggestive of an intellectual game in which the primary (obviously

23. Although I have not included Martin Buber in this discussion, one should not forget his significant contribution to philosophical deliberations on self, other, and the dialogical relationship of I and Thou. See Theunissen (1984).

never stated) purpose is to be more clever than one's predecessors. Without detracting from this erudite masterpiece, one might also take seriously Gabriel Marcel's reproach of Sartre's pretentious assertion to the media (where spectacle and sound bite preclude substance) that God is dead, in contrast to Nietzsche's trembling and private admission. (Marcel 1963, 63–64)[24]

Handelman succinctly clarifies the roots and implications of Levinas's perspective:

Levinas is making all persons 'survivors' responsible without ever having decided to be so and before any voluntary act is undertaken. There is no escape. . . . All of Levinas's writing, with its difficulty and complexity, is a direct refutation of any attempt to relieve anyone of responsibility — from even such tangentially involved figures as de Man to the notorious Klaus Barbie, who at his trial for war crimes said, "I've forgotten about it. If they haven't, that's their concern." But even more, it also makes responsible everyone who excuses him- or herself precisely because he or she is not a Klaus Barbie — every one of us, even every reader of Levinas." (1991, 212)

Coming from the genealogical and political background that I do, I understand that this passage is intended to extend far beyond the context of genocide and inhumanity — it is a prescription for everyday life. The Holocaust was a culmination of a system of values and attitudes savage at the core. How one conducts him/herself with others (subordinates, equals, whomever one is in relation to whether stranger or intimate companion) is relevant, significant, and should be grounded by ethical obligation: *we are always responsible.*

With the completion of his major three-volume project on mythology, Lévi-Strauss responded to Sartre. In his conclusion to *Origins of Table Manners*, Lévi-Strauss contends forcefully

If the origin of table manners, and more generally of correct behavior, is to be found, as I think I have shown, in deference towards the world . . . [i]t teaches us, at any rate, that the formula "hell is other people," which has achieved such

24. It is not polemical but political to note that my readings are influenced by a firm conviction that philosophical reflections acquire meaning and command respect *not* as theory, but as praxis; *not* as intellectual exhibitionism, but as a basis for concrete action that always manifests a commitment to integrity. Without this commitment, radical and constructive social change is not possible (Alinsky 1972).

fame, is not so much a philosophical proposition as an ethnographical statement about our civilization. For, since childhood, we have been accustomed to
fear impurity as coming from without. When they assert, on the contrary that
"hell is ourselves," savage peoples give us a lesson in humility. . . . [S]ound
humanism does not begin with oneself, but puts the world before life, life
before man, and respect for others before self-interest. (1978, 507–8)[25]

In a variation on the preceding perspectives, Seyla Benhabib similarly
argues against traditional philosophy's presentation of the autonomous
self as always already an adult. Instead, she displaces this autonomous
self with the moral self, an embedded and embodied being that recalls
the constitution of self in Levinasian terms. Benhabib defines an embodied identity as a mode of being in one's body and of living the body: "The
self becomes an *I* in that it appropriates from the human community a
mode of psychically, socially and symbolically experiencing its bodily
identity" (1992, 152).[26]

25. One might argue, convincingly, that the link between Levinas, Lévi-Strauss,
and Arendt is a specifically Jewish one. The foundation on which a Jewish people
came into existence resides precisely in privileging the relationship between autonomous subjects, between individual subjects and God, and, finally, between a collectivity of autonomous subjects (who then become a community with a past and a
future) and God. The autonomous subject is — *always already* — defined in relation
to others, that is, comes into being as a subject whose subject position is an inherent
product of social interactions. To argue that there is an intellectual tradition out of
which both Jewish thinkers and thinkers who are Jewish emerge and, to push the
limits of this abstract possibility further, suggest an element of predictability, is to
follow Lévi-Strauss's matter-of-fact response to the comment that "he's the very
picture of a Jewish intellectual." Lévi-Strauss, a partisan of assimilation, replied, "I
admit that certain mental attitudes are perhaps more common among Jews than
elsewhere. Attitudes that come from the profound feeling of belonging to a national
community, all the while knowing that in the midst of this community there are
people — fewer and fewer of them I admit — who reject you. One keeps one's sensitivity attuned, accompanied by the irrational feeling that in all circumstances one
has to do a bit more than other people to disarm potential critics. It doesn't upset me
if this effort, explicable as it is, gives offense" (1991, 156). Parenthetically, Zygmunt
Bauman, whose contribution to critical social thinking has been invaluable, echoes
these sentiments in response to similar questions (1992, 225 ff.). Lévi-Strauss's remarks should be kept in mind when considering the issue of Jewish identity, membership, and community in chapter 4.

26. This is very reminiscent of Bourdieu's notion of the habitus as inhabited

Benhabib argues that with the paradigmatic shift from a focus on consciousness to the interrogation of language, the self-reflecting self has disappeared into the subject, who in turn "dissolves into a chain of significations of which it was supposed to be the initiator" (1992, 214). Consequently, in contrast to Cartesian *dis*interest in the gendered and racial positions characterizing the autonomous and disembodied self, postmodernist theoreticians *deconstruct* gendered, racial, and religious positions and extol what feminist philosopher Susan Bordo repudiates as "the epistemological fantasy of *becoming* multiplicity" (Bordo 1990, 145). This fragmentation, I suggest, is the other side of assimilation in consequence.

Starting from the same premise as Benhabib, that the Hegelian dialectic reduces the other to the same, Yedullah Kazmi focuses on the resultant subordination of difference to identity. Kazmi's reading (that the other is that who is not me) directs him against the analogy between self and other as inherently asymmetrical. The other in his/her difference lacks something and consequently is in need of re-formation in my image. He states that "[t]his is the dialectic of identity; that which is different is defined as abnormal, and then is assimilated — the negation of negation. And that which cannot be assimilated (cannot be normalized) is excluded" (Kazmi 1994, 71).

Regardless of Kazmi's intentions, the discerning reader may notice the trace of Lévi-Strauss's reproach against the ethnocentric sociologization of the cogito — the others are not like us: we can dominate them and finally we can enslave them. In the status of slave, the other is dehumanized, excluded from the realm of humanity yet indispensable for the slave-master's identity.[27]

Benhabib and Kazmi, as well as Arendt and Levinas, depreciate the value and critique the intellectual and moral efficacy of an approach in which identity is relational *and* conditioned by negation — the Jew is *not* a Gentile; the Black is *not* white; the woman is *not* a man. It is through exclusion from this "spectator model of the self" that each

---

(1977; 1991). See, for example, his discussion of working-class men, linguistic competence, and the relation between articulatory styles and the body.

27. See Fanon's chapter "The Negro and Recognition" in *Black Skin, White Masks*, which responds to Hegel's paradigm of the master-slave relationship (1967).

group is defined, marked, and dehumanized (Benhabib 1992, 207). Not surprisingly, Hegel can pronounce the following: "What we properly understand by Africa, is the Unhistorical, Undeveloped Spirit, still involved in the conditions of mere nature" (quoted in Benhabib 1992, 235n.31).

I want to intervene here and shift explicit attention to Jewish identity negatively defined. In *The Anti-Semite and the Jew*, Sartre contends that "Anti-Semitism is not merely the joy of hating; it brings positive pleasures too. By treating the Jew as an inferior and pernicious being, I affirm at the same time that I belong to the elite" (Sartre 1965, 19).[28] In other words, an essential component of the identity of the anti-Semite is founded on distinguishing him/herself from his/her opposite other and defining the other differently. If the Jew is inferior, the anti-Semite confirms his/her own superiority. The Jew functions as the model of indifference.[29]

Fanon draws on Sartre's analysis to argue that just as anti-Semitism is not a *Jewish* problem, "[i]t is the racist who creates his inferior" (1967, 37). Thus, the emancipation of the Jews in the French Revolution on the basis that they were human beings — not because they were Jews — makes salient the refusal of many sectors in France to acknowledge the legitimacy of Jewish identity.

Clearly, identity is relational — that is, at the individual or the collective level, an identity presupposes the unique and the particular. It is the condition of negation that is at issue, and here cultural studies analyst

28. Sartre's ambition for the assimilation of the Jews without, however, questioning French identity is challenged by Harold Rosenberg who argues against Sartre's denying Jewish history and continuity (1970).

29. Sartre gives little attention to the role of theology. One of the major American Protestant theologians of the century, Reinhold Niebuhr, was a vocal critic of Protestant anti-Semitism in the United States. As early as 1933, Niebuhr had alerted his audience to Protestant German support of Hitler, and he protested the *racial* basis of the Nazi policies against Jews (Ross 1980). Note, as well, Mary Douglas's observation that Christian influences were a powerful force in shaping stereotypes of Jews: "living in the interstices of the power structure." Their social status was viewed with ambivalence as their economic role in the society was significant. Resentment of Jewish prominence in the commercial arena was fueled by theological antagonism, because "their real offence is always to have been outside the formal structure of Christendom" (Douglas 1970, 104).

Lawrence Grossberg makes a salutary intervention. He too begins with difference as constituting a negative relation to the identity of someone else (1933). However, Grossberg draws a theoretical differentiation between two distinct but related notions: *difference* and *otherness*. Difference is adversarial in that I define myself *against* the other whose identity, in turn, depends totally on their relation to mine. This echoes Sartre's conflict-ridden and circular relation of self and other:

> At the origin of the problem of the existence of others, there is a fundamental presupposition: others are *the Other*, that is the self which *is not* myself. Therefore we grasp here a negation as the constitutive structure of the being-of-others. (1966, 312)

In other words, "the for-itself is not what it is and is what it is not" (Sartre 1966, 472). Here surfaces a dissimilar approach to otherness as both hypothesis and practice between Sartre's depiction of other and the differentiation Grossberg advances: otherness, in contrast, is positive in that it recognizes the other in his/her own place, independently of any specific relation of difference (Grossberg 1993, 10).[30]

Consider Sartre's comments on the paradox that the more the individual Jew tries to assimilate, the more his/her being a Jew is confirmed. If for Jews assimilation is both tenuous and in bad faith, nevertheless, *"a Jew, white among men, can deny that he is a Jew but from black skin there is no escape"* (Sartre 1963; italics added). In that context, then, one may summon the examples of anthropologists Franz Boas, Melville Herskovits, and Hortense Powdermaker, less as individuals troubled by their identities, and more as examples of Jewish intellectuals grappling with the tension between universalism and particularity.[31]

---

30. This reformulation of alterity as respectful of the distinct autonomy of self and other is reminiscent of Merleau-Ponty's observation that "Myself and the other are like two *nearly* concentric circles which can be distinguished only by a slight and mysterious slippage" (1973, 134).

31. A comparison of scholars' theoretical orientations may illuminate how personal histories informed the constitution of areas of study as well as the conceptualization of notions of race and ethnicity in the social sciences in general and in anthropology in particular (Melnick 1993; Whittaker 1990; Whitten and Szwed 1970). For instance, an effort to secure a sense of identity through assimilation may have conditioned the foci and treatment of anti-Semitism, racism, and race relations

In 1921 Boas flatly asserted in the *Yale Quarterly Review*, "It would seem that man being what he is, the negro problem will not disappear in America until the negro blood has been so much diluted that it will no longer be recognized just as anti-Semitism will not disappear until the last vestige of the Jew as Jew has disappeared" (quoted in Lewis 1988, 138; Jackson 1986, 98). As Ellen Messer stresses, Boas was basically an assimilationist who believed that Jewishness was an unnecessary otherness and by analogy, he was not sympathetic to nurturing a separate Black racial identity (Messer 1986; Stocking 1968, 149–50). Racism and anti-Semitism would disappear, in his view, through intermarriage.[32]

Although Boas's views were intended as an antiracist position, I see no reason to excuse or bracket (and thus not hold him accountable to) the illusory anticipation and expectation of the voluntary disappearance of the Jewish community.[33] In the context of his own era, the

---

in America by Boasian anthropologists, who were also important to the conceptualization of the field of Afro American anthropology (Cerroni-Long 1987; Fraser 1991; St. Clair Drake 1980). Thus, one might situate these scholars specifically into the historical context of immigrant and first-generation Jewish Americans and African Americans who grappled, independently and in concert — and occasionally in contest — with civil rights issues and with their shifting political, legal, social, and economic status and positioning in the wider and dominant white Protestant culture (Edgcomb 1993; Harris 1968; Kuper 1988; Stocking 1986).

Martin Jay's appraisal of the Frankfurt School is applicable to the Jewish circle of anthropologists, some of whom also joined the Ethical Culture movement: "If one seeks a common thread running through individual biographies of the inner circle (of the Institute), the one that immediately comes to mind is their birth into families of middle or upper-middle-class Jews. . . . If one were to characterize the Institute's general attitude toward the 'Jewish question,' it would have to be seen as similar to that expressed by another radical Jew almost a century before, Karl Marx. In both cases the religious or ethnic issue was clearly subordinated to the social. . . . In fact, the members of the Institute were anxious to deny any significance at all to their ethnic roots" (quoted in Outlaw 1990, n.35).

32. Leonard B. Glick presents a careful examination of Boas's refusal to recognize and identify with Jewish cultural identity, and the manner in which his biographical background — as a German Jew — notably informed his ideas about culture and assimilation (1982).

33. See Jacob Katz's essay "Misreadings of Anti-Semitism," in which he comments, "the predicament of emancipated Jewry and ultimately the cause of its tragic

politicization of Jewish identity in Europe, especially with the Zionist movement, and Boas's own encounter with German anti-Semitism, which stimulated his emigration to the United States, all compel a negative evaluation of Boas's opinion.[34] Ber Borochov (1881–1917), one of the first Russian Jewish Marxists to apply a Marxist analysis to the European situation of Jews, provides a refreshing refutation of Boas's statement:

Death and suicide are the most radical solution to the Jewish problem. If there were no Jews, there would be no problem. . . . No honest statesman or idealist ever attempted to solve, for example, the Polish question by suggesting that the Polish people should cease existing. . . . Only to us Jews have self-appointed "physicians" had the audacity, the shamelessness, to preach national suicide. (Borochov 1937, 85)

One might link Boas's sentiments to a careful reading of the relevant section of Hortense Powdermaker's *Stranger and Friend* in order to

---

end, was rooted not in one or another ideology but in the fact that Jewish Emancipation had been tacitly tied to an illusory expectation — the disappearance of the Jewish community of its own volition" (1983, 43).

34. Unlike Boas, Zionist Marxists, such as Dov Ber Borochov and Nahman Syrkin, analyzed anti-Semitism against the structural position of Jews as the alien Other within a capitalist system. Syrkin, whose doctorate in Philosophy was from the University of Berlin, had called for a Socialist Jewish state in 1896, arguing that full civic rights would not solve the anomaly of the Jewish middle class. Historian Walter Laqueur writes of Syrkin: "[he] was not a fully fledged Marxist but he regarded the class struggle as one of the central themes in Jewish history, reflected both in the Pentateuch and the Prophets. The history of ancient Judaism as he interpreted it was the unfolding struggle of the Jewish toiling masses for a Socialist way of life" (1972, 273).

Ber Borochov pushed the Marxist analysis further than Syrkin and delineated a structure in which the Jewish laboring class was at the apex of an inverted pyramid, whereas most Jews were involved in mental labor, trade financing, and money lending (Borochov 1937). I should add that between 1967 and 1970 I was a member of Hashomer Hatzair, the Marxist Zionist youth movement under the wing of the Socialist Kibbutz Movement in Israel. In addition for a brief period in 1969, I participated in the New York–based Jewish Liberation Project. In both organizations, Ber Borochov's ideas were pivotal to their principles. Not parenthetically, during this period I was also one of the founders of the Black Students' Council at the Brearley School.

highlight her motives behind the choice of a Black community in Mississippi over Edward Sapir's suggestion that she study a community of Hassidic Jews (Powdermaker 1966, 131). Anthropologist Gertrude Fraser suggests that Powdermaker's romantic view of a cultural authenticity among the immigrant Jews reflected her own dis-ease with assimilation and the snobbish attitudes of the reform German Jewish community into which she was born (Fraser 1991, 405–6; Powdermaker 1966, 21–22). Yet a former student, Erica Bourguignon, recollects that Powdermaker "never mentioned her Jewishness" (Bourguignon 1991, 421). Powdermaker believed Jewishness could be deferred by dealing with the American Negro: "Her proposal for the Mississippi study emerges as if it had been formed out of whole cloth, pulled out of the sub-conscious, and arrived at by a set of oppositional strategies — not Jews, not Native Americans, but 'Negroes' " (G. Fraser 1991, 405).

Turning to Melville Herskovits, as historian Walter Jackson points out, one finds a first-generation American Jew, born in the Midwest who also defers his own ethnic identity by focusing on Blacks. As a scholar, Herskovits would eventually become an avid spokesperson for acknowledging the retention of African cultural elements among american Blacks. Yet like Boas, he would also argue for the virtues of assimilation of Jews and Blacks. Despite (or because of) his encounter with anti-Semitism during his first years at Northwestern University, Herskovits insisted on the insignificance of his Jewish identity (Jackson 1986, 110).[35] During this same period, his academic research interests were concentrated on Afro American and African peoples. Implicitly if not explicitly, however, his attitude about his own identity actually attested

35. Before finding the intellectually comfortable milieu at Columbia University, Herskovits initially explored the possibility of becoming a rabbi, studying Hebrew and theology at the Reform Movement's Hebrew Union College in Cincinnati. This brief interlude was followed by a virtual withdrawal and aloofness from Jewishness (Jackson 1986). Historian August Meier, a first-generation American Jew, attributes his own interest in mixed-race ancestry to Herskovitz. Meier, who grappled with the tension between an ethnic identity and anti-Semitism, was raised to think of himself only as American, assimilationist, and anti-Zionist. This alienating intellectual orientation provided a departure point for Meier's immersion in literature on race relations and the Black experience. Eventually, when he went to teach at Tougloo College, he found it "helpful" to join the Unitarian Church (Meier 1992).

to an ambitious desire for recognition as an acculturated — white — American: "[N]either in training, in tradition, in religious beliefs, nor in culture am I what might be termed a person any more Jewish than any other American born and raised in a typical Middle Western milieu" (quoted in Jackson 1986, 101).

Jackson calls attention to the criticism Herskovits articulated against chauvinism and racial prejudice among Jews and to his early disapproval of the emergence of (Negro) race consciousness, which, during the 1920s, asserted itself as a resistance to assimilation (e.g., the Harlem Renaissance, the Garvey Movement, and the early Pan-African Congresses). Convinced that cultural pluralism, advocated by Horace Kallen,[36] was political myopia, Herskovits wrote:

The social ostracism to which (the Negroes) are subjected is only different in extent from that to which the Jew is subjected. The fierce reaction of race-pride is quite the same in both groups. But, whether in Negro or in Jew, the protest avails nothing, apparently. (quoted in Jackson 1986, 102)

In the 1920s and '30s, a new emphasis on researching common links across a Black diaspora served the purpose of a project of vindication. By the 1940s, Herskovits's ideas of acculturation shifted and evolved to focus on the survival and diffusion of African culture within the Black slave population and inherited by their descendants (Mintz and Price 1976; Szwed 1974). Unfortunately, his theoretical approach also channeled interest away from the process of interracial cultural dynamics.[37] In the context of the United States, that approach encour-

---

36. Kallen, who was Jewish and a vocal advocate of cultural pluralism, emphasized hyphenated identities and the legitimacy of ethnic affirmation in the public sphere (Walzer 1990). He was also one of the founding members of the journal *Judaism*.

37. I am not suggesting that among sectors of the African American community in the United States different types of cultural articulations — what perhaps may be more usefully seen as styles — and specific institutional structures did not develop that were significantly different from those of various white European American communities. I do, however, insist that these are practices and productions that need to be specified, contextualized, and problematized — not presumed. Instead, texts dealing with African Americans have tended to romanticize, mystify, or dramatize behaviors as culturally distinctive *Black* practices (Azoulay 1996).

aged a conceptual segregation of Blacks and whites that became more ubiquitous than spatial segregation.[38] What is interesting, however, is that although Herskovits could conclude that slavery did not completely erase the legacy of African cultural patterns, he was unable to discern the patterns that reproduced, in a diaspora that extended from Europe to Africa and Asia to America, a recognizable Jewish identity for two millennia. More than that, Jackson notes that Herskovits argued that Jews "possessed no common language, culture or religion, and that their only common experience was a sense of being vaguely different from those around them" (Jackson 1986, 101).

Herskovits devoted his attention to the Black diaspora and neglected the parallels with the Jewish diaspora. Nonetheless, I suggest that identities take shape or surface at the moment when their potentiality are denied. Although most of the people I interviewed placed little weight on the significance of *being Jewish*, nevertheless all but one did indeed reveal a moment in which *being a Jew* — not doing (content) — evidences an identity that demands recognition and refutes erasure. This revelation is usually expressed in a projection of the past. I asked one (white) woman, who describes her children as "mixed-race," whether she had raised her children to be consciously Jewish and she said no. Yet each year they celebrated Passover and within this observance the subject of slavery and liberation linked the Jewish experience to the Black experience in metaphors of exile and diaspora, Moses and Pharaoh. Nonetheless, Nina insisted she did not believe in God and had no affinity to Jewishness as an ethnicity. After a little more questioning, however, she finally declared, "well look, if tomorrow they start handing out yellow stars, I'll stand up and be counted. So yeah, I guess you could say being Jewish to me is more a political identity."

Referring back to Boas's solution to the problem of anti-Semitism and racism, and more contemporary attitudes on transcending racial identities, Lewis R. Gordon provides a refreshing assertion relevant to

---

38. In a conversation remembering Herskovits, his student James Fernandez points out the tension facing all of Boas's students, "that Afro-Americans would assimilate, that the African past was past and could make no difference. On the other side, there was the argument of cultural persistence" (Launey 1988, 8).

both Jews and to american Blacks (and which echoes Borochov's comments on national suicide):[39]

Do black people have a right to exist? Since I don't know of any group of human beings who can make a viable response to such a loaded question, a question loaded in the sense of playing on the bare fact that existence in itself justifies nothing save that one faces the choice to go on or the self-defeating resort of suicide, we can see the oppressive nature of the demand. Yet, black people face this demand everyday. To be black in the United States is the ever-present call to justify still being around. (1995b, 43)

39. In his acknowledgments, Lewis R. Gordon provides this critical autobiographical detail as part of his legacy and identity, "[to] my maternal grandfather Edgar Solomon, who did not live long enough to know that his daughter had a child in 1962, a child who has become known as the living embodiment of his spirit. I never met Edgar Solomon, yet I have always known him. A man of African and Jewish parents, his death away from 'home' signified the two forms of diaspora that he embodied" (1995a, xiv).

2

CONTEXTS, SOCIAL CATEGORIES, AND

CONDITIONS OF POSSIBILITY

This chapter serves three functions. It is prefaced by a delineation of the three conditions of possibility that permit a discussion of Jewish Black identities.[1] The first section presents a brief historical overview of the experience of Blacks and Jews in the United States, calling attention to several points of similarity and difference. The second section maps out the difficulties of defining the meaning of a Jewish identity since the emancipation of Jews in Europe. The chapter ends with a discussion on the significance of racial/ethnic identity in the Jewish and in the Black communities.

Black *and* Jewish *and* Interracial: Conditions of Possibility

"Black and Jewish" as a reference point for commenting on identity is an event in need of explanation. In retrospect, three conditions needed to be met in order to confer specificity on this particular conjunction. Each of these was necessary, but alone none would have been sufficient. First, in 1967 the Supreme Court decided in favor of the Lovings (Richard Loving and Mildred Jeter) in their appeal against the state of Virginia. Until then, marriage across the color line was prohibited by law throughout the American South. Although Jews seemed to have

1. It must always be kept in mind that the context in which I am focusing on the convergence of interracial, Black, and Jewish — as an aspect of identities that can be named — is specifically as a characteristic of the discourse on interracial marriage that is peculiar and distinctive to the United States. The only other country in which this particular focus could be applied (and serve as a useful comparison) would have been South Africa under apartheid. Because of the racial structure and strict enforcement of sexual apartheid, the situation was very different. There are Jewish South African women (of European origin) who are married to Black South Africans, but

been conceptualized (literally) and understood (metaphorically) more as "honorary" whites than "authentically" white, they have also been included and counted as part of the white population (Baldwin 1970; Baldwin and Mead 1971; Lincoln 1970; Stepan and Gilman 1993).[2]

Second, American attitudes about race have always marked Blacks as different — the primary racial other. As historian Nathan Huggins — who was Jewish, Black, and interracial — pointed out, "black-white dualism has always been manifest in American life" and therefore Black "cultural boundaries are very loose and must be seen in the broader context of American history" (Huggins 1971a, 16–17).[3] The saliency

---

these marriages took place outside the country. The case of South Africa, for both Jews and Blacks, deserves very careful attention and therefore any further comment would be unsatisfactory. Parenthetically, it is notable that in *A Sport of Nature* (1987), Nadine Gordimer deals more directly with Jewish references than in any of her previous novels. The theme of deliverance marking the holiday of Passover is given prominence, and the daughter of Hillela — the character around whom the novel develops (with a deliberately identifiable Jewish name) — and her African nationalist husband, is named Nomo, after Winnie Mandela (Schwartz 1987). Although Nomo disappears in the text, eventually growing up to become an international model, her presence as a character is no more accidental or incidental than the calculated name Gordimer chose for Hillela. Nomo, in sum, is Jewish and African.

2. Horace Mann Bond describes how deeply ingrained theological anti-Semitism can surface without second thought in a forty-eight-year-old childhood recollection. Called "Nigger" for the first time in his life by a six-year-old (Bond was twelve), he responded sharply, "You Christ-killer" and "the little boy burst into tears, and I have felt badly ever since" (1965, 4). Reflecting as an adult on the incident, Bond points out that nothing in his background consciously prepared him to think "how this 'bad' word came into my vocabulary," and he attributed it to the indirect influence of the vocal Southern white anti-Jewish atmosphere surrounding the lynching of Leo Frank. Whereas Bond accentuates a relation between anti-Semitism and class competition between Jews and Negroes, the Leo Frank affair evidences that if for Black Christians, Jews were "just another variety of white" exploiters, for white Christians, Jews were a *racial Other* in addition to often being a political irritant. A contemporary illustration of this is found in the film *Driving Miss Daisy* (1989), which captures poignantly the anomalous position Jews occupied alongside the well-defined white and Black Christian populations (Lucius Outlaw, Haverford philosophy professor, born in Mississippi into a working-class Black family, responding in a private conversation with me to Black criticism of the movie).

3. For a moving portrait of Nathan Huggins, who was sincerely reluctant to accept Harvard's invitation, see Lawrence W. Levine (1993). My thanks to Professor

of an America marked first and foremost by the Black and white context, into which migrants and immigrants are *subsequently* incorporated, integrated, or excluded, is petitioned by educator William Pinar. In an instructive essay entitled "Notes on Understanding Curriculum as a Racial Text," he poses the question "Who are we as Americans?" and answers that the "African-American's presence informs every element of American life. For European American students to understand who they are, they must understand that their existence is predicated upon, interrelated to, and constituted in fundamental ways by African Americans" (1993).

Pinar's emphasis on the profound effect of the inseparable, intertwined historical experience Black and white Americans share includes the necessity of contextualizing this association within the relationship between the North and the South. Historian John Philips also underscores these insights in a provocatively titled essay, "The African Heritage of White America": "[O]ur understanding of white American society is incomplete without an understanding of the black and African impact on white America" (1990, 237).

Cornel West's reiteration of the need for an examination of ways in which Whiteness is "a politically constructed category parasitic on 'Blackness' " is a project Toni Morrison effectively carries out for literature in her book *Playing in the Dark* (West 1993a, 19; Morrison 1990). Morrison contends,

Explicit or implicit, the Africanist presence informs in compelling and inescapable ways the texture of American literature. It is a dark and abiding presence, there for the literary imagination as both a visible and an invisible mediating force. Even, and especially, when American texts are not "about" Africanist presences or characters or narrative or idiom, the shadow hovers in implication, in sign, in line of demarcation. *It is no accident and no mistake that immigrant populations (and much immigrant literature) understood their "Americanness" as an opposition to the resident black population.* (Morrison 1990, 46–47; italics added)

In sum, although demographic transformations have complicated the fundamental racial binary, american Black as the Other continue to be

Sydney Nathans, in the History department of Duke University, for bringing this reference to my attention.

the standard against which domestic social groups, such as poor whites and Native Americans, as well as successive waves of immigrants have been measured. Lewis Gordon is right on target when he argues that

in the context of the United States, the black/white dichotomy functions in a far more determining way than is acknowledged in the current rhetoric of equal-opportunity discrimination. This is because, in the United States, *racism* means *antiblack racism*. All other groups are assessed and ultimately discriminated against or favored in terms of the extent to which they carry residues of whiteness or blackness. Thus to articulate the racial situation in the United States without focusing on blacks leads, ultimately, to *evading* American racism. (Gordon 1995b, 41)[4]

The consequence of slavery and confrontations with Indians (for Black people and Native Americans) was that with rare exceptions (including passing), color was "regarded as an indelible sign of the individual's identification . . . Membership in their groups is not merely the result of a voluntary decision; it is thrust upon them by the prejudice of the whole society" (Handlin 1965, 14). Accents, dress, behavioral norms, and styles can be learned, but skin color cannot be erased.

White-skinned Jews, unlike other European immigrants, have not comfortably seen themselves or been seen as "white," although the binary division characterizing the American racial structure facilitated the mobility and leverage of white-skinned ethnic groups, including Jews, on condition that they adapt to the norms set by the dominant group, white Anglo-Saxon Protestants.[5] Conforming to this model made it possible for individual Jews to aspire to and attain successful assimilation. Jews could internalize white American racism, for "in color-conscious America, one's pigmentation has been incomparably more

4. Gordon's comment is not original or profound, although it is well stated: the insistence on remembering that Third World immigrants to the United States do not have the history of slavery experienced by those people of African descent who have been in the country for three hundred years.

5. Note the distinction between WASPs as a dominant group who have managed and administered definitions of norms, standards, and values and the absence of a demographic majority that can claim a distinct or authentic American heritage: "the term *minority groups* has come to be applied to those groups in the United States who face certain handicaps, who are subject to certain discriminations, and who are the objects of the prejudices of most other people. There is no one *majority group* with a distinctive history and a special claim to the land" (Rose and Rose 1965, 3).

important than one's religious persuasion in determining social accept-ability and vocational success" (N. Friedman 1969; see also Gilman 1986). An ever-present Christian inflection in American secularism and civil religion did, however, impose an Otherness that Jews as a collective and some Jews as individuals could never completely escape.[6] Greg Tate, a Black cultural critic who writes for the New York *Village Voice*, wrote a revealing reaction to *Schindler's List*:

> After seeing *Schindler's List*, I finally understood why some Jewish folk don't consider themselves "white." Forgive the lightbulb that went on over my dome but now I dig: The Holocaust didn't happen to white people, because the Nazis decided they weren't killing human beings when they killed Jews. (1994, 22)

Moreover, Jews, as a social category of otherness, have defied at-tempts to classify them. In one sociological textbook published in the mid-1960s, the editors compromise in one broad sweep falling on reli-gion as a point of convergence:

> The Jews constitute a fairly unique minority in that there is no adequate single basis for categorizing them. Their racial, nationality and language characteris-tics and backgrounds are about as diverse as possible. . . . The most satisfying way of describing them is to say that for all of them, their recent forebears are known to have believed in the Jewish religion. (Rose and Rose 1965, 5)

One cannot overemphasize that pivoting a definition of "the Jews" on religion remains contentious, even in the State of Israel.[7] The multiple images embedded in a notion of Jewishness in the American context,

6. Despite the official separation of state and religion, the existence of a *state* religion in America continues as evidenced by the prayer service for the victims of the Oklahoma bombing in 1995 led by Evangelical Billy Graham with the active presence of the presidential family.

7. In 1969, Norman Friedman commented that "the 1960s will go down in American Jewish history as the decade of symposia on the *Jewishness* of Jews who have made names for themselves in American intellectual life" (1969, 6; italics added). Actually, there has been no decade in which a proliferation of organized discussion on the meaning, significance, fate, and future of the Jews, Jewishness, and Judaism has not taken place. In the 1990s the tradition of symposia on Jewish identity focuses on the same theme: "the gap between Jewishness as identity, Juda-ism as religion, humanistic perspectives and community-particularistic self-interest orientation" (Goldberg and Krausz, 1993). See Shlomo Kahn's well-titled essay, "Israeli, Hebrew, Jew: The Semantic Problem" (1970) for a brief but informative essay on the links between political unity and semantic clarity.

however, were expressed more eloquently if rhetorically, by journalist Jim Sleeper:

Perhaps it began as a curiosity. Jewishness becomes intriguing when you try to make sense out of the fact that as a Jew on the current scene you are a slumlord to blacks, a civil rights worker to Southern whites, a white-heeled business school opportunist to hippies, a student radical to WASP conservatives, an Old Testament witness to Vermont Yankees, an atheist to Midwestern crusaders, a capitalist to leftists, a communist to rednecks. (quoted in Porter and Drier 1973, xlvii–xlviii; Sleeper and Mintz 1971)

From the mid-1960s to the mid-1970s, Jewish radicals were bitterly critical of the organized Jewish establishment, which, they claimed, has "consistently fought against the inclusion of questions on religion in the U.S. Census" (Porter and Dreier 1973, xxxix ff.).[8] Others were frustrated by the way the census facilitated the definition of Jews as a religious group rather than an ethnic entity. They scorned what the establishment saw as an advantage: being defined *only* as a religious group was an expeditious strategy for assimilation — it *deemphasized* Jewish *difference* from white Christians. The activists who identified themselves as Jewish and as radical did not limit their criticism to the Jewish establishment, but, in response to anti-Semitic rhetoric from the Black nationalist camp, they were equally scornful of Jews who internalized a white identity and, from *that* standpoint, sought acceptance as radicals (Lamm 1970). This perspective appeared in a scathing letter to the widely circulated (then still considered radical) New York weekly *Village Voice*: M. J. Rosenberg castigates "the Jewish Uncle Tom" with

8. See Jack Nusan Porter and Peter Dreier (1973) whose book, "Dedicated to the men and women of the radical movement, both here in the United States and abroad," opens with the political statement that characterizes the revolutionary vision of prophetic Judaism: "If I am not for myself, who will be for me? And if I am only for myself, what am I? If not now, when?" (quoting Hillel the Elder, *Ethics of the Fathers, I, 14*). This collection of essays is a significant reminder of the passion that engaged and linked intellectual thought and politics of the 1960s, particularly when contrasted to the paralysis of spirit and dampened political fervor of the 1990s characterized by what Brian Palmer caustically described as "a retreat from moral and political authority into a narrow academic discourse: a kind of academic word-playing with no possible link to anything but the pseudo-intellectualized ghettoes of the most self-promotionally avant-garde enclaves of that bastion of protectionism, the University" (1990, 199).

an aspiration of becoming a WASP for encouraging negative stereotypes about Jews:

[H]e does not and will not understand that his relevance is as a Jew, a fellow victim, and that his only effectiveness is as such. . . . In relating to blacks, he will not come on as a Jew but as a white; he is hardly ready to relegate his precious whiteness to a secondary position . . . [T]he black militant comes into contact only with these self-hating Jews; it is not hard for him to realize that any man who cannot accept his national identity is hardly likely to honestly accept any other man's. (1973, 6–7)

This radical perspective combined political perspicacity with an acute sense of Judaism, thereby providing a moral and spiritual structure that permitted — indeed encouraged — "not simply a universalist or particularist but multiparticularist" attitude (Waskow 1973, 25). Radical Jewish activists advocated and represented the Jewish commitment to social justice *without* necessarily an adherence or allegiance to religious expression.

Finally, but not least in significance, the third condition needed to produce *the idea* of "Black and Jewish," as a specific and unique identity, results from the political activities of Jewish radicals, particularly in the labor movement of the 1930s and '40s, the Communist Party (CP) of the 1950s and, most important, the civil rights movement of the 1960s (Cruse 1967). Of my eight interviewees, two had parents who met through their membership in the CP (the Communist Party actively encouraged interracial marriages)[9] and three of them had parents who met through their political activities on civil rights issues. Sociologist Nathan Glazer estimated that although one-third of the CP members were Jews, a high proportion by any measure; this does not take into account an even wider base of supporters who were Jewish. In addition, the main constituency of the Socialist Party was Jewish unions (Glazer 1961; 1969).[10]

9. Finding documentation on this point was difficult, and here I rely on the numerous testaments of friends and family who were close to, or members of, the Communist Party.

10. See Vivian Gornick's *The Romance of American Communism* (1977), a title that poignantly captures the intense feelings members had for the Party. Gornick presents a well-deserved challenge to preceding sterile, abstract, and often antago-

A dominant proportion of these activists were Jewish by descent but more often they exemplified Isaac Deutscher's trenchant expression "non-Jewish Jews" (Deutscher 1968).[11] This phrase came to signify, derisively and with cheerless contempt, Jews whose political commitments did reflect the prophetic tradition of Judaism oriented toward emancipation and liberation yet who rejected or negated the value of a Jewish identity. This was an internationalist perspective that complimented Jewish values (social justice), but refused any obligation to acknowledge Jewishness. In other words, being Jewish — from a political standpoint — was a necessary but insufficient reason to be on the side of the oppressed. Ironically, this attitude stands out against anti-Semitic stereotypes equating radicalism and sedition with Jews, itself a result of the disproportionate number of Jews in social movements on the political Left.[12]

Jews and Blacks shared similar concerns when it came to the politics

---

nistic portrayals and misinformation that American Communists were "a uniquely evil group of people, a terror 'from across the sea.'" Gornick, who traveled cross-country to interview former CP members and record their recollections of the emotional meaning of the political experience in the Party, writes: "I learned that something I had been taught all my young life but had actually never believed was, in fact *true*: the Communists came from everywhere. Secretly, I think I had always believed along with J. Edgar Hoover that the Communists were all New York Jews of Eastern European origin" (Gornick 1977, 23).

11. Isaac Deutscher (1907–67) was a Polish Jew noted early on for his poetry; he was expelled from the Polish Communist Party, which he had joined in 1927, and organized the first anti-Stalinist faction. In 1939 Deutscher emigrated to England and eventually became an academic specializing in studies on the Soviet Union, its leaders, and the Revolution. He lectured before wide audiences in both Europe and the United States and participated in the Berkeley Teach-In on Vietnam in 1965.

12. This phenomenon repeats itself in radical and liberal movements throughout Europe, Latin America, and South Africa from the 1917 Russian Revolution and through to the antiapartheid movements of South Africa. Nowhere is this example illustrated with such precision as in the case of Joe Slovo. Slovo, of Lithuanian Jewish background, who spoke only Yiddish until he was six years old, headed the military wing of the African National Congress. With the dismantlement of the apartheid regime and the legalization of the Communist Party of South Africa, Slovo went from being vilified as a dangerous pariah to celebrated as an exemplary hero within the Jewish community. Among the official eulogists at his funeral in 1994 was one presented by the Chief Rabbi of South Africa.

of group identity and attitudes toward its reproduction. Lenora Berson underlines a persistent theme: both Jews and Blacks have a strong ambivalence about assimilation, "the terror of being swallowed." At the lightest end of the color spectrum within this caste system based on shade differences is white-skin, and "[t]he fairest black men of them all have become all too often colored white men consciously acting out a pathetic and macabre parody."

To Jews too, the dilemma of assimilation is very real. Though they bear no visual physical mark to identify them, there is an internal brake . . . guilt, a guilt that so many Jews have sought to expiate by embracing, if not the Negro, then his cause. Still these Americanized Jews can never quite avert their inner eye from the archetypal image of the old man in his kaftan and tallis, (orthodox Jew in prayer). . . . It is a memory of failure. (Berson 1971, 205–6)

Although numerical figures for interreligious marriages in general, and interracial marriage between Jews and Blacks in particular, are not available,[13] one of the sites in which Jews and Blacks came into close contact were politically motivated social movements. Again there are no statistics available—simply impressions such as the following by Berson, who, unfortunately, does not provide either references or a bibliography.

Among interracial marriages, Jews figure prominently as the white partners. These marriages are most frequently among the best educated whites and Negroes. They are often the end result of college romance. A complex of reasons makes Jews more likely than other whites to marry Negroes, Jews seek higher education in greater numbers than other groups. They are more inclined to be intellectual and committed to civil rights. They are frequently in rebellion against stifling family bonds. Breaking the taboo against marriage with an outsider is a tempting form of revolt. A Negro partner represents extreme defiance. In addition, Jews suffer from feelings of generalized guilt which tends to make them identify with Negroes. (Berson 1971, 205)[14]

13. Concerns with demographic trends and the impact of interreligious marriage on Jewish survival have remained high on the Jewish agenda. For an early article on this topic, see Samuel Lieberman and Morton Weinfeld (1977).

14. A fuller discussion on the trend of interracial Jewish Black marriage appears later, in the section "Jews and Intermarriage."

Jews and Blacks in America

A cursory glance at some historical moments is useful for highlighting parallels and divergencies of the Black and the Jewish experience in the United States. The most immediate difference between Blacks and Jews is obviously the route along which their presence in the United States was established. Whereas Africans came to Virginia in 1619 as involuntary slaves, Sephardic Jews who immigrated from Brazil to New Amsterdam in 1654 entered on their own volition in order to escape the oppressive authority of the Catholic Church that directed Portuguese rule.[15]

Contrary to popular misconceptions, Jews were not accepted as white. For instance, in sifting through Virginia's laws pertaining to miscegenation, one finds evidence that Jews were not conceptualized as merely a religious group, but were specifically marked as a nonwhite race.[16] In October 1705, one of the bills passed under the "Act concerning servants and slaves" stated that "no negroes, mulattos and Indians or other infidels, or Jews, Moors, Mahometans or other infidels, shall, at any time, purchase any Christian servant, nor any other, except of their own complexion" (Guild 1936, 49). The same legislative section prohibited these groups from intermarrying with white Christians. Although these restraints were framed in religious terminology, the infusion of race thinking is evidenced by the explicit mention of "their own complexion," a phrase that consciously and expressly distinguished

---

15. The historical-political context is carefully presented by Michel-Rolph Trouillot (1991a). He situates the inauguration of European constructions of otherness in the fifteenth century. He notes that 1492 marks the fall of Muslim Granada, the expulsion of the Jews, the consolidation of political borders in Europe, and the concentration of political power in the name of a Christian God. In retrospect, Trouillot privileges the contemporary significance of these events over Columbus's arrival in Antilles. See also Tzvetan Todorov (1984, 34–50).

16. This refutes the claim made by Jacob Rader Marcus in his history of American Jews that "there was probably not a single law in the land, in the eighteenth century, that had been enacted for the purpose of imposing a disability on Jews alone" (Marcus 1961, vol. 2, 526). The Virginia bill did not, it is true, single out Jews alone for attention. However, this legislation does highlight that Jews, along with North Africans and Muslims, were *racial others* and not, as some would believe, *merely* an ethnic religious minority.

Jews and other non-European Christians from the white colonial community (Martyn 1979).[17]

Prior to the American Civil War, northern states had varying legal policies that structured Black participation in white American society: John Hope Franklin spotlights 1919 as the worst year of racial violence in the North (Franklin 1988). Comparisons between Jews and Blacks begin with the biblical narrative of exodus, liberation, and redemption, but from an early period, actual events seemed to provide inescapable parallels. Anti-Semitic pogroms in eastern Europe and white racist violence against Blacks in the North provided immediate examples.[18]

The massive entry of eastern European Jewish immigrants at the turn of the century coincided with the mass migration of southern Blacks in search of improved opportunities, and possible economic prosperity, in the expanding markets of northern urban centers. Unlike the established German Jewish community, Jews from eastern Europe stood out because of their clothing, language (Yiddish), mannerisms, and religious customs. They were physically distinct — a result of poverty, climate, and poor nutrition (Boas 1962). Sander Gilman persuasively demonstrates how "the Eastern Jew had come to fill the position of the 'primitive' in the popular anthropology of Western Jewry," a field dominated by Jews of German Jewish origin (Gilman 1985, 176; Powdermaker 1966, 21 ff.). Stereotypes reminiscent of the Shylock image, reinforced through Shakespeare's *Merchant of Venice* and imprinted on the European imagination, persisted in America, in part because of the high visibility of small businesses owned by Jews (Lester 1992). Conditions of poverty generate similar problems — prostitution, gambling, squalor, and crime. Middle-class German Jews and Blacks alike were

17. This racial distinction would figure in a Supreme Court decision that ruled that Jews and Arabs were racially distinct from Caucasians, based on nineteenth-century classifications: *St. Francis College, et al. v. Majid Ghaidan Al-Khazraji*, and *Shaare Tefila Congregation v. William Cobb et al.*, 18 May 1987. For a discussion of the ritual reproduction of race in the United States, in which this decision plays a role, see Barbara Jeanne Fields (1990).

18. In a discussion on white Americans' racial behavior, Anna J. Cooper [(1892) 1988, 97] protests the concern for the scandalous Russian pogroms of Jews at the expense of attention to the appalling treatment of american Blacks, which is casually accepted.

appalled by the possibility that their struggle to be accepted in spite of racism and anti-Semitism would be undermined by the visibility of such "problem-ridden" communities with which they were associated in the public mind (Lewis 1988).

Self-identity had little to do with the manner in which the dominant society chose to ignore *diversity* among Jews or Blacks. Educated and economically advantaged sectors within each group, self-conscious of their class position, hoped to escape the stigma of being associated with stereotyped images of their community. Historian David Levering Lewis discusses the common horror and humiliation of northern black intellectuals and wealthy Jews of German Jewish descent in the face of southern black migration and eastern European Jewish immigration respectively at the turn of the twentieth century. Both groups feared an escalation of racism and anti-Semitism and the erasure of small gains ("we all suffer for what one fool will do"), and both groups implored their constituencies to become civilized Americans, speak English properly, and conform to hygiene standards (Lewis 1988).

Discrimination against Jews and against Blacks was not the same, chiefly because one group was always visible by skin color and the other could carefully conceal its background. Nonetheless, there is an unavoidable parallel to be drawn between Jews seeking entry into circles that excluded Jews, and African Americans who were light enough to pass as white. In both cases, all links to one's kin and history had to be carefully concealed. The majority of Jews, however, did not "pass" or change their last names. Moreover, whereas Blacks faced legislative racial discrimination in addition to social discrimination, in general Jews were confronted only by the latter.

It would be a mistake, however, to understate the violent aspect of anti-Semitism in America and the way in which it intersects with the history of racism against Blacks. Although violence against Jews was never as prominent as that perpetuated against African Americans — particularly with regard to physical violence — a numerical comparison diminishes and obscures the manner in which expressions of animosity intersected with racist violence.[19] Furthermore, it is the *possibility* of

19. See chapter 3, note 29 for reference to white supremacists and their revolutionary ambitions (Ferber 1995).

violent anti-Semitism that, in varying degrees, Jews keep in the back of their minds, and it is this fear that grounds being Jewish to a *political* identity regardless, and especially in the absence of, religious or cultural feelings of affiliation.[20] In this respect, Fanon's reminder that the anti-Semite is also a racist can never be overstated.[21] People of color and those who could be distinguished as Jewish by their manner of dress were easy targets in cities in the North.[22]

The 1915 case of Leo Frank astutely illustrates Fanon's anecdote as well as the potential for extreme anti-Semitism in America (Lindemann 1991). Frank was an ordinary, nondescript Jew from New York who made the mistake of going South, married into a Jewish family in Atlanta, and became the first white man to be convicted of murder on the basis of a Negro's court statements.[23] This event inescapably brought Jews and Blacks into an intimate link and more important, it accentuated the association between Blacks and Jews in the public arena.

Frank was found guilty on the testimony of a Black janitor at a time when Black testimonies against whites were unheard of. However, this northern Jew, represented as the actual murderer of the white woman, Mary Phagan, filled the demand for "a villain blacker than any Negro could ever aspire to be" (Berson 1971, 38). Frank's lynching and mutilation were deliberately intended as a warning: "The Next Jew Who Does What Frank Did is Going to Get Exactly The Same Thing We Give to Negro Rapists" (Weisbord and Stein 1970, 12). Lenora Berson provides an excellent summation of the significance of this event.

20. This point came up in nearly all the interviews I conducted with people who are Black, Jewish, and interracial.

21. See chapter 1.

22. One need only recall the fate of Youseef Hawkins in Bensonhurst and Yankel Rosenbaum in Crown Heights. Cornel West points out that one of the axes around which identity is thought and therefore should be discussed is death. "Identity is about binding, and it means that you can be bound—parochialist, narrow, xenophobic. But it also means that you can be held together in the face of the terrors of nature, the cruelties of fate and the need for some compensation of unjustified suffering: what theologians used to call the problem of evil" (West 1993a, 164; Dyson 1993, 142–43).

23. See Morris N. Schappes (1952, 291) for the account of a double lynching of a black and a Jew in Tennessee, 1868.

The lynching of Leo Frank was a kind of shorthand symbolism, enacting the nightmares that troubled the sleep of the white Southerner. In this action was caught the twisted myths of sexual perversity and sexual superiority of the alien and the blood paranoia of a thousand years of European anti-Semitism. It was transmogrified into that peculiar American tradition of lynching, the orgiastic sacrifice by the frustrated and politically impotent mob. (1971, 30)

America provided a nebulous refuge from the burden of imposed and internalized anti-Semitism. Racism and anti-Semitism were not merely manifestations of nativist white Americans who were apprehensive of people who seemed culturally alien and racially different.

Jewish Identity

In 1970, in the wake of a strong anti-Semitic undercurrent in the organized and vocal anti-Zionist movement, Emil Fackenheim, a renowned expert on Hegel and one of the leading contemporary Jewish philosophers, pointed out that whereas Blacks, as individuals and as a community, were generally marked by skin color, Jews tended to look like the people in their host countries and therefore they (potentially) could disappear through assimilation. A great deal of denial underlies the belief that Jews as a group may disappear into the dominant society, even if the individual Jew may succeed in doing so (inauthentically). In this context, the following lengthy passage from historian Walter Laqueur, provides a valuable intervention. Laqueur does an excellent job in mapping out the problem of emancipation and assimilation at the individual level, underlining the fact, exemplified best by Karl Marx, that even the converted remains marked as a Jew:

Marx felt himself anything but a Jew; so did Lasalle whom he loathed. Marx's exchange of letters with Engels is replete with references to the 'Jewish Nigger' Lasalle, his lack of tact, his vanity, impatience, and other 'typically Jewish' traits of character. But to the outside world men like Marx and Lasalle remained Jews, however ostentatiously they dissociated themselves from Judaism, however much they felt themselves Germans or citizens of the world. Well-wishers saw in Marx a descendant of the Jewish prophets and commented on the messianic element in Marxism; enemies dwelt upon the Talmudic craftiness of the Red Rabbi; there was no getting out of Borne's 'magic circle.' It was above all this hostility on the part of the outside world, and in particular Christian opposition to emancipation and later on the antisemitic movement, that prevented the total disintegration of the Jews as a group. (1972, 19)

Fackenheim does not take into consideration the stereotypes of Otherness that have marked the Jew as *racially different* throughout Christian societies, a theme Sander Gilman has eloquently and meticulously explored throughout his scholarship:

[T]he association of the Jews with Blackness is as old as Christian tradition. Medieval iconography always juxtaposed the black image of the synagogue, of the Old Law, with the white of the Church. The association is an artifact of the Christian perception of the Jews which has been simply incorporated into the rhetoric of race. But it is incorporated, not merely as an intellectual abstraction, but as the model through which Jews are perceived, treated, and thus respond as if confronted with the reflection of their own reality. (1992, 7)

The Jewish *dilemma* — rather than "identity crisis" — in the diaspora, then, has been created through participation in the dominant society.[24]

Fackenheim examined the question of the survival of Jewish people and tradition against a diasporic history marked by persecution, and he concluded that "to account for Jewish survival is possible only in terms of Jewish faith." It was faith that coalesced a collective body of people, who in turn reproduced a tradition and group loyalty (Fackenheim 1970, 253). Paul Ricoeur proposes that Israel becomes an object of faith as well as an object of history constructed by faith in which each generation reinterprets the foundations of tradition: the identity of Israel "is inseparable from an endless search for a meaning to history and in history" (Ricoeur 1974, 46).

The biblical documents, exegesis, and commandments provide the links that ensure the survival of the collective group. They are the

24. Sander Gilman argues that Fackenheim fails to recognize "the special position anti-Jewish feeling has within the history of Europe and the Americas. Seeing the Jew as black reflects the protean nature of all perceptions of difference" (1992, 12). See Gilman's discussion of Jewish intellectuals (including Erik Homburger Erikson and Sigmund Freud) who internalized — at the same time they attempted to deflect — the specifically racial image in order to construct an alternative sense of identity.

resources from which to reproduce and reinforce Jewish identity, and Fackenheim pivots this on God and faith. Once these are called into question, in his perspective, the meaning of being Jewish has to be painstakingly rethought (1970, 261).[25]

Political freedom enabled (limited) participation in the public sphere, but the price for acceptance was negation of difference. For the first time Jewish identity was secularized, but illusions about the meaning of emancipation would be brutally and irrevocably disrupted with the Holocaust. Throughout the eighteenth and nineteenth centuries, however, the Emancipation (inspired in large part by the Enlightenment, this was a gradual movement toward secularization on the part of Jews and a lifting of restrictions on Jewish lifestyle and occupations by European rulers) facilitated meditations about reason and faith among a wider circle of Jews inclined toward skepticism. At the same time, anti-Semitism remained influential in reinforcing Jewishness as a mark of difference. In fact, one might see religion and racism as mutually compatible buttresses to Jewish identity and Jewishness as difference.

Garry M. Brodsky proposes a resolution to the tension of secularism, and its inherent ambiguity on the issue of continuity, by suggesting that intellectual and postmodern Jews are conscious of the intellectual and political history of anti-Semitism and Jews in Europe of the nineteenth and twentieth centuries. He points out that the issue of history and dialectic was challenged in the concentration camps, a perspective that flows throughout the philosophy of Levinas, who himself was a survivor. Brodsky states that "Being a liberal can be and is a way of being both a Jew and a person for the postmodern Jew" (1993, 261).[26]

As has previously been noted, in *The Anti-Semite and the Jew*, Sartre contends that an essential component of the identity of the anti-Semite is founded on distinguishing himself from his opposite other and defining him differently. If the Jew is inferior, the anti-Semite can confirm his own superiority. The Jew, therefore, functions as the model of difference, illustrating the condition of negation.

25. See chapter 4.

26. In 1969, sociologist Nathan Glazer, who was very critical of the New Left, had already remarked on the compatibility of Jewishness and social consciousness. Thus Brodsky's remarks are an opportune echo from debates of radical Jews in the New Left during the late 1960s and into the early '70s.

Stuart E. Rosenberg defines Judaism as a religious system "a religion of a specific people — the Jewish people. Much of its religious culture, custom and tradition is interwoven with the national history of the Jews . . . [this is a] national, religious civilization of a corporate conventional community" (1985, 30). The collective experience is initially manifested at Mount Sinai in a covenant between God and a people, and this event conditions the possibility of a Jewish people coming into being (Fackenheim 1970, 255).[27]

From this moment, the perennial Jewish existential theme, which continues to preoccupy Jewish Israeli thinkers, centers on the explicit recognition that whereas all people are equal, the Jews are compelled by a special covenant with God and thus are challenged to reconcile a commitment to the group without, however, having it come at the expense of others. The covenant established the ground rules and functioned as a call to action at the individual level and as a collective action that challenged the group. Thus although all people are linked to God, participants in the Jewish experience view the covenant as profound and unique in spite of its universal application. Here, I would like to refer back to Grossberg's distinction between difference and otherness in order to underline that a Jewish perspective, informed by the particularity of the covenant, carefully — indeed cautiously — delineates clear boundaries (group and territorial) not merely as significant, but also as essential, for the recognition of identity as conferring legitimacy and respect to otherness (Grossberg 1993).

Jews and Intermarriage

The common theme, across time, in conferences convened by the representatives of the established Jewish community is the quality and con-

27. See Paul Ricoeur's discussion of the historicity of founding events that constitute a tradition, "We are confronting a historical interpretation of the historical; the very fact that here sources are juxtaposed, schisms maintained and contradictions exposed has a profound sense: the tradition corrects itself through additions, and these additions themselves constitute a theological dialectic" (1974, 46). Note that there are a number of covenants, but the one at Mount Sinai is usually viewed as the most significant. Although Jewish thought tends to be extraordinarily present-oriented, there are some Midrashic interpretations that suggest that Abraham was informed of the future.

tent of Jewish life in America. The question of assimilation has figured prominently in the discourse on the continuity of the Jewish people. Thus the dilemma of the secular Jew is not seen as an individual, personal predicament. Rather, it is linked to a history in which the Jewish people have been marked as different, been discriminated against, or have come under pressure to convert. Jewish resistance to these forces has depended on and been seen as a conscious continuity in spite of these efforts at annihilation. Without reproduction, the notion of peoplehood disintegrates (Gibel 1985).

Two white Christians, D. H. Lawrence and Michael Novak, offer a useful consideration of the pressure in middle-class America to lose identities, and their statements provide a supporting intervention in the discussion on the dilemmas of assimilation. Gary Gossen (1993, 451) quotes from an essay of D. H. Lawrence: "Men are freest when they are most unconscious of freedom. The shout is a rattling of chains, always was." Lawrence's comments were inspired by his observation that America was composed of (European) immigrants escaping from some place and some other identity. The problem that faced generations of American immigrants was how to *discard* rather than *incorporate* identities. Whereas the issues of memory and forgetting have been crucial to the immigrants' experience, it is the strategy for "becoming" an American that is significant. One had to discard features that mark one as different.

The subject of the Americanization of identities and the immigrant experience was treated in a play whose title became an American household word: *The Melting Pot*, by British-born Jewish author Israel Zangwill. The play opened in Washington, D.C., in 1908 and applauded the social melting and reformation of identities, "all the races of Europe," in the American Crucible.[28] It would only be with the rise of Black Power, and the drive for Black consciousness and self-esteem, that Jews and other ethnic groups would begin to—publicly—readdress and question the price of assimilation and the meaning of identity.[29] As

28. For an interesting discussion of the dilemma of the assimilating Jew, see Shumsky (1975).

29. Note that questions of a public Jewish identity were never an issue for the ultra-Orthodox but always a problem for the upwardly mobile, Reform, many Conservative, and most secular Jews who sought acceptance in mainstream Protestant American arenas.

Michael Novak, a Slavic Catholic intellectual, noted in 1972, "People uncertain of their own identity are not wholly free" (quoted in Rosenberg 1985, 32).

An enduring question that has troubled the leadership of the non-Orthodox Jewish community in particular has been how to make Judaism morally and spiritually relevant. The issue of assimilation and the disappearance of the Jewish community is usually bemoaned as "a crisis." One is born a Jew, and on this core definition the generation and reproduction of a people is possible. From the nineteenth century, the question facing Jews who felt no religious commitment has been whether and how to reconcile social assimilation and a cultural identification with Jewishness. This is a central issue for a minority that tries to maintain a separate cultural and religious identity in a society where the pressure to assimilate and integrate is high. One key to discussions about Jewish survival is the central problem of Christian hostility to Jews. Fackenheim contends, and six of my eight interviews will later be shown to evidence his assessment, that in the post-Holocaust era,

if a single generalization may be safely made about the contemporary Jew, it is that he still regards Jewish survival as a duty, to be performed whether he likes it or not. He may not have the slightest idea why it should be a duty; he may even consciously reject this duty. Still he feels it in his bones. (1970, 262)

The symbolic significance of anti-Semitism, therefore, whether or not it is salient in a given situation, is the motive and background against which to understand Jewish antagonism and discomfort with intermarriage. Emancipation provided European Jews with the opportunity to gain access to both Christian and secular Christian circles. This loosening of imposed boundaries — spatial, not merely metaphorical — that enclosed Jews from the outside gave license to assimilation, which in turn threatened the collective self-definition. Assimilation then becomes a problem that can be countered only through a conscious Jewish response. This was demonstrated as an increasingly emphatic trend toward closing ranks.

In terms of biblical narratives and historical situations, Judaism, which was not a proselytizing religion, discouraged marriage outside the community in favor of maintaining lines of endogamy, continuity, and reproduction of Jewish collectivity.[30] By the mid-nineteenth century, most of Europe introduced civil marriage as one of the consequences of the separation of religion and the state. Intermarriage proved to be a strategy for discarding Jewishness. Instead of integrating as a Jew and being accepted as a Jew, the Jewish partner exchanged his/her old identity for the privilege of being accepted *in spite of* his/her being a Jew.

After Emancipation, the earliest interreligious marriages in Europe involved mainly Jewish men and Christian mothers. Consequently, the children were not Jewish, and thus this combination immediately represented the disappearance of the Jewish family and was a potential foreshadowing of the dissolution of the Jewish community. The problem was also that social mobility and economic advancement in Gentile circles seemed at odds with traditional Jewish life, with its rituals, rules, and customs that interfered unnecessarily; a Jewish religious affiliation was increasingly seen as irrelevant to modern life.

In the United States, interfaith marriage was opposed on religious grounds by the three major Jewish religious modes of thought: preservation of the Jewish home, Judaism, and Jewish people. Again, the focus was always on the tension between individuality and particularistic identities, although nothing in the Bible sanctioned ranking or hierarchies among human communities. Preservation of a Jewish identity through an insistence on loyalty to traditions did not detract from or diminish a commitment to the value of all human beings (A. Gordon

30. Famous biblical intermarriages include Moses and the Cushite, Boaz and Ruth, and Esther and King Ahasverus, whose reign extended from India to Ethiopia (Esther 1:1). An examination of rabbinical interpretations here would be interesting although outside the scope of this project. The specific case of Ruth is particularly relevant because she will be the foremother of King David and thus, according to the *Tanakh*, of the Messiah. Emerging from the story of Ruth, the issue will be how to gain membership and then be recognized as a *full* member of the group. Conversion becomes a process that entails more than simply casting one's lot with the destiny of a people. For this to happen — and more important, to abort speculation on David's Jewishness — the exchange between Ruth and Naomi, Ruth's mother-in-law, comes to be interpreted by some rabbinical authorities as the moment of instruction and induction. My thanks to Rabbi S. Saeger of Beth El Synagogue in Durham, North Carolina, for pointing this out to me.

1964a, 183). Even Mordechai Kaplan, the founder of Reconstruction-ism—a *not* unorthodox rethinking of Judaism within the context of twentieth-century America—expressed his strong reservations against marrying out of the Jewish community: "Since Jews are a minority and Judaism is exposed to tremendous disintegrating forces from the non-Jewish environment . . . it cannot approve of uncontrolled intermar-riage with non-Jews" (quoted in A. Gordon 1964a, 225).

One of the primary reactions to individuals who marry out of the community in both the Jewish and Black communities is a charge of disloyalty.[31] In part, this can be attributed to an interest in holding on to a sense of group solidarity because of the history of racism. Among sec-ular Jews who are relatively indifferent to religious aspects of Judaism, the Nazi objective to annihilate the Jewish people provides an incentive to preserve the continuity of a Jewish presence in the world. Perhaps the most famous statement on this was expressed by Fackenheim:

[T]here now exists a 614th commandment—Jews are forbidden to give Hitler a posthumous victory . . . if we live as if nothing had happened, we imply that we are willing to expose our children or their offspring to a second Holocaust—and that would be another way of giving Hitler a posthumous victory. (quoted in S. Rosenberg 1985, 31)[32]

31. This does not presume that only Jews and Blacks are concerned with the relation between intermarriage and assimilation. Sociologist Teresa Kay Williams, self-described as "biracial, bicultural, and bilingual, binational Japanese-European-American," uses her experiences as a practical and theoretical resource for analyzing racial images and representations. A main source of consternation is Japanese aver-sion to intermarriage in favor of monoethnicity and consequently the exceptional manner in which her own relatives, particularly her grandmother, accepted her while at the same time not quite resolving "the love-hate pendulum" toward what she terms "mixed-blood." For further references on (Japanese-Other) interracial marriage and interracial children, see her references in "The Theater of Identity" (1995, 79–96, n.9).

32. Fackenheim proposed this stance during a symposium sponsored by the Jewish quarterly *Judaism*, on Purim, 26 March 1967, entitled "Jewish Values in the Post-Holocaust Future." At that time, he stated that whether one is agnostic or atheistic, "if the 614th commandment is binding upon the authentic Jew, then we are first, commanded to survive as Jews, lest the Jewish people perish." Survival, remem-brance of the 6 million martyrs, resistance to despair, or denial of God are, for Fackenheim, four "imperatives" against handing Hitler posthumous victories. To

In 1964, at the height of the civil rights movement, Alfred Jospe, a delegate to a conference on the subject of intermarriage among college students stated, "some of our best human material can be found in the forefront of the civil rights struggle yet turn their backs on the synagogue and other institutions in the Jewish community" (Jospe 1964, 93). The civil rights movement seemed to fill a vacuum for young adults who were Jewish by birth but were alienated from involvement with Jewish life. Despite the fact that the overall percentage of Jewish youth were actually involved in social activism vis-à-vis the Jewish community, their participation in relation to their percentage in the larger community was high. As in other countries and other periods, social activism might be interpreted as an attitude toward life that exemplified the best Judaism had to offer.

What is particularly interesting, however, is that at about the same time that some college students who were Jewish had joined the civil rights movement, Albert I. Gordon (1964a) researched the issue of intermarriage and found that although 91 percent of his Jewish respondents would not favor interracial marriage, only 50 percent would object to interreligious marriage. In other words, race was more than a significant factor in the manner in which Jews — at least the participants in Gordon's study — also viewed themselves. One must infer from this that while marrying a white Christian was unfortunate and resulted in the (at least potential) loss of a family from the larger Jewish community, assimilating into white America was less threatening than disappearance into Black America.

Is it possible to dismiss the relevance of Jewish influence on the political behavior of people who merely happen to be born Jewish? In 1964, Jospe was challenged by Rabbi David Golovensky, who claimed that the commitment of the activists was limited to a short period after which they returned to their parents' suburban homes. For Golovensky, the activism was merely late adolescent rebellion and a display of emotionalism, not an indication of either political engagement or a reflection of Jewish values (COI 1964, 111). Five years later, sociologist

---

obey them, "requires the endurance of intolerable contradictions. Such endurance cannot but bespeak an as yet unutterable faith" (quoted in "Jewish Values in the Post-Holocaust Future" 1967, 272–73).

Nathan Glazer, sharply critical of the anti-Semitism that characterized the New Left and noting the disproportionate number of Jewish activists in their camp, stressed that they were not really in rebellion against their parents because a tradition of (Jewish) radicalism was already established.[33] In fact, he argued, unlike mainstream white American youth, Jewish radicals were acting in continuity or overcoming their parents hypocrisy/complacency,

If their parents were once radicals, the children often see themselves as carrying out the heritage from which their own parents were deflected by fear or lack of sufficient strength. Let us not underestimate the significance of this heritage. Perhaps half of the American Communist Party in the 1950s and 1960s was Jewish. (Glazer 1969, 129)[34]

In fact, Jewish intellectuals and activists had found — consciously or not — alternatives to religion that were compatible and indeed expressed the ideals of Jewishness. The ideological principle of social justice and struggle against oppression, central tenets of socialism and communism, were not a contradiction to Jewish codes. For instance, Hettie (Cohen) Jones, the first wife of LeRoi Jones/Amiri Baraka, was rejected by her parents following her marriage. In her memoir, *How I Became Hettie Jones*, she writes of becoming the "white" mother of interracial children:[35] "And white I would be, because I knew the Jews — mine at least — would give me up" (Jones 1990, 52–53). Today, according to her daughter, Lisa Jones, she officially defines herself as "Semitic American mother of black children" (Jones 1994, 32). The un-Jewish racism of her parent's position was, however, challenged by the rabbi of her synagogue.

33. The relationship of Jews to the Left in general and the Communist Party in particular requires its own focus. However, Vivian Gornick reminds us of a singularly significant point that cannot be overemphasized: "of this party it could rightly be said, as Richard Wright in his bitterest moment did, nonetheless say: 'There was no agency in the world so capable of making men feel the earth and the people upon it as the Communist Party'" (1977, 7).

34. Glazer's estimate may be inflated. See chapter 2, note 10 for Vivian Gornick's contrasting observations (Gornick 1977).

35. Hettie Jones (born Cohen) adds quotation marks to the world "interracial" (Jones 1990, 52).

[T]his is the last service, I remind myself, the last Kol Nidre,[36] I'll ever sing here. On the pulpit stands the rabbi, my onetime teacher. In a few months we'll meet, in a car, outside the Theological Seminary. . . . He'll tell me the baby's color is of no concern to him. As long as it's a Jew, he'll say—and I won't believe him. [Years later, on the front page of *The New York Times*, he will be seen welcoming Anwar Sadat to America.] (H. Jones 1990, 61–62)

In contrast to the experience of Hettie Jones and her daughters is that of one of my collaborators, Jared Ball. When his mother married his father, the grandmother on his mother's side, who was born in Palestine and brought to America as a little child by her parents, welcomed him without hesitation.

I mean my grandmother was a Communist, like their whole family was into Communism and they were somewhat radical I believe, you know, as far as the average person was during that time and—oh just allowing my mother, not just for them necessarily allowing but *accepting* a Black man into that especially in the '50s, '60s, that open-minded thinking was probably what led to the way my mother raised me and tried to teach me things and then which left doors open for me to educate myself. So I guess indirectly she's responsible (for his having a Jewish identity).

Although Hettie Cohen Jones's example was all too common, one cannot discount the type of examples provided by Jared Ball's grandparents or the elderly grandmother of my mother's dear lifelong—and probably only completely apolitical—friend, Rita Kaufman Michel. When I was two, my mother brought me to visit "Tante Rita's" family. Rita's grandmother, who never learned English, played with me and held me on her lap, then turned to my mother and asked in Yiddish, "she *will* be raised Jewish, right?" When reassured by my mother, she said, with satisfaction, "Good."

By the 1990s, the question of Jewish identity resurfaced as a problem that secular Jews no longer wanted to escape but rather sought to resolve satisfactorily. In a collection of essays on Jewish identity, Laurence Thomas, a Jewish person of African American descent, pushed the

36. The prayer at the evening services of the most important Jewish holiday, Yom Kippur. This is the one day of the Jewish calendar when synagogues across the world overflow, even with Jews who have no other affiliation with organized religion.

meaning of Jewish identity back to its roots and implicitly raised the question of memory and forgetting (unknowingly echoing Michael Novak), which has been an important part of the American immigrant (voluntary and forced) experience: "without a narrative a people cannot maintain a sense of identity" (Thomas 1993a, 163). In a complementary tenor, Alan Montefiore (1993) focuses on the process of assimilation as a dispossession of memory and self-understanding, which therefore makes one an outsider to oneself. Loss of memory is usually a disorienting and traumatic experience, and in this light it becomes evident that assimilation inevitably results in an individual's exclusion from a social, cultural, and historical experience. This is alienating although it may not necessarily be experienced by the individual in these terms.

In 1990 the Council of Jewish Federations (JF) conducted a study of demographic trends in the American Jewish community. According to their survey, marriage to non-Jews had reached an all-time high, with one of every two Jews marrying a non-Jew. In addition, the children of most of these marriages were being raised without any affiliation to Judaism or were receiving a Christian education.

The Logic of Coupling: Jewish and Black

Albert Gordon's 1964 study focused on attitudes of college students toward intermarriage, a general phenomenon that included marrying outside their religious, ethnic, or racial group. In addition he examined specific attitudes toward particular communities. Gordon refers to the conclusions of a doctoral project from 1960 on interracial couples in New York City, conducted by Charles Smith (Teacher's College at Columbia University): of the twenty-three marriages, half were between Jewish and Black partners. To relate this figure to the total sample, it should be noted that 59 percent were interreligious, and 57 percent of the couples reported no religious affiliation. The Smith study received some media attention and was reported in the *New York Times* on 18 October 1963 (Cahnman 1967, 11). The figures were never intended to be statistically accurate; and private observations, according to sociologist Werner Cahnman (Rutger's University in New Jersey), indicated that "between 70% and 80% of all white spouses of Negro men in the New York metropolitan area are of Jewish derivation" (Cahnman 1967, 11).

In a separate section entitled "Negroes and Whites," Albert Gordon presented the narratives of three couples — all included a Jewish partner.[37] In one case the husband was Jewish and the wife was a Panamanian Negro, and the couple focused primarily on the problem of religion rather than race. The husband, Henry, was one of four children and a first-generation American Jew whose parents emigrated from Russia. His home environment was nominally Jewish, but the level of religiosity was minimal. Three of the children (including Henry) are married to Christian whites. Henry and the wife, who considers herself a Catholic, were married in a church much to the distress of the husband's parents. In his editorial comment, Gordon notes that the parents were far more disturbed by Henry's marriage than by his siblings because the wife was not white.

The following cannot be overemphasized and in no way is an assertion of false modesty: to seek attention for interracial Jewish children in America is by no means original. Precisely because the topic has surfaced in the past, its obscurity indicates a political and perhaps ethical predicament, which is less an enigma than a negligent omission (A. Gordon 1964b; Gibel 1965; Roditi 1967). In June 1967, Cahnman wrote a critical essay entitled "The Interracial Jewish Children" for the biweekly *Reconstructionist*, a publication of the Jewish Reconstructionist movement. Pointing to the unsuccessful efforts of Louise Wise Services, a large adoption agency affiliated with the New York chapter of the Federation of Jewish Philanthropies, which, since 1953, tried to place interracial Jewish children with Jewish families, his discussion explicitly addressed and linked the issues of first, relations between Jews and Blacks, and second, the insincerity in the racial attitudes of Jews who defined their politics as liberal. Most important, however, he anchored his argument in Jewish law and underscored the internalization of American racism at the expense of and in flagrant contradiction to *Halakhah*:

37. The section on Negro Jewish marriages was republished in the journal *Judaism* (A. Gordon 1964b). In the same journal, see Gibel (1965) for a critical response to the issues raised by Gordon's approach and conclusions.

It is abundantly clear that color, not religion, is the determining factor in the adoption of Jewish children . . . [A]ccording to a report published in *The New York Times* of October 11, 1959, and headed "Religious Rule on Adoption Bars Many in State," it is clear in the case of Negro children that religious lines are crossed regularly because it is "standard practice" to place Negro children outside their religion "where the designation is Jewish." In other words, Jewish couples in New York are frustrated in their desire to adopt white babies irrespective of their religion (and, shall we say, irrespective of their ethnicity), but they are reluctant to adopt babies of their own faith, on the sole ground that they are colored. The conclusion is inescapable. The Jews of New York are thoroughly Americanized, as far as their racial attitudes are concerned. (Cahnman 1967, 8)

Cahnman was particularly sharp in his appeal to and criticism of the Orthodox rabbinate whose silence on the issue of Jewish racism against Jews was reprehensible. Although Cahnman's reproach reached the Rabbinical Council of America and was put on the agenda of committee meetings and plenary sessions of the Commission on Synagogue Relations of the Federation of Jewish Philanthropies of New York, all three rabbinical denominations — Orthodox, Conservative, and Reform — "remained silent" (Cahnman 1967, 9).

The relevance of including racial variables in the question of inter-religious marriage constitutes, perhaps, a reflection of a particular period in American race relations in general and its impact on ways in which the Jewish community publicly discusses Jewish and Black relations on the one hand, and Jewish attitudes to interracial marriage on the other (Gibel 1968, 22; Melnick 1994, 108–7). The 1990 CFJ study of demographic trends, mentioned in the previous section, was carried out by the Graduate Center of CUNY as part of a larger project on religious identification. Of concern to the CJF was the finding that marriage to non-Jews had reached an all-time high, with one of every two Jews marrying a non-Jew (J. J. Goldberg 1992), and that the children of these marriages were being raised without any affiliation to Judaism or were receiving a Christian education. It is not incidental to note that without reproduction and formal membership in Jewish associations and organizations, the establishment itself loses its foundation of support. In short, and without being facetious, one should note that if there are no members, there is no money for the organizations to continue operating.

In mid-October 1994, I called Dr. Barry Kosmin, a researcher at the Graduate Center of CUNY and asked him whether questions of race were included in the CJF population survey. They were not. However, during the screening process, questions of race and ethnicity were asked. A small but nevertheless surprisingly larger-than-expected number of people who described themselves as Black or African American also self-defined themselves as Jewish. But whether they were Jewish through conversion, birth, or affiliation with a sect such as the Black Hebrews was unknown, as there was no follow-up on this question. As an area for further investigation, then, the association between Blacks and Jews was a nonissue for the researchers or CJF. The key questions around which the survey was based were a statement of religious identity, whether a person considered him/herself Jewish (self-identity), whether s/he was raised Jewish, and whether s/he had a Jewish parent. The large number of (although statistically small) people who were not self-classified as "white," and yet self-identified as Jewish, raised some concern that respondents or interviewees may have provided false answers. Kosmin said, however, that a review process established that people were giving answers they thought were true. Nonetheless, there was no effort to establish whether all the respondents who said they were Jewish were really of "legitimate Jewish origin."

In the survey conducted on the Jewish population, including race as a component of the questions to ask people was dismissed completely for several reasons. One reason is that the formal inclusion of the Ethiopian Jewish population and their emigration to Israel reinforced a polite taboo on attending to skin color or ethnicity as a variable when looking at criteria of Jewish identity.[38] There was therefore a deliberate

38. Difficulties in the integration of Jews from Ethiopia, particularly the Orthodox, within Israeli society are more complex than explanations based on color suggests. For instance, compare a 1992 report on the hostility to Russian Jewish immigrants placed conveniently, or fortuitously, next to an article on the Ethiopian *kesim* (religious priests), whose authority has been challenged by the rabbinical authorities (Halevi 1992). Four years later, color-based prejudice, along with a racialized language that speaks — in Hebrew — of white Jews and Black Jews, has led to "a kind of defiant Ethiopian identity" among the youth. Halevi notes that "[F]or

decision not to ask about race, for this might have been interpreted as an antagonistic infusion of race thinking, transplanted from American racial prejudices, into an examination of the content and quality of contemporary Jewish identities.

Let us dwell on this event: In an expensive brochure published and distributed in 1985 by the Israel-Africa Friendship Society, effort went into highlighting "the Black Jews of Ethiopia" in order to downplay Israeli ties with South Africa. American Jewish organizations were encouraged to assist in this counter-propaganda (more tactfully described as diplomacy) that stressed the "rescue of the black Jews of Ethiopia and their migration to Israel is a clear illustration of the *non*-racist nature of Zionism."[39]

An illustration of cooperation between American Jews and Israeli officials to underscore the presence of Ethiopian Jews as evidence of the multiracial — indeed, nonracial[40] — character of the Jewish people was reported in the *Baltimore Jewish Times* in October 1994 by Melinda Greenberg, under the eye-catching headline "Exhibiting Unity: Ethiopian Jewry group takes its artifact show on the road, to show that blacks and Jews don't have to be disparate" (Greenberg 1994, 24). The Israeli Consulate had specifically asked the North American Conference on Ethiopian Jewry to circulate the exhibit throughout american Black communities, accentuating the diversity of Jews, accentuating at the same time, the diversity of Africans, and, finally, strategically evidencing the links that unite Blacks and Jews.

Albert Bedell, who is Jewish and has been active in black causes for many years, served on the Baltimore committee for the exhibit. (Bedell is executive secretary for the Maryland Academy of General Dentistry.) He believes blacks and Jews

---

an alienated minority, a Black African identity is becoming a substitute for a failed sense of Israeliness — an ironic reversal of their parents' insistence on being Jews, not Ethiopians" (1996, 19–20).

39. To their credit, the Likud governments under Menachem Begin and Yitzhak Shamir took seriously, and indeed carried out, their commitment to bring the Jews of Ethiopia to Israel, unlike the policy of benign neglect of the previous "liberal-socialist" Labor-headed governments.

40. Nonracial is used here as it was by antiapartheid activists in South Africa. Its meaning is more problematic in the United States, but this subject is out of the bounds of the immediate topic at hand.

will see this exhibit and realize that Ethiopian Jews forge a common bond between the two groups. "These are people who live in huts and look very much like Africans in every other country in Africa. But they are also Jews and they have been for 2,700 years. This exhibit, I hope, will make people understand that Africans come in many ways—Christian, Muslim, traditional religionists and Jews." (Greenberg 1994)

A second reason for not including race-related survey questions, and of equal importance, is that the issue of race remains a sensitive one for Jews expressly because of Nazi ideology and the ways in which Jews have been defined and designated as a race or a racial group.

These are valid and significant arguments against focusing special attention on a link between interracial children and its Jewish dimension. What essential difference should it make whether the non-Jewish partner is white or Black? And yet in the anecdotal material available, it clearly has made a difference for people with this background. I would suggest the possibility of another factor for evading a specific focus on race. Many of the Jewish social scientists and researchers who work on projects related to Jewish identity are, as Dr. Kosmin implied, seriously committed to the ideals of social and racial equality. If in the African American community Black Consciousness was a pivotal moment for thinking about Black identities, among Jewish radicals and those who considered themselves to be of a leftist persuasion, greater consciousness about the meaning of Jewish identities was also crucial (Carmichael and Hamilton 1967; Carson 1981; Dolgin 1977).[41]

41. Dolgin's study of Meir Kahane's Jewish Defense League (JDL) may seem a curious inclusion; however, it should be remembered that the JDL was a proletariat antiestablishment organization that embarrassed the Jewish establishment and middle-class suburban Jews. When the league members initially began their activities, the nationalist direction of their politics closely and consciously paralleled those of Black nationalists—in particular the Black Panthers: "There is no question that despite the effort to paint us as racists—which is incredible nothingness—we certainly do feel and understand a great many of the things that, for example, the Panthers say. . . . And we don't differ with the Panthers in the sense that if after asking for 300 years for things from the government—federal or local—it becomes necessary to use unorthodox or outrageous ways. There is no question. On this we don't differ. We don't differ on their wanting to instill in their young people ethnic pride. Not at all. Where we do differ with them is where we think that nationalism

Racism in the Jewish community could be criticized and chastised by pointing to the diversity of the Jewish Diaspora, particularly in Israel, where there is an "in-gathering of the exiles." In this context, then, the Ethiopian Jewish community was extremely important precisely because they were black-skinned Jews who were "authentic" Africans: tangible evidence that Jews were neither a race nor a racist community that discriminated on the basis of skin color. Consequently, if there were individual Jews who happened to be white-skinned and happened to be racist, this was not a manifestation of Jewish identity but was directly in contradistinction to Jewish values. Under these circumstances, the directors of the North American Jewish Data Bank, with the agreement of the Council of Jewish Federations, concluded that to isolate and give attention to people who embodied dual heritages ignored the centrality of a Jewish identity, on the one hand, as far as a Jewish community was concerned, and, on the other hand, put emphasis on a racial identity that was marginal to the constitution of a Jewish identity.

The avoidance or evasion of dealing specifically with interracial Jewish people in the United States invites closer attention as interest in what constitutes a multiracial and a multicultural background increases. It is not a question of disinterest but a tactical policy motivated by a concern to frustrate accusations of racism. Yet within the American context, *not* directly examining the interracial dimension of intermarriage leaves untouched and undocumented the importance people may attach to two independent cultural identities whose significance and definition are often contested and debated on the merits of preserving memory for the sake of those who struggled against oppression. Here a reiteration is necessary, and I take it a step further: to ignore or overlook this dimension is to suppress the potent possibilities of the political and personal significance people can (even when they do not) attach to these two particular cultural identities whose raison d'être is memory and survival (continuity).

During the time that I was working on this project, friends periodically called to tell me about someone "whose name I have forgotten"

crosses the boundary line and becomes Nazism." See the 1971 interview with Meir Kahane and two responses in Porter and Drier (Lowenthal 1973, 277–87; Littman 1973, 278–295; Porter and Drier 1973, 296–300).

seen on television "yesterday." A number of comedians have used their interracial, Jewish, and Black identities as material for their performances. In reflecting on the ambivalence of some grandparents, who otherwise continued to be in contact with their interracially married children and offspring, there is one old joke: A "white" Jew is sitting on the subway when a Black man sits down near him. The latter takes a Yiddish newspaper out of his pocket and begins reading. The first man leans over and asks the second, "Excuse me Mister, you're Jewish?" to which the second Jew replies in Yiddish, "*noch dus durf ich haben?!*"[42] One comedian spoke of being every real-estate person's nightmare: in which neighborhood do you integrate a family which is Jewish and Black? An old joke no longer unusual enough to be amusing is "How do you fill three quotas at once? Hire a woman who is Black and Jewish."

In his introduction to Marian Wright Edelman's *The Measure of Our Success*, Jonah Edelman, her son, pays tribute to the importance the civil rights movement had on his life. In his estimation, the struggle against racism also created transformations in cultural identities such that

[i]n the absence of the civil rights period, the person I have become — the cultural mulatto, the well-to-do Black liberal wary of the political process, the sheltered Bar-Mitzvah boy who struggled with his blackness — never could have existed. Society, I do not believe, would have allowed someone of such a diverse heritage to develop. (Edelman 1992, x–xi)

Contrast this statement again with Franz Boas's flat assertion that only assimilation within the dominant population — articulated in the metaphor of blood — would solve the problem of racism and anti-Semitism. Intermarriage would dislodge the potency of these twin evils in his view. Yet half a century later, we have a young lawyer, Jonah Edelman, who takes pride in the fact that he is the product of an interracial family and distinguished by being both Jewish and Black.

Another public affirmation of the link between Jewish self-identity with Black self-identity is displayed by Justin E. Warfield, a young rap singer, who dedicated his album (*My Field Trip to Planet 9*) to his

42. Translation: "I need that too?!"

grandmother Betty Ann Haimowitz (Warfield 1993). Rap music appeals to its audience through its play on words as well as rhythm. The fact that Warfield is a Black man is documented by the photo on the album cover and evidenced by his music. If an identity informed by *Blackness* may also be assumed by the association of rap music and black identities in the public media (Spencer 1991; Gilroy 1993), Warfield intentionally notifies his audience of the complexity of identity through lyrics. In his song "Pick it Up Y'all," he firmly declares — and thus stakes his claim to — self-identification as a Jew: "the J to the W but Even in the middle the JEW is my initials / not a controversial riddle." As a declaration insisting on recognition and therefore respect, to whom is this addressed?

Rap singers such as 2 Live Crew have come under criticism from a broad range of groups — from Black women who are outraged by their misogyny to politicians who view the music as a stimulant for violence (Sinclair 1990). In playing with the initials of his name, J-E-W, in "Pick it Up Y'all," Warfield has woven into his music and made audible the existence of a public persona who is both a Jew and a Black: "I'm black as a panther and a lyrical Jew." At one and the same time, he is informing Jewish listeners that his Black identity is significant and that he is also a member of the Jewish community. This kind of public insistence echoes those integrated into the comedy acts of "multicultural" artists. In fact, it encapsulates a marvelous example of Stuart Hall's notion of "coupling." Warfield cannot be accused of anti-Semitism or self-hatred when explicitly professing his self-identity as a Jew. At the same time, he is reminding his Black audience of the cultural and racial diversity of the american Black experience.

The panther as a symbol of Black pride elicits from the listener an immediate association with the Black Panther Party of the 1960s. Interestingly, Warfield and many of his audience may not be aware of the existence of the Black Panther Party in Israel, which was founded by Jews of North African background protesting against ethnic discrimination and inequality. Founding an organization with this name itself was an intentionally provocative move, suggested by several American-born social workers who understood the political implications of adopting a name with symbolic capital and thus advancing an identity that might — it was hoped — attract the attention of American

Jews.[43] Once again, then, we find between Jews and Blacks a link that is uneasily dismissed as mere coincidence. This is not to suggest that one should overinterpret the significance of parallels that may be artificially imposed in order to gain access to the Israeli political center and thus place a domestic Israeli problem on the government's political agenda. However, it should also not be overlooked. How the issue of racism in America channels itself into the discourse of ethnicity in Israel illustrates the way ideas and theories travel at the level of popular opinion as well as between members of the academy (Behad 1993).

The emergence of a discussion on "biracial" identity does indeed evidence the coming of age of a new generation. Edelman uses the term "cultural mulatto," but, despite my own personal political reservations about the notion "biracial" as an affirmation of a positive identity, it is not possible to negate the validity of a position that disrupts the reductionist dichotomy of racial categories. This move was made possible by the civil rights movement, and one might interpret it as an indication of a dialectical process transcending white racism and the *anti*–anti racism represented in the Afrocentric circle of the Black Power movement.

In the 1960s and early '70s, the emphasis was on "Black is beautiful" — lighter-skinned African Americans were no longer privileged and instead often found themselves adopting styles of dress and hairstyles that required an investment in time and money to project an image that prevailed over their racial ambiguity.

The initiative of a younger generation of people, born since the late 1960s, to organize themselves around an issue that is public, political, and cultural also brings under challenge previous thinking about what it means to be biracial and multicultural. The demand for a redefinition of labels and categories that deny the complexity of biological genealogy and self-identification with racial, ethnic, and cultural heritage manifests a new confidence and a bold affirmation of plural identities. This development, it cannot be overstated, has evolved at the same time that the media has highlighted and focused attention on racial polarization.

Although the negative associations of "mixed-race" are not yet dis-

---

43. See Shlomo Swirski (1985; 1984; 1981), Ella Shohat (1988), and Inge Lederer-Gibel (1984) for critical discussions of ethnic discrimination in Israel.

lodged, they are under assault precisely because this discussion is taking place in the public arena. The next chapter probes identity, self-referentiality, and "biracialism" from a slightly different perspective and provides a brief introduction to the issue of miscegenation and "multiracialism."

3

BLACK, JEWISH, AND INTERRACIAL (I)

Racial categorizations may be untenable scientifically; however, their political significance remains a salient aspect of American life. The idea of racial ambiguity is, in this context, not an apolitical notion but linked very intimately to the history of racism in the United States.[1] Official racial designations have not been stable but have been slightly modified throughout American history as a whole and specifically in different states. What has remained consistent over time, however, is the law and social custom stipulating that "a drop of blood" determines that one is Black. Although I have been deploying the terms "biracial" and "interracial" interchangeably, it needs to be stressed that I have done so with a discomfort and even deliberate inconsistency. Given the limitations of a language infused by race thinking, I cannot find another way to signify people who have one parent identified by society as Black and one parent identified as white. This criterion is completely arbitrary given the fact that many socially defined Blacks can point to European and Native American Indian ancestry. Nevertheless, it is a definition that coincides with current conventional understandings of the social definition of racial identity.

Leaving aside, for the moment, any discussion on the political semantics and significance of the term, I want to briefly highlight a number of social, historical, and political aspects that impact on the representation of "biracial" people. My intent here is not to compose a coherent overview of the history of romantic interracial relations or "miscegenation." Instead, the purpose is to call attention to a range of notable factors that may inform or affect — even tangentially — the experience of those whose plural heritage, as a product of a politicized

1. A loosely parallel phenomenon to racial ambiguity at the level of individuals and social definitions is the political occurrence of "deracialised politics," which Manning Marable and Leith Mullings ascribe to Black politicians who "minimise or downplay their racial identity or affiliations with institutions within the African-American community" (1994, 64). Kwame A. Appiah offers a credible elucidation of the nuanced distinctions between racialism and racism (1992).

biological genealogy,[2] have been an object of legal regulation and social scrutiny.

Race relations between Blacks and whites have never been a private affair in the United States, and this is particularly evident in the legislative intervention into that most personal sphere: the domain of marriage.[3] The first legislative intervention against interracial marriage was carried out in 1661 when the General Assembly of the Colony of Maryland decreed that children of white mothers and slave fathers would carry the status of the father, contradicting prevailing English law regarding mothers and children.[4] In addition to this punitive act, the status of the white wife was reduced to that of a servant. In effect, for the remainder of her husband's life, the wife would become the master's temporary property. In 1705, Virginia became the first colony to impose a total ban on marriages between Blacks and whites.

Colonial laws regarding marital relations between whites and Blacks provided the legal and social foundation from which to restrict the evolution of a recognizable intermediary group between whites and Blacks. At the same time, law and social custom reinforced the permanent institutionalization of a biracial society. One was Black or one was white, but one could not be both. For a brief period, the criteria for being legally Black was flexible enough to accommodate the possibility that a free-born individual, known in society as a Black, could nevertheless be legally white (such as the 1785 Virginia definition that did not look for Black ancestors beyond one's grandparents). During the colonial period, marriage between Blacks and whites was not prohibited by

2. Again it should be emphatically stressed that racial categories are unscientific, arbitrary, and meaningless. The development and social consciousness of racial formations in the United States, however, is *not* arbitrary, and therefore race is a social fact that has been shaped by legislation, politics, economic sanctions, and social custom. Sexual relations, marriage, and procreation across the color line are thus singled out here for special attention.

3. I am indebted to Joel Williamson's study (1980) for ideas contributing to this discussion. For more comprehensive studies on the history of "miscegenation," see John G. Mencke (1979) and Bryon Lurti Martyn (1979). Mencke's dissertation was supervised by Joel Williamson. For a brief review, which neglects any reference to the *Americanness* of american Blacks as a common denominator with white Americans, see Phil Brown (1989–90).

4. Virginia followed suit in 1662.

law; however the status of the children in terms of public opinion remained ambiguous. In 1678, the Maryland Assembly passed an act that sanctioned officially ignoring the existence of children of interracial marriage. This decision had less to do with prevention than with social etiquette. The "Act for Keeping a Register of Birthes, Marriages and Burialls in each Respective County" (1678) legally exempted the registration of births, marriages, and deaths of "Negroes, Indians and Mulattoes" from all public records (Martyn 1979, 31). The ambiguity of who qualified as "mulatto," however, threatened to destabilize the definition of a white identity and was eliminated rather quickly.

Although the social definition of being Black, imposed by the one-drop rule, was adopted as an affirmation of a political identity during the 1960s, the very expression "to look white" indicates the explicit invention of a category whose meaning cannot exist on a visual level but only as an ideological construct. Gunnar Myrdal's momentous project, *An American Dilemma*, makes this point very clearly in laying out the definitions of the racial terminology used in the study. "There are also American Negroes with the clearest of white skin, the bluest of blue eyes, and the long and narrow head which happens to be both a Negro and a 'Nordic' trait" (1944, 114).

Fifty years ago, when some contemporary social constructionists were still in diapers and others were waiting to be born, Myrdal and his coauthors had already insisted that "[t]he definition of the 'Negro race' is thus a social and conventional, not a biological concept. The social definition and not the biological facts actually determines the status of an individual and his place in interracial relations" (Myrdal 1944, 114). Beginning in the colonial period but with increasing anxiety by the beginning of the Civil War, "looking like" a white person had to be distinguished from actually "being" a white person. This was in fact a crisis because there were more and more white-looking slave children who also remarkably resembled their masters.[5]

5. There are innumerable family histories, but one that has persistently troubled the white (particularly southern) American imagination is the relationship between Sally Hemings, a light-skinned slave, and her "owner," Thomas Jefferson. Barbara Chase-Riboud created a storm with her literary account of Thomas Jefferson's slave mistress and their children, who were light enough to leave the South and pass as white. The book, *Sally Hemings: A Novel* (1979), so upset the preservers of the

It was the *invisibility* of Blackness that became a threat to white self-identity. Because whiteness could only have significant meaning in juxtaposition to Blackness,[6] if this opposition proved to be an illusion, the entire cornerstone for attributing significance to separate racial group identities would be destroyed. Not only did this have economic implications, there were profound ideological and moral ramifications to legitimizing a rupture in the schema of a rigid, binary-race-based social order.

The obsession with skin color reveals a preoccupation with identity and the manner in which identity is represented. The issue of appearance has always played a significant role in the discourse of race. The one-drop rule, however, defined and confined people with African ancestry — however remote — from being designated white unless they moved to an area where they were able to conceal all traces of their family background (Myrdal 1944; Davis and Gardner 1965).

Passing as white meant cutting ties with the past and with genealogy, and once skin color lost its significance as a visible indicator of race only legal definitions of race could be relied on to protect and safeguard racial boundaries. Race as a legally binding category had to be reconceptualized and thus invented. Laws needed to be imposed in order to maintain social order. As historian Eva Saks points out, appearance (looking like) and being (without Black ancestors) brought the legal system to an "epistemological loop" (Saks 1988, 58). Reading through the miscegenation cases, Saks found that once physical appearance no longer provided reliable evidence for racial identity, and given the fact that the metaphor of blood lacked an external observable referent, the courts eventually had no alternative but to consider legal race as a problem of representation. Consequently, one finds a series of linguistic

---

Jeffersonian image that it became one of the only novels ever written to have fueled controversial academic rebuttals. See, for instance, Moss and Moss (1987), Dabney (1981), and Burg (1986). The novel was used as the basis for the film *Jefferson in Paris* (1994), which disappeared from Durham, North Carolina, as fast as it arrived. Chase-Riboud has written a follow-up novel, *The President's Daughter* (1994), in which Sally and Thomas's daughter, Harriet, leaves Monticello in 1822 at the young age of twenty-two and moves to Philadelphia, where she passes for white.

6. For pertinent interventions that destabilize the construction of a white history of the United States, see Philips (1990) and Pinar (1993).

acrobatics in the legal discourse of miscegenation as jurists try to formalize "referents and *referentiality* for race" (Saks 1988, 61).[7]

In theory and in practice, the Supreme Court decision in *Plessy v. Ferguson* (1896) stands as the landmark for a legal definition of what constitutes a Black person (Thomas 1997). In this case, Homer Plessy had argued that he was visibly white and therefore should be allowed to sit in the train's white section. Overriding his skin color as an indicator of *not* being a Negro, the Court instead took "judicial notice" of the fact that a Negro is *any* person known to have Black ancestry.[8] *Plessy v. Ferguson* is well known as the case that legalized segregation. More significant, however, is that by extending judicial approval to a racial definition based on common knowledge, the decision set a legal precedent by endorsing, rather than dismantling, racial categories. Eighty-seven years later the U.S. Supreme Court refused to review its position.[9]

Antimiscegenation laws have reflected social attitudes about descent and underline the very public nature of family and kinship on the one hand and race on the other.[10] The term "miscegenation" was coined in 1864 by David Croly, editor of the *New York Daily Graphic* (Saks 1988, 42). The notion of biracialism could only exist as an ideological

7. A further example of the continuing discomfort with racial ambiguity was the Hollywood casting of Alex Haley's slave great-grandmother in the film production of his autobiographical account, *Queen.* Instead of locating a phenotypically white, African American, the producers cast a brown-skinned (although interracial) actress. Writing about the (mis)casting of mixed-race Amerasians, Teresa Kay Williams points out that "the complexities of multiple racial identities cannot be imaginatively portrayed in a world where caricatures define reality" (1995, 87).

8. The decision, 6 March 1857, voided the 1820 Missouri Compromise and essentially gave legal support to proponents of polygenesis by denying "persons with Negro blood, because of their African slave heritage" citizenship or "protection guaranteed by the U.S. Constitution and the federal laws based on the Constitution" (Martyn 1979). For a discussion of the exclusion of american Blacks from the political community and the different meanings of the bicentennial for Black and white Americans, see A. Leon Higginbotham (1988).

9. See chapter 4 for discussion of the Phipps case.

10. Myrdal (1944) is particularly informative on this topic, and special attention should be directed to the meticulous footnotes in volume 2, pages 1203–12, which painstakingly review all the current research including (but not only) the investigations of E. Frazier, Melville Herskovits, and Edward Reuter.

and political concept whose meaning was constituted through associating metaphors of blood and heredity with disease and pathology.[11]

Miscegenation became of obsessive interest to the white public in the nineteenth century, in part due to the increased importance of social Darwinism (Saks 1988; Brown 1989–90). During the nineteenth century, scientists provided legitimacy to popular notions about blood and heredity. The obsession with classifications and categories became a crucial tool for calculating and defining the racial composition of people. Application of a terminology of fractions — in which genealogy was pivotal to the composition of a legal definition for race — reflected both the authority of science as objective and neutral and the ideological concern with racial purity that permeated the manner in which scientists approached their research.[12]

In the public arena, science and racist ideology coincided in providing a basis for demarcating and legislating social boundaries and individual identities. The "mulatto," being neither Black nor white, was deviant: "the offspring of these unnatural connections are generally sickly and effeminate" (*State v. Scott*, Ga. 1869, quoted in Saks 1988, 64). Newspaper editorials helped to fuel and sustain public concern with the issue of miscegenation. At the Arkansas Constitutional Convention of 1868, for instance, the conservative white newspaper persistently condemned white delegates in the Radical element for advocating "miscegenation and mongrelism" (*Arkansas Daily Gazette*, 1 February 1868, quoted in Palmer 1965, 111).

Fears about racial equality were exploited and equated with interracial marriage. Prejudice could be appealed to by reminding fathers of their paternal responsibility to protect their daughters. Delegate W. D. Moore of Ashley County, Arkansas, warned that enfranchisement meant Negroes will "marry their daughters and, if necessary, hug their wives" (quoted in Palmer 1965, 118). A week later (8 February), the *Gazette* petitioned its white male readers:

Poor white men of Arkansas, think of this! Reflect that when you send your children to the public schools they will not only be compelled to sit side by side with negroes in obedience to radical laws, but the radical party encourage the

11. See Saks (1988) on the manner in which antimiscegenation laws were formulated through a figure of speech dependent on metaphors of blood.

12. See the collection of essays in Harding (1993a).

latter to aspire to win the affections of your youthful child with a view to matrimonial alliance, by refusing to provide in the fundamental law against miscegenation. (quoted in P. Palmer 1965, 117)

As late as 1957, thirty states had legal restrictions on interracial marriages, ranging from total prohibition to heavy fines, although the criteria for a legal definition of Negro varied. Marriage between people legally and socially defined as Black and white were only legalized in 1967 in the case of *Loving v. Virginia*. In this case, the Supreme Court overruled state laws prohibiting interracial marriage on the basis of these laws' being unconstitutional. Since 1967, reported interracial marriages have more than doubled, although there are no reliable statistics due to the manner in which the U.S. census is conducted. Estimates, however, suggest that 20 percent of all interracial marriages in 1993 were between Blacks and whites.[13] The formal decriminalization of interracial unions, however, has not gone hand in hand with social attitudes toward marriage across the color line.[14] In this vein, Spike Lee's *Jungle Fever* cleverly unmasked the extent to which interracial marriage remains a controversial issue for both Blacks and whites.[15]

13. *Newsweek*'s cover story "What Color is Black?" (13 February 1995, 72) included four articles as well as a table of statistics from the U.S. census indicating that between 1970 and 1993 the total of interracial marriages in the United States had gone from 310,000 to 1,950,000. The actual referent for this figure is unclear, as it is standard for "interracial" marriage to designate, exclusively, marriages between whites and those designated as "not white." According to the *Newsweek* estimate, 20 percent of the interracial marriages were between Black and white partners. For interracial marriages in general, Hanna Rosin (of the *New Republic*) cites the figure 1.2 million, or 2.2 percent of all marriages (1994, 12). The *Wall Street Journal* (27 January 1993) reported a sevenfold increase in interracial marriages since 1960, when the estimate was 157,000, to the current census figure of 1.1 million. Russell, Wilson, and Hall note that in 1970, 1.5 out of every 1,000 (or 65,000) marriages were Black/white, whereas in 1990 the figure has risen to 4 out of every 1,000, or 218,000, of which 71 percent are between Black men and white women (1992, 116).

14. Every year articles appear in popular magazines and newspapers under titles such as "Black-White Marriages Rise but Couples Still Face Scorn" [*New York Times* (2 December 1991, B6)] and Sylvester Monroe, "Love in Black and White" [*Elle* (March 1992, 94)].

15. Lee's film and his usual cryptic interviews that set up a controversial atmosphere before the release of his films opened up months of discussion and debate on

I suggest that the difference between nineteenth-century biological notions of race and the late-twentieth-century recognition that these are social definitions that have no basis in science is crucial but not critical to the way race and racial identities are understood. Although contemporary social propriety inhibits anyone from publicly employing biological justifications against interracial marriage, the idea that race is a salient social phenomenon continues to be a significant factor in interpersonal relations, particularly at the intimate level. The terminology of race is displaced by culture, and coded language serves to veil racial prejudices. This is evident in the continuity of the language of racial identity: biracial, multiracial, and mixed-race. It is a language from which we cannot escape, but the persistence of these terms, unsurprisingly, reflects a legacy of biologized thinking.

The emergence of a discussion on "biracial identity" represents a generational change made possible by the civil rights movement and its offshoot, the Black Power movement. Since the mid-1980s, a younger generation of people has initiated and founded associations that bring together and demand recognition of biracial and multiracial people. Many of their parents came to maturity during the heyday of 1960s social movements — a period marked by diligent articulation of social identities. This was an emotional and political period, as well as an era in which discussions about identities in general, and racial and ethnic identities in particular, became significantly more public and the desirability of assimilation came increasingly under question.

Embedded in the very concept "biracial" is an inescapable duality that seems to determine the alternative ways of thinking about positioning oneself. And this, I think, is a problem that is imposed and can be internalized by people whose parents are of different racial backgrounds.[16] There is a subtle but pernicious social dictate that expects

---

his depiction of Black male attitudes toward Black women, issues of skin color, and gender relations (and, as a theme that surfaced in *Do the Right Thing*, his exploration of the tension of racial identity among working-class Italian Americans).

16. Deborah J. Johnson, a professor of psychology at the University of Wisconsin at Madison, argues for more widespread research on biracial children, as a third group in empirical studies of racial preference (attitudes and identity formation) of Black and white children (1992). Note also the publication of magazines such as *Interrace* and *New People*, directed at multiracial families.

the individual to position oneself publicly. The growing momentum to refuse these slippery directives is taking place at the same time that definitions of *Blackness* are being debated and deconstructed, reassessed and resurrected.

The current under-thirty generation has increasingly called for a redefinition of labels and categories that confine them to identifying with only part of their heritage. The proliferation of biracial and multiracial student groups on campuses throughout the country, as well as the growing refusal of young people to mark only one racial category on official documents, suggests a new confidence and a bolder affirmation of the complexity of identity and self-referentiality than may have been possible previously. Interestingly, this development has taken place at the same time that the media have called attention to an increasing racial polarization [see "What Color Is Black?" (1995) cited earlier].

During the first two hundred years, the U.S. census' racial classifications for people who are counted as *not* white have served as an indicator of fluctuations in contemporary social and political attitudes about race.[17] In the 1890s, the light-skinned sector of the African American community was subdivided officially under the terms "Mulatto," "Quadroon," and "Octoroon"—categories that loosely paralleled social and class divisions. One hundred years later, opponents of the "multiracial" category point back to this earlier racial fragmentation (Wright 1994). Indeed, there is no contradiction between the assertion that race is an ideological construct and an acknowledgment that race has meaning as a social fact. Under these circumstances, the maintenance of a unified stable racial designation that includes everyone of African descent—in other words, *Black people*—suggests a feasible

17. The first census was conducted in 1790, and the purposes of racial categories were to distinguish free whites from indentured servants, African slaves, and Native Americans. From 1850, racial distinctions on the census, for the population that was not *perceptibly* or socially defined as white, were influenced by supposedly scientific work on anthropological classifications, phrenology, and cranial measurements on the one hand, and a social discourse articulated through metaphorical conceptualizations of race, blood, and pollution, on the other hand. For a brief, but informative, genealogy of racial classifications and the history of census-taking, see David Theo Goldberg (1995).

political strategy with regard to allocation of resources and the implementation of civil rights laws.[18]

In the mid-1970s, a branch of the federal government introduced Directive 15 to standardize racial and ethnic categories for the purpose of statistical evaluations, implementing legislative correctives, and administering policymaking.[19] The problem with these official categories, however, is that aside from their strictly political advantages, the continued deployment of racial classifications neglects the complexity of individual genealogies even in areas as important as monitoring a particular group's susceptibility to certain diseases.[20] Furthermore, a careful examination of the classifications demonstrates that they are often an arbitrary and unreliable index, especially for medical research. As James Shreeve wrote in a special issue on race in *Discov-*

18. See Nikki Giovanni (1994) and Dan Danielsen and Karen Engle (1995, 63–122).

19. Office of Information and Regulatory Affairs at the Office of Management and Budget (OMB) — they make final recommendations on census reclassification revisions. OMB Directive 15 establishes the categories used by all federal agencies in order to have a standardized criterion for data: "This Directive provides standard classifications or recordkeeping, collection and presentation of data on race and ethnicity in Federal program administrative reporting and statistical activities. These classifications should not be interpreted as being scientific or anthropological in nature, nor should they be viewed as determinants of eligibility for participation in any Federal program. They have been developed in response to needs expressed by both the executive branch and the Congress to provide for the collection and use of compatible, nonduplicated, exchangeable racial and ethnic data by Federal agencies." The full directive is reprinted in Zack (1995, 206–9).

20. See J. Jarrett Clinton (1993, 2158): the AHCPR (Agency for Health Policy and Research) recommended universal screening for sickle cell disease because "it is not possible to determine reliably an individual's racial or ethnic background by physical appearance, surname, presumed racial heritage or self-report" (quoted in Lawrence 1995, 36). In 1993, I caught the tail end of a news report on a press conference regarding the initiation of testing the entire population for sickle cell disease because not all the people who self-identified as white were in fact "white." By the time I absorbed this information, it was too late to tape but I assumed it would appear in the next day's newspaper. The admission that more than a few white people might, in fact, *not* be white, seemed quite newsworthy considering the fact that this communiqué took place in the atmosphere of Pat Buchanan's complaints against the "browning of America." In fact, however, until I came across Lawrence's essay, I had heard no further mention of the AHCPR report nor could I find anyone who had heard anything about it.

ery, classifications of the global population might more accurately be done along the lines of digestion or fingerprints (Shreeve 1994). The issue, however, is not the *validity* or continued viability of racial classifications, but *the manner* in which these designations manifest (and impose) political significance and social meaning for individuals in a given society.

During the last decade, individuals whose parents are of different "racial" categories, have voiced exasperation with the manner in which these labels impose a choice of formally identifying with only one of their parents. In addition, parents of "mixed-race" children have mobilized together in order to gain recognition of this in-between category under the label "multiracial." The term "multiracial" is as problematic as other labels (e.g., biracial, mixed-race, interracial) that signify kinship lineages across color lines. The reaction to this campaign, therefore, has been mixed.

At the intersection of private lives and the public domain, the issue of naming and definition has always been political. The literature on interracial marriages and interracial children has generally presupposed a problem of marginality (Rosner 1993). The overriding concern lies in how and where the children of a Black/white union will be situated. With whom will they identify? And how are they to be identified? The negative implications of these studies are somewhat inverted by advocates for a multiracial category.

The popular movement to promote multiracialism has coincided with trends in the academy, where postmodernist fragmentation of identities and social constructs have become fashionable. Multiracial does not signify an end to race thinking but is suggestive of a diminishing affirmative attitude toward blackness. Thus the resurrection of a middle category seems to be threatening just at a time when renewed attention is being paid to the link between problems of structural inequality and racism. Within the american Black community, caste consciousness and concern with racial features have influenced marriage patterns, particularly among educated American Negroes, exemplified best in the "Blue Vein" societies (Gatewood 1990; Frazier 1957a; Myrdal 1944; Russell, Wilson, and Hall 1992).[21]

21. Members of these societies supposedly had to be light enough for their veins to show through their skin as noticeably blue. Attitudes in the Black community

The issue of a multiracial category has stimulated questions about who should be included. The significance and meaning of "multiracial" reveals the persistence of racial terminology representing an abstract idea but which is probably applicable to nearly every Black American who has been in this country since the slave period. (This is in addition to other ethnic and racial groups including Blacks from the Caribbean, Latin America, and Mexico.) One of the questions that has been raised is whether the institutionalization of an official category would include subcategories according to how people register a breakdown of their heritage. Undoubtedly this would eventually disrupt the conceptual foundations on which the classifications were constructed.

The issue of identity and racial classifications revolves around identifying oneself as a member of one or more groups. The critical aspect to which I want to call attention is that for people whose immediate heritage places them in a position to identify with more than one group, the fluidity of group boundaries is a pragmatic and practical facet of their system of self-reference. Therefore, while the semantics of racial terminology highlight an individual's ancestry or network of kinship, in the public sphere the politics of this discourse unveils a myriad of intergroup linkages that invisibly mark any apparently homogeneous sector of the population (Haizlip 1994; T. K. Williams 1995). At the same time, ethnic and race-based communities of meaning, which have historically been subordinate groups within the wider society, are troubled by porousness at the boundaries — a porousness that I suggest facilitates and fosters assimilation. Specifically, among Japanese, Jewish, and African Americans, endogamy, or the question of "marrying out," is neither taken for granted, encouraged, nor approved.[22] A significant reason refers directly to attitudes about historical legacy and cultural continuity.

In sharp contrast to advocates of "multiracial," Carol Camper —

---

about color and skin tone are treated in Spike Lee's film *School Daze* (1988) and by Kathe Sandler's *Question of Color* (1992).

22. The issue of *tolerance* after a marriage has taken place is a separate question altogether and therefore should not be confused with approval. On Japanese attitudes toward interracial marriage, see Teresa Kay Williams with special attention to references in footnotes 9 and 10 (1995, 79–96). Williams, a sociologist, writes from the position of a bilingual, bicultural, Japanese European-American.

editor of *Miscegenation Blues* — writes in her introduction, children of "mixed marriages" do not repudiate the history and heritage of the parent who happens to be a member of the dominant group by identifying with the politically/socially subordinate group to which the other parent belongs. Thus the refusal to adopt an assimilationist disposition manifests political opposition against the threat to annihilate existing racial groups, their histories and cultures as if they were obsolete (1994, xxiii).

Contemporary notions of "passing" have changed because ascriptive legal definitions of racial identity no longer play a central role in social definitions of race. In the starkest terms, passing used to require a deliberate erasure of memory, although the individual might always fear that someone from the past would appear and threaten their adopted identity.[23] In the 1990s, racial ambiguity has taken the place of passing.[24] Skin color is at the crux of this predicament. And I use the word "predicament" deliberately, as it suggests the possibility of different options (Cross 1991; Russell, Wilson, and Hall 1992; Scales-Trent 1995).

When a biracial person presents a persona that imitates what is stereotypically labeled "acting white" — in dress, speech, and gestures — s/he may encounter hostility from other Blacks who interpret this as a denial of heritage.[25] This raises the problem of what constitutes heritage and how it is linked to a personal sense of identity that is voluntary — as opposed to mandatory. Susan Graham, a white (that is how she publicly identifies herself) and Jewish woman married to a Christian Black man, canvassed and established a group under the title Project Race: Reclassify All Children Equally. The objectives of Project Race, which has

23. For examples of the life-threatening consequences for passing and remaining in the South, where family genealogies were easily known on both sides of the racial divide, see Davis and Gardiner (1965); for a classic Hollywood rendition of the "tragic mulatto" and the personal cost of passing, see the two film versions of *Imitation of Life* (1934/1959).

24. For example, consider the controversy over the racial identity of singer Mariah Carey and its attempted erasure by CBS Columbia. See L. Jones (1994).

25. Anecdotal references can be found over the years in *Ebony* and *Essence*. One recent personal account of this phenomenon as it is subjectively experienced, published as an opinion piece accompanying *Newsweek*'s cover story "What Color Is Black?" (February 1995, 16), was by Brian A. Courtney and entitled "Freedom from Choice: Being Biracial Has Meant Denying Half of My Identity."

branches in thirty-six states, are to (1) advocate for legislative directives instituting a multiracial classification on all state and federal official forms and to (2) promote multiracial pride based on the assumption that self-esteem requires racial identification with both parents.

Cultural critic and theomusicologist, Jon Michael Spencer, a vocal opponent of the "multiracialist" movement, challenged Graham with a fascinating anecdote during a talk show on KCRW ("Which Way L.A.?") hosted by Warren Alden in Los Angeles: "Around mid-century, the daughter of a prominent black composer in Los Angeles came home from grade school and asked her Jewish mother what color they were. And the Jewish mother said, 'we are a colored family.'"[26] Graham's rather unimaginative response completely overlooked the nuanced question of whether Jews are white. Undoubtedly, however, this instances a typical response from most American Jews of European background who have internalized a "white" racial identity because they have white skin and feel they have successfully assimilated into mainstream America.

First of all, let me tell you that my daughter has a Jewish mother also and my daughter is not black, my daughter is multiracial. . . . Let me also point out that it is not that I do not want my child to be black, my child right now is White on the United States Census because they told me she should be white, that she has their blessing to be White; it is not that I want her to be White; I don't want her to be White nor do I want her to be Black. I want her to be what she is — multiracial.

The irony of Graham's comments is that there are countries where not too long ago Jews were officially designated as a race. Under the logic of white supremacy her children's "multiracial" status is not due to being white, but to being Jewish. More to the point, however, is that Graham positions herself first and foremost as a white woman — she has assumed the "racial" identity of being "white." In fact, it is Professor Jon Michael Spencer, the Black scholar, who with conscientious precision suggestively offers her a subtle distinction between Jewishness and white-

26. KCWR, Santa Monica 89.9 FM, broadcast this program on 8 April 1994. I called Professor Spencer to ask the source for this anecdote, and he told me it can be found in Arvey (1984).

ness.[27] Graham, however, fails to pick up the cue for momentary self-reflection.[28] Whiteness and Jewishness are not co-terminous, a subject to which I will return in more detail. For anti-Semites, even in contemporary America, white and Jewish is an oxymoron![29]

Where light skin was once taken as a valuable asset, the 1960s was a period when the emphasis on "Black is beautiful" seemed momentarily to reverse traditional attitudes toward skin color within the Black community. The idea of claiming a biracial identity as if it were a source of pride was unthinkable and in contradiction to notions of what it meant to be Black and proud. Self-perception and social definitions could not coincide precisely because of the prevailing rigidity of the significance of racial identity as a source of pride. Any insistence on the validity of claiming white heritage was seen as a sign of betrayal.

As people of biracial background become more visible and vocal, exemplified by the number of talk shows focused on interracial children and the proliferation of literature written by and about biracial children, one common and recurring theme is misperception as a result of appearance. One who is phenotypically Black or has distinctive features that mark him or her as African American does not undergo the same experience as someone whose racial background is ambiguous.

27. I confirmed this interpretation with Professor Spencer, who agreed that I had accurately apprehended the exchange.

28. Contrast, for example, anthropologist Elliot Liebow's experience in the early 1960s while doing fieldwork. In his retrospective reflections (1967), Liebow points out that although his being Jewish came up only twice during his fieldwork, both times evidence his being marked as other than white. He could not have been more succinct: "We had been talking for some ten minutes or so when (a soldier in a local bootleg joint) asked me whether I was 'Eyetalian.' I told him I was Jewish. 'That's just as good,' he said. 'I'm glad you're not white' " (252).

29. Abbey L. Ferber writes of one example: *The Turner Diaries* by Andrew MacDonald, "a novel widely read by members of various white supremacist groups," which anticipates a revolution in which absolute racial segregation is violently imposed. Ferber quotes a horrifying passage describing the "horribly bloated, purplish face" of white women hung for the transgression of sexual involvement with racial others: "There are many thousands of hanging female corpses . . . all wearing identical placards around their necks. They are the White women who were married to or living with Blacks, *with Jews or with other non-White males*" (Ferber 1995, 165–66; italics added).

An African American racial identity seems obvious and the issue of explaining one's background is almost incidental (at least in initial encounters with strangers), whereas a light-skinned person mistaken for white will usually be cognizant of the gap between how they are perceived and how they perceive themselves.[30]

The issue of how one appears — what one looks like — has an extraordinary impact on the interaction between self-identity and social identity. Whatever label one chooses to use, the existence of physical characteristics that mark one as a person of color are immediately visible. Therefore, an obviously brown or black person is not usually mistaken for a white or Hispanic person. The issue of racial or ethnic background surfaces only where there is racial ambiguity. Holly Devor's research (1989) with women who are mistaken for men provides interesting insights.

Devor explored the rupture between self-perception and the perception of others that occurs when the way a person thinks of herself is contradicted by the way she is thought of by others. Devor began with a careful distinction between two conceptual categories — sex as a biological status and gender as a social identity. Although the women whom she interviewed were at ease with their sex identity as biologically female, they did not conform to prevailing social definitions about women. Their appearance and the way they carried themselves contradicted both male and female expectations of femininity. Devor found that despite their refusal to conform to social definitions of what it means to be a woman, the women she interviewed were acutely sensitive to their encounter with other women and men. Each time the women became self-conscious of being misrecognized as a man there was an unpleasant "disjunction between I (as subject) and me (as an object)" (Devor 1989, 60).

Devor proposes that when people become self-conscious about being seen differently from the way they thought they should be seen, there are three possible reactions. A person may try to accommodate herself to others' expectations and thus attempt to alter her own self-definition.

---

30. This predicament applies as well to those who are not biracial, although the difference resides in the question of choice as a result of the discourse of "mixed-race." See Adrian Piper (1992), Toi Derricottee (1993), and Judy Scales-Trent (1995).

Alternatively, she may attempt to alter other people's attitudes in order that they not only accept but recognize — thus confer legitimacy — to her own expectations. The third option, which may be the most satisfying, leads one to search for other people who conform to and confirm one's own self-image.

Although most of the women Devor interviewed were uncomfortable when women or men mistook them for men, they were also unwilling to alter their appearance or behavior in order to conform to social expectations. At the same time, Devor also noted that the women themselves had internalized many of the values that they rejected. Ideas about femininity, for example, paralleled standard ideas about the convergence of biological sex and gender.

The issue of racial ambiguity slightly parallels gender ambiguity, for in both cases the issue of self-identity is intimately linked to others' perception. In both cases, there is a moment in which one chooses to affirm or negate the misimpression created by appearance and in both instances this decision is a self-conscious political position.[31] Although "race" is an arbitrary ideological construct without scientific legitimacy, "sex" remains a reference to a valid biological fact — most people are born with distinct sexual organs that generally distinguish males from females, and it is only women who are physiologically equipped to bear children. But what is called into question here is not whether race and sex/gender[32] exist in reality, but rather the social definition deeply ingrained in the way society and its members think about racial and gender identities. In a society that places value and confers a social

31. One ingenious example is artist and philosopher Adrian Piper, who is famous for handing out cards that state she is Black. In November 1993, the City Gallery of Contemporary Art in Raleigh, North Carolina, displayed a special exhibition of her work.

32. I am deliberately calling attention to the affinity between both words because as far as I have been able to ascertain, it is only in the English language that two separate words have been created to differentiate biological and social notions for the social definitions of male and female. This semantic differentiation diverts attention away from the conception of the body as "a surface of social inscription and as the locus of lived experience" Elizabeth Grosz (1993, 188). For several other illuminating discussions of sexual difference and the politics of developing theories that account for embodied, engendered subjectivities, see Naomi Schor and Elizabeth Weed (1994).

status based on appearance, denying or confirming the opposite of what one looks like is more than a matter of reducing social categories to hypothetical essences; it is transformed into a political stance precisely because of the benefits or losses that result from this affirmation.

Misperceptions are not only seen as irritating but are sometimes described as provoking hostility. Some of the personal experiences expressed by biracial people include the pain of being rejected by Blacks because of intraracial color prejudice while being more readily accepted by whites. The sense of social isolation in such a situation can be dislocating. For instance, in *Black, White, Other*, a collection of interviews from people of biracial background, edited by Lise Funderburg, those who identify as Black, but are misidentified as white, frequently complained about having to prove themselves (Funderburg 1994).

In the next chapter the focus will be on the interviews I conducted with eight individuals. As a prelude to this discussion, I want to consider the experiences of the five interracial adults included in Funderburg's survey who had a Jewish parent and a Black parent. In the early 1990s, Funderburg was one of a few people of interracial background who were interested in collecting, and succeeded in publishing, the narratives of other people who shared their experience of having parents who were socially considered to be of different racial backgrounds. The specific experiences of individuals with biracial heritages differ, although the experiences share some common aspects and the individuals have encountered similar situations. The primary impetus for (re)-presenting self-portraits to the public has been to rectify the absence of our voices and to speak in our own names. Funderburg's interviews were of interest to me personally — at the subjective level — as well as in relation to my own research into how interracial people define and situate themselves. As I will discuss further, the themes that emerge in the narratives of the people who collaborated with Funderburg were very similar to those in my own interviews.

Kimani Fowlin, a twenty-four-year-old from New York, has a background vaguely similar to my own (Funderburg 1994, 54–58). Her father is Jamaican, and her mother is Jewish. West Indians, and people linked to any of the other Caribbean islands, tend to be conscious and proud of their island heritage. My own experience has been that anytime I have met someone connected to Jamaica, whether they were an immigrant or a first-generation American, there has been an immediate sense of common identity that has nothing to do with camaraderie. Fowlin's parents met in Greenwich Village, New York. She described her maternal grandparents as very conservative, white middle-class Jews. Her father's family were "middle-class-sort-of-bourgeoisie Jamaicans, assimilated to white American standards" (1994, 56).

Fowlin was closer to her mother's family, although there were disagreements with the grandmother over race issues. Fowlin portrayed her mother's adoption of a Black persona in public as "false pretense." Her critical stance, communicated by the derisive characterization of "false pretense," is the opposite of Frantz Fanon Walker, one of my collaborators, who expressed delight in the ambiguity of his mother's telephone style:

She's been around Black people so long I think if you talked to her on the phone you wouldn't be sure what she was. She doesn't really talk like — if you spoke to her you couldn't tell what she was, Black or white or Jewish.

Among American Jews, the initial assumption is that only white-skinned people are Jewish, despite the knowledge that not all Jews are either white or European. This is an example of the gap between having information and yet maintaining preconceptions. Fowlin's satisfaction in undermining stereotypes Jews have about Jews was shared by all my interviewees as well as myself. In addition, as can be seen in the following passage, she recognizes the advantages of having a plural heritage while at the same time feeling handicapped by an illiteracy for which her parents were responsible:

When I'm around Jewish people I love to shock them and say, "Yes, I'm Jewish." And at times I get this overwhelming feeling of how lucky I am to come from such diverse cultures. I can really say that *this* is me and *this* is me. But because I really haven't delved deeply into each one, I'm not really a part of it, and that's where I think I'm losing. I wish I had grabbed onto one — actually I wish I'd grabbed onto both — but I took the superficial aspects of both. I think that's partly because of my mom and dad. I get angry at them a lot for that because I wish they had directed me. (Funderburg 1994, 58)[33]

33. The tactic of shocking people into confronting their stereotypes or preconceptions is a repeated theme in my interviews. See chapter 4.

One of my interests is in the manner in which the terms "Jewish" and "white" are used interchangeably. In the preceding passage, Fowlin is quite explicit about claiming Jewishness as an identity but she later uses "white" as an aspect of identity in her discussion: "Usually right off the bat with white people I let them know, 'Hey, I'm also half of you,' so I can have the liberty to make comments and things they think I shouldn't say but I can" (Funderburg 1994, 58). The phenomenon of identifying simultaneously and unself-consciously as "white" and as "Jewish" is problematic although, on an everyday level, it generally does not assume the weight of its historical significance. Nevertheless, when use of identifying labels slip between "white" and "Jewish," the opposition between white and Jewish and the correlation of Black and Jewish is masked, and indeed indicates a discontinuity or loss of historical memory.

Pam Austin (age thirty-four) was abandoned by her Jewish mother at a very early age and raised by Black Christian relatives. She describes being taunted by her godmother's brother and their mother, who would call her "half-white bitch" or "Jew bitch" (Funderburg 1994, 225). In high school, where racial integration did not coincide with social relations, Pam was isolated in the middle and became lifelong friends with "the other class reject" — "a nice middle-class Jewish kid with an Afro" (Funderburg 1994, 227). Her Black high-school peers complained that she distanced herself from them and associated with Jews. Austin's response was that her Jewish friends treated her better. At eighteen, Austin visited Israel for five months.

It is standard fare in Israel for people to encourage Jewish teenagers from abroad to *make aliya* (immigrate). Austin encountered the same proposition, which is usually offered with genuine sincerity. Israelis are also not known for their tact or discretion but are straightforward and direct. Austin's contacts mentioned in the narrative were not with Israelis, but with Jewish teenagers from the United States who imported their American prejudices into Israel. (A sizable percentage of right-wing nationalists who have settled the West Bank were American, although this observation overlooks the fact that the Israeli peace camp also has a strong American-born constituency.) Austin was offended by the American Jewish kids' display of prejudice against Arabs: when "they made jokes about the Arabs, well, they're the same nigger jokes

I've heard all my life" (Funderburg 1994, 239). The racism expressed by these kids eventually dissuaded her from seriously considering the suggestion that she should make aliya. Moreover, such comments as "it wouldn't matter here that your father was Black. At least he wasn't an Arab" (Funderburg 1994, 239) also prompted her to decide that it was time to leave.

It is reasonable to speculate that Austin visited Israel as an exploration of one aspect of a cultural heritage that was not cultivated during her youth but to which she felt some affinity. Although Austin was raised as an African American in an African American family and community in which two of the adults in her household made periodic insulting references to her Jewish identity, she appears to have transcended that mental abuse. One of the ways in which Austin subverted the negative effects of abandonment and the negation of part of her history seems to have been her independent cultivation of a positive attitude to a multicultural inheritance.

Outside the United States and other countries where racial divisions do not inform national politics, the social meaning of race and the significance of a Black identity lost their particularity. In Israel, Austin resented the parallels she found between Jewish prejudice against Arabs and white prejudice against Blacks that exists in America. Her experience in Israel seems to have reinforced her resistance to having a monocultural identity imposed on her.

As with many interreligious/interracial marriages, sometimes the issue of religious or cultural affiliation is effaced altogether as in the case of forty-two-year-old Bernette Ford (Funderburg 1994, 207). She has a Jewish father whom she resembles, and she states that strangers usually assume she is Jewish. This description of background is the only indication of awareness of a potential link to the Jewish community, but it is also merely incidental. Ford's narrative contains no other references to Jewishness. Ford specifically declares that she identifies as an African American and notes that her parents raised her as Black.

Unlike Fowlin and Austin, whose mothers were Jewish, Lisa Feldstein's father was Jewish, and therefore by Jewish law his marriage to a non-Jewish woman precluded his having Jewish children without her conversion. The father had been raised in an Orthodox family, and Feldstein's contact with this branch of the family appears to have been negligible. Her father was estranged from his brothers after his marriage because of race and because of "marrying out." One of his brothers sat *shiva* (ritual mourning for a dead person) because he married a Black woman, while the other brother grieved because he married a Christian (although it is unclear whether she was a *practicing* Christian). The adoption and internalization of American racism refute the lessons in the biblical story of Moses' taking an Ethiopian (Cushite) wife. Brought up to contemporary times, the radical act of sitting shiva because of racial prejudice is fundamentally challenged, as it is recalled that Miriam was severely punished for speaking against Moses' wife.

In Feldstein's case, the only legitimate sympathy that might be extended to the father's siblings is on the basis that for a man to marry out of the community effectively ends the continuity of his line of descent as a Jew, for the children of a non-Jewish mother will not be Jewish. This however, does not necessitate pronouncing him dead, and as we will see from my interview with Chelsea Steiner, one of my collaborators, the child of a Jewish father can also decide to claim and actively affirm a Jewish identity. Furthermore, as adjustments are made to accommodate Jewish life in the diaspora, Reform Judaism and in some cases Reconstructionist Judaism have become more lenient about recognizing Jewishness along patrilineal descent lines.

Feldstein grew up in New York's Spanish Harlem, but she felt different from her neighborhood peers in that she was interracial, middle-class, and educated. The theme of being an outsider and not being recognized as a member, or of having one's membership in a community under constant suspicion, is also raised by nineteen-year-old Lindsey Smith, one of my informants. In that situation, Lindsey and her sister, both phenotypically white, spent parts of the year with their Black father in a low-income housing project in New Jersey. There, the Black children often ostracized the sisters because of their light skin. Neither their mother not their father took an active role in socializing them into any particular identity, although when their parents had married, one of the links between them was a political consciousness. Lindsey explained that unlike her sister, she had learned how to counter and thus neutralize this antagonism. Her sister's resentment at being rejected and excluded on the basis of her visible physical appearance prompted her to distance herself from — though not deny — a "Black identity." According to Lindsey, this expressively manifested itself in her saying that "I'm Jewish *but* my father is Black." The emphasis on the conjunction "but" always signaled a noncommittal acknowledgment of her position vis-à-vis the Black community in contrast to a declaration of identification as a Jew.

Lisa Feldstein also explicitly stated that her parents did not inculcate in her any racial, religious, or cultural identity. She points out that she does not think of her mother "as culturally being terribly identified with anything" (Funderburg 1994, 132). Her father was the civil rights activist in the 1960s while her mother watched soap operas. Feldstein's impression of the lack of any directed identity formation is partially contradicted by appreciation that her father encouraged her to apply to the Black college from which her mother graduated. Whereas Mr. Feldstein was able to resign his Jewish identity (also recalling Sartre's observation on Jewish inauthenticity), he did try to foster a Black identity in his child. Blackness cannot be discarded and retreated from as easily as Jewishness, however.[34]

A closer look at Feldstein's critical assessment of her parents indicates that what she perceived as her mother's apoliticism in fact reflects a traditional integrationist perspective. This inclusionist vision[35] does not deny historical memory, but it is opposed to sentiments favoring racial particularity. It is a political position that does not require active promotion, and therefore it can often be mistaken for neutrality or quiescence. The mother discouraged Lisa's application to a Black college, arguing that Lisa had not been raised in a way that would have prepared her for an all-Black southern environment. What Feldstein's narrative illustrates is that a salient consciousness about the significance of race and class and a sensitivity to the regional particularism of the South are learned attitudes and that these were absent from the social environment of the Feldstein household, partially by chance and

34. An argument can be made that an easier retreat from Jewishness, as compared to Blackness, is historically untrue as evidenced by the Holocaust and the virtual impossibility of escape. However, the suggestion here is that skin color, as a visible mark, is difficult to erase whereas the traditional markers of being Jewish (apart from circumcision) — names, attire, and language — can be abandoned.

35. Note the model of racial ideology put forth by Manning Marable and Leith Mullings (1994).

partially by choice. Whatever the cause, it also seems evident that the Feldstein parents were not unaware of the manner in which they introduced politics into the house. I would underline this by pointing to the fact that although the family belonged to the middle class and Lisa was educated outside of her neighborhood, the choice to live in Spanish Harlem does evidence a politically informed decision and not merely an economic expedience. The issue I am highlighting here has nothing to do with a loving home environment — this clearly existed — but I would suggest that cultural identity is something that has to be explicitly nurtured and instilled in the home. It is the conscious expression and transmission of identity that provides a person with a tangible sense of community one can identify with or rebel against.

At college Feldstein refused to position herself with the Black students. When they attempted to "recruit" her, she insisted on her right to associate freely with white students without being dismissed as disloyal, but her interactions with Black college peers were "pretty much consistently negative experiences" (Funderburg 1994, 131). In addition, Feldstein refuses to identify as merely Black, and when she is misidentified she responds by saying, "Actually I'm half-black and half-Jewish" (132). Although she had no apparent ties with her father's family, and he seems to have conveyed nothing more than a nominal link to Jewishness, Lisa Feldstein does lay claim to it as part of the way she publicly identifies herself. Yet ultimately that identity is empty of content and therefore dissatisfying: "To me, a lot of being black-identified is cultural — like being Jewish is cultural or being Mexican-American is very cultural — and I didn't really grow up in that culture so I don't identify with that culture" (132).

Of all the Black Jewish individuals with whom Funderburg met, the one with a definite and distinct sense of self-definition — identity/ies — was a fifty-year-old woman named Sandy Lowe. She is a second-generation American whose maternal grandparents were immigrants from the Ukraine. Her father was an american Black and the child of racial/ethnic diversity: his father was Cuban Chinese, and his mother was African American. Lowe identifies herself specifically as Jewish, and in her narrative she tersely refutes the widespread association of Jewishness with whiteness. She was raised in a family where politics were a central topic of discussion, and her political education was reinforced in summer camps closely affiliated to Jewish leftist circles. In contrast to Feldstein's early association, Lowe's provided a solid and definite sense of self linked to community and history:

To me, Jewishness is not just a religion, it's a culture, and I come from that part of the culture that was oppressed, that connected its oppression with the oppression of everyone else, that developed an ethos and a theory around what it meant to be thrown out and disposed in the world. That's what it means to me to be Jewish. (Funderburg 1994, 245)

When called upon to identify herself in the public sphere, Lowe states, "I'm black, I'm a lesbian, and Cuban, Chinese and Jewish" (245). It is a public statement of complexity that insists on the recognition of difference as a positive affirmation. Lowe makes a sharp distinction between the categories of white and Jewish: "I think of myself as being Jewish, not white. I don't think of Jews as being white because they're Semites" (245). This historical perspective, which emphasizes Jewish ethics and values and a sense of peoplehood that transcends the geographical dispersion, is crucial. By dissociating Jews from European American Christians, Lowe has eliminated the racial dichotomy that underlines the thinking of many of the biracial participants in Funderburg's collection. The term "biracial," which linguistically reflects a notion of duality—and makes possible the idea of being half this and half that—has no meaning in Lowe's self-identity or in the way she (re)presents herself to the public.

As a conclusion to this chapter and a preface to a discussion of my own interviews in the following chapter, a brief synthesis of background information on the demography of American Jews will establish an ethnographic context in which to situate the people I interviewed.

The U.S. Constitution institutionalized an official separation of church and state; therefore no census has ever included questions of religious identity.[36] Furthermore, "when efforts were initiated by some groups to introduce such a question during hearings of the U.S. Immigration Commission (1907–10), representatives of the Jewish commu-

36. In 1654, some twenty-three Jewish refugees of the Inquisition arrived in New Amsterdam (N.Y.), and since then the number of Jews in America has only been estimated.

nity were among those voicing the strongest objections" (Goldstein 1990, 1). This was also a period in which some Jews changed their last names in order to escape any distinctive ethnic mark. In a report on methods and problems in counting Jewish populations, the researchers note that "last names were used to keep out Jews and other southern Europeans under the 1924 National Origins Act, which mandated classifying last names from censuses 1790–1890 according to ethnicity" (Kosmin, Ritterband, and Scheckner 1988, 214). Studies on the American Jewish community are often compared with the Canadian one. Unlike the United States, Canada does have a census question and category for Jews by religion and by ethnicity. The particular value of the Canadian census is the finding that the number of Jews who self-identified by ethnicity was significantly higher than those who marked religion (Kosmin, Ritterband, and Scheckner 1989, 207).

The Council of Jewish Federations' National Jewish Population Survey (NJPS) estimated that in 1993 Jews made up approximately 2.3 percent (5.8 million) of the entire U.S. population, with 41.2 percent of the Jewish population located in the Middle Atlantic region. According to the *American Jewish Yearbook*, "In determining the Jewish population, communities count both affiliated and nonaffiliated residents who are 'core' Jews as defined in NJPS [Born Jews who report adherence to Judaism, Jews by choice, and born Jews without a current religion ('secular Jews').] (Kosmin 1994, 207).

The CJF research team reports that the census proxy indicators are race, country of origin, and mother tongue. He notes that "since Jews are overwhelmingly white" one method of estimating fluctuations in the size of the Jewish population is through the use of statistics on deaths and the death rate in comparison to the general white population. The advantage of this morbid procedure is that as a "definite proxy indicator" (Kosmin, Ritterband, and Scheckner 1988, 207) Jews who die, even if they were not practicing Jews, find their way to funeral homes, and it is unusual for the deceased to be buried outside a Jewish cemetery.

In the reports published by the CJF as well as literature from other Jewish organizations, "intermarriage" often is used interchangeably with "mixed" or "interfaith." However, "interfaith" deemphasizes the specificity of inter*religious* unions (faith being distinct from religion).

Researchers at the North American Jewish Data Bank report that "rates of Jewish intermarriage have had to be estimated largely from special studies of the Jewish community *per se.*" Since the mid-1960s, there has been a steady increase in the number of Jews marrying non-Jews, with conservative estimates of a 13 percent to 15 percent rate of intermarriage. In one recent survey, researchers were startled by the discovery that although Jewish friends and being older were a predictor for endogamous Jewish marriage, the effect of Jewish education or generational status (how many generations in America) were not significant variables in predicting marriage patterns (Kosmin 1989): "As acculturation took its course, the question of Jewish identity arose, not just as a religious or communal concern but as a practical research question" (Kosmin, Ritterband, and Scheckner 1988, 218).

The material collected in the North American Jewish Data Bank does not contain sufficient information for their analysts to ascertain whether American Jewry is moving toward greater "ethnic assertiveness" or "join[ing] the mass of white America as just another church." However the evidence that has been collated and analyzed indicates a "particularly intriguing group is the non-denominational (27%), most of whom are 'Just Jewish.'" They appear to be growing particularly among the young adult population (31 percent) (Kosmin 1988, 28). With this in mind, and remembering that the American Jewish population is small,[37] geographically concentrated in the Northeast, and exhibiting a steadily rising rate of interreligious marriage, my decision to settle for only eight interviewees needs some explanation.

As I noted in the prelude, the people with whom I met were located through word of mouth. Initially, I intended to have fifteen interviewees, some of whom were affiliated and active in a Jewish framework.

---

37. The 1990 National Jewish Population Survey estimates that the Jewish descent population — anyone with Jewish ancestry, excluding approximately 185,000 converts (Jews by choice) — to be 6.6 million people. According to the NJPS's demographic analysis, "the total population includes all 8.1 million persons currently residing in 3.2 million households where some identify themselves either ethnically or religiously as Jewish . . . (including) 16% of unqualified persons (Gentiles)" (Kosmin and Goldstein, et al. 1991, 6). Note, too, that discrepancies of figures are due to alternative typologies from the core statistical data collated from the population survey.

After interviewing eight people, however, a general pattern emerged, which, based on my reading of anecdotes that appear in the press and in the recent publications of "biracial" people, seemed fairly consistent and in accord with the analysis of research data from surveys conducted through the CJF. There may be religious tolerance or complete secularism within interreligious marriages, but all the indications suggest that children are not raised with a strong Jewish identity nor are they in social settings where such an identity might be inculcated. In this respect, interracial *seems* incidental to, or has no effect on, the religious/cultural environment of an interreligious home. The conclusion of Ehrich Rosenthal's 1963 report "Jewish Intermarriage in the U.S." continues to be applicable: "It was found that well over 70% of the intermarried couples raised their children as non-Jews. Intermarried families in which the wife was Jewish were even less inclined to raise their children as Jews" (Rosenthal 1965, 280).

Despite this evaluation, and particularly in the context of the 1990s, a decade in which the idea of *microdiversity* (Zack 1995) and the proliferation of multiethnic/racial organizations are evidence that people of "mixed backgrounds" are more self-assertive and resistant to devaluing identity categories, I hypothesize the following: that *there might be* more *likelihood that a Jewish child in an interracial marriage would be more sensitive to (1) the disjuncture between people's stereotyped equation of Jews having white skin and the true variation that exists and (2) the politics of claiming an affinity to two histories with legacies of violent oppression and legal discrimination.* In other words, Jewish children who are socially defined in America as Black and defined as Jewish according to the Halakah are more likely to refer to their Jewish heritage than are "white" children of a Jewish intermarriage. This hypothesis cannot be substantiated at the moment, and until Jewish demographers cease trying to outdo liberals who (offensively) claim not to see color,[38] periodic surveys will proceed without questions that relate to race or ethnicity of the non-Jewish partner.

38. It is noteworthy that sight/vision are as socially constructed as language. Cultural socialization will naturalize and thus prestructure some categories of knowledge, which in turn shape the way one sees (Berger 1972; Gilman 1985; Mudimbe 1988, 9). In a society as racialized as the United States, skin color is not an arbitrary, inconsequential phenomenon of melanin. It is a politically charged variable embedded in race as a social fact. As such, "not seeing" race is another facet of the invisibil-

My first four interviews took place during the weekend of 14 October 1994, in New York. Two of the people I interviewed were acquaintances from childhood who had grown up in the city. Belinda Peters introduced me to her friend, Claire Jackson, who agreed to be interviewed partially as a favor and partially out of curiosity. Both women asked that I not use their real names. A third interviewee, Elinor Tatum, is the daughter of the publisher of a prestigious Black newspaper. Her father is married to a Jewish refugee and has been involved in several public and controversial debates between the Jewish and Black communities in New York City. The fourth interview was with an independent businessman, David Lincoln, whom I've known for many years. He also preferred that I find a pseudonym rather than use his real name.

Three interviews took place a few weeks later in Maryland. Although the people I met had spent most of their lives in the state, their parents were originally from the Northeast and they themselves had lived for short periods in other regions or abroad. Franz Fanon Walker and Chelsea Steiner resided in Baltimore, and they both described the city as racially segregated although individually they had friends of different racial and ethnic backgrounds. Jared Ball had grown up in Columbus, which, he pointed out, was a reputed haven for interracial families, though he questioned the romantic sincerity behind some of these interracial liaisons. The eighth person, Lindsey Smith, was living temporarily in Durham but had grown up spending half the year in a public housing project in New Jersey and the other half in an affluent, predominantly Anglo, California suburb.

Of the eight interviewees, five were college graduates, and two were currently in college; the youngest interviewee had taken a year off after recently graduating from high school. Two people were married, one was divorced, and all three of these interviewees were parents. All the interviewees, except one, had a Jewish mother, and two of the men were raised only by their Jewish mother. The exception had a strong sense of Jewish identity, although (and therefore) she refused to con-

---

ity of whiteness. Omi and Winant highlight that "One of the first things we *notice* about people when we meet them . . . is their race. We utilize race to provide clues about *who* a person is. This fact is made painfully obvious when we encounter someone whom we cannot conveniently racially categorize. . . . Such an encounter becomes a source of discomfort and momentarily a crisis of racial meaning" (1986, 62).

template going through a formal conversion process. She is married to a man of mixed background (racial and ethnic) who was adopted and raised in a monoracial (white) family.

It has become fashionably impolite to articulate previously prevalent racist stereotypes regarding interracial marriages[39] and partners, although periodically this does surface and acts as an unpleasant reminder that the linkage between race and sex continues to be an obsession for some sectors of Americans. Furthermore, it is a mistake to presume that those who agonize over interracial liaisons are ancient relics of a reactionary era, a deception shattered by essays and anecdotes from adult children of interracial marriages.

Jewish Americans are not immune from racial prejudice, and one indication of attitudes can be found in the classified personal sections, where advertisements are placed for partners.[40] If there are any doubts that race matters — even at the most intimate interhuman level — in contemporary America, these ads should suffice to refute them permanently. Here I am less concerned with the "regular" *white seeks white/ Black seeks Black* type but rather wish to draw attention to the phenomenon of ads in which Jewish and white are specifically coadjectives or where it is taken for granted that Jewish assumes the respondent will also be Jewish and that both will be "white." I was unwilling to experiment, but I am confident that there is a presupposition that the respondent to a "seeking Jewish partner" ad will not be Black, even if Jewish. I did spend an afternoon looking through the New York–based *Village Voice* personals and found no "SBJF" or "SBJM," that is, Single Black Jewish Fe/Male. To offset criticism of my own preconceptions, I refer back to the research conducted by the North American Jewish Data Bank, which takes for granted comparisons of American Jews with white Americans (i.e., will they "join the mass of white America").

Bracketing completely all personal attitudes to personal advertise-

39. Nowhere is this more evident than with Supreme Court Justice Clarence Thomas.

40. Although I am an admirer of Sander Gilman's research on representations of Jews, my interest in Jewish self-representation in the classified personal sections preceded my discovery of his work. We share, then, along with radical Jewish activists in the 1960s, an interest in exploring and exploding the question "Are Jews white?" See Gilman (1991, 169–93).

ments, we may ask the question, How would Tzipporah, Moses' wife, have been listed or received as a respondent (Numbers 12)? The Bible is a useful source from which to hypothesize an answer, for it is the originating basis on which interpretations of Jewish law rest.[41] According to the *Encyclopedia Judaica*, the rabbinical interpretations identify Tzipporah as the "Cushite woman whom Moses had married" (Numbers 12:1). Tzipporah is first mentioned in Exodus 2 as the daughter of Reul, the priest of Midian. (In Exodus 18, the priest is named Jethro. Since the purpose here is not biblical exegesis, I leave it to the curious reader to independently pursue questions regarding different names.)[42] The point to be underlined about Tzipporah is that the Rabbis draw an analogy between her black skin and her virtuous deeds and say the former is a mark of the latter (see Midrash 16b).[43]

Numbers 12 has always appealed to me, and coincidentally or not, it was the weekly biblical portion that my son Ron Marcus read for his bar mitzvah. So I am always gratified by the opportunity to point out that this short chapter is entirely devoted to the apparent race prejudice Miriam articulates against Moses' "Cushite wife" and God's severe punishment (leprosy), which is modified only by Moses' intervention on his sister's behalf. The end result, however, is that the journey of the liberated slaves is subsequently held up by a week while Miriam endures her penalty (Numbers 12:15).

These lengthy prefatory remarks, including the detour through the Bible, introduce a discussion that moves from the language of race to the issue of double-consciousness and visibility/invisibility and finally to questions of community and negotiation of identities.

41. In fact, hermeneutics originates in the homiletic explications of the biblical text and are found in the Talmud and Midrash, which together comprise the Halakhah, from which this interpretation was adopted from the *Encyclopedia Judaica Yearbook*.

42. Moses escaped to Midian after slaying an Egyptian overseer who had beaten one of the Jewish slaves. Reul provided Moses with shelter and, sometime after, with his daughter (Exodus 2:15–22). They had two sons: Gershom (a name signifying *stranger*) and Eliezer (whose name is a combination of "God" and "help," signifying the liberation) (Exodus 18:3–4).

43. One might also want to refer to the Song of Songs, a paean to a dark-skinned woman.

BLACK, JEWISH, AND INTERRACIAL (II)

The Language of Race

As noted in Chapter 3, in order for me to be able to think, speak, or write about interviews with biracial people who are also both Jewish and Black, my labels, descriptions, and presuppositions were constantly shifting, both during our meetings and in my own thoughts, reflecting (and in fact demonstrating) that language *is* a social institution. The language of race, the key words that are manipulated and utilized, has been destabilized in academic thinking as well as in popular discourse. The words used to signify racial identities — African American, Black, biracial, mixed-race, and so on — seem to be selected with greater self-consciousness and play than in previous time periods. There are simply more words from which to select, each with its proponents who insist on its legitimacy as a reflection of the diversity of Black experience (Houk 1993; Smitherman 1991).

For those of us whose biological parents are of different racial backgrounds, I think there is a self-conscious discomfort with, or defiance against, the limitations language imposes on our definitions of self as a subject. This concern parallels feminist deliberations on a reconceptualization of the subject as a site of multiple subjectivities and competing identities. Teresa de Lauretis observes, "what is emerging in feminist writings is . . . a subject that is not divided in, but rather at odds with, language" (quoted in Fuss 1989, 33). Nowhere is this dissatisfaction better illustrated than by the scorn my interviewees felt for official forms demanding a single designation of race.[1]

First-generation people of "mixed background" is a cumbersome way of describing "interracial." This problem of language is com-

1. In terms of defining oneself as Jewish, there is also a slippage of meaning that makes salient the dilemma secular Jews confront when defining "Jewish" as an identity; the dilemma of what "Jewish" means, then, represents an ambiguous stance and affiliation vaguely associated with culture, religion, history, and politics.

pounded when one is confronted by requests for self-definition according to official classifications. We cannot simply follow the directive "Mark One" on the official racial/ethnic lists except as a political statement and even choosing among the options has now become a dilemma. If previously there was a political motive to marking "African American" or "Black," now marking all the applicable categories has become an assertive statement and rebuttal to official directives. Frantz Fanon Walker, raised by his Jewish mother, has lived most of his life in a predominantly Black and working-class neighborhood of Baltimore and is at first rather mild in his reaction to the question "How do you describe your racial identity?"

I describe myself as mixed — cause I always have. The language — I always think it's like a silly issue. You know everybody's always trying to name this and label that — I don't take time to think about it. I just think it's silly you know. Call yourself whatever you want to call yourself. I realize that that kind of nonsense has to go on. People are always gonna do that; so I kinda let them do it.

His complacency is rustled, however, by official demands for self-classification. The tactic of rebellion is to mark as many boxes as possible, "Anything just to not give them satisfaction (*laughter*)." The extent of the absurdity in these category/classification name games was called to my attention during a visit to a university, where I was told that application forms now include the category "blended"! — not merely *instead of* but *in addition to* "other."

Elinor Tatum, one of my interviewees from New York, had a typical reaction, which reflects a refusal to comply with the arbitrary imposition of classifications:

It depended on what the choices were. And if the choices weren't there, I'd make them up. I'd add things in. I'd make comments on those sections. I'd say this is what I am, I'm not gonna put one or the other down.[2] I'm gonna put both down. And there was no one who can tell me I can't because it's what I am. I

2. In the coda I will discuss Andre Gluckman's work on Socrates and the meanings and implications of interruption/contestation (Gluckman 1980). From Elinor's comments, one may consider the self-identity of biracial people as a challenge and as a refusal to accommodate to categories made up by people who used their own homogeneity (as an idea) to set a standard — a norm — against which everyone else is different.

mean they've got Hispanic, they've got White Non-Hispanic and all these but they don't have Black and Jewish so they don't have mixes and matches so I make them.

The "Race" labels and classifications impose their own limitations and constraints when "interracial" people converse about and among themselves. They compel an interrogation of the language of race, posing an incessant challenge to those who wish to divest (white) racism of its power and authority. I interviewed two friends at the same sitting, and occasionally one would interject a remark during the other's interview. An example of divergent opinions on the significance of labels was captured in the following passage from the interview with Belinda Peters. There were several instances during both interviews when Belinda referred to a correspondence in perspectives with Claire Jackson, which the latter promptly corrected. Belinda concedes halfheartedly when her friend reiterates a position that an emphasis on the universal ("we are all humans") should not exclude recognition of particularity.[3]

Belinda: Oh, by the way, I don't use the term "interracial," I truly, I am truly of the school that we are all humans. I feel like Claire, you know, names are names. I don't care what they call it, you know if you really want to start separating things, I don't know how many people you'll find that are all one thing or any persuasion — anymore.

Claire (intervenes): I think it is important to say, to call people multiracial. It doesn't have, I don't care what you, I don't care whether

Belinda: I don't care, I don't really like multiracial.

Claire: you call it multiracial or biracial or whatever racial but I do think it is important that you have a category.

Belinda: Okay, if you have to work within a framework of the way the government wants to have forms — and why they still feel the need to categorize you with anything but an American citizen — then if you must use the term I prefer: *mixed heritage.*

At one level, the very words "biracial," "multiracial," "mixed heritage," and so on manifest conditions of possibility peculiar to and inherent in American conceptions of race since the slave period. At

3. I will refer back to this passage later in relation to racial ambiguity.

another level, these words as signifiers paradoxically represent both a capitulation to and an appropriation of classifications created from American white racism, with its binary opposition of Black and white.[4] This is subsidized by a legacy of social custom and judicial fiat converting, conflating, and connoting the phenomenal appearance of shades of blackness and the referential category of "the Negro" (defined as anyone with a trace of African descent).

Metaphors of "intermixing" reflect, and are made possible by, the scientifically false notion of different races.[5] As a consequence, however, these words facilitate and perpetuate the construction of a category of alterity that was already in place during the slave period. In actuality, as pointed out in the previous chapter, the referential category of the "Negro" has had little to do with the phenomenon of skin color; thus, the binary racial opposition of the American South was persistently destabilized by the presence of "mulattoes," ranging in skin color from brown to white. This in-between group "were a sore upon the social sight of white Southerners; each was a living indictment of the failure of the strictly biracial society envisioned by the white Southern ideal, a walking, talking and mocking symbol of a white man's lapse in morality" (Williamson 1971, 216).

Although there is clearly no ontological basis to the *construct* of being Black, the *idea* of Blackness operates as *more* than just a symbolic metaphor or trope. Unquestionably, the Black/white binary has been under increasing pressure as other groups have entered into the racial hierarchy. Nevertheless, Blackness is *experienced*. As expressed by Jacquie Jones:

For many of us, this notion of a nation divided, one black, one white — separate, hostile, unequal, the whole thing — is the way we experience the world. And for many more of us, race as black and white, and encounters with blackness, specifically, are the only shared calibration for what we have come to call

4. This is not to ignore race classifications of other racially divided societies. My concern in this project, however, is deliberately limited to the United States, where, in the words of sociologist F. James Davis, "not only does the one-drop rule apply to no other group than American blacks, but apparently the rule is unique in that it is found only in the United States and not in any other nation in the world." (1991, 13).

5. The association of Blackness with negative ideas inherited from, although not originating in, the Middle Ages received new meanings in nineteenth-century discussions of pathology and insanity. See Gilman (1985).

reality . . . [A]bandoning externally imposed boundaries of blackness means, in essence, risking erasure. (1995, 10–11)

It is not only — or even necessarily — skin color, but also "common knowledge" about genealogies that factors into a person's position in any given social field in the United States (white-skinned Negroes were still members of the Black community according to the U.S. Supreme Court decision in the 1896 case of *Plessy v. Ferguson*). This knowledge continues regardless of whether it is a constant intrusion or an always potential interruption.[6]

In a 1983 law suit in Louisiana, Susie Guillory Phipps sued to have her racial classification changed from "coloured" to "white." The state exploited a large sum of its budget and traced her genealogy. They "proved," conclusively, that Phipps was *legally* Black because she was 1/32 Black, with a lineage traced back to 1770. At that time, her great-great-great-great-grandfather, a French planter, entered into a sexual relationship with a slave. Phipps appealed successive Louisiana court decisions until she reached the U.S. Supreme Court in 1986, where her appeal was "dismissed for want of a substantial federal question" (107 Sup. Ct. Reporter, interim ed. 638, quoted in Davis 1991, 10). The highest court in the country refused the opportunity to overturn the 1896 decision taken in the case of *Plessy v. Ferguson* whereby racial designation accords with common knowledge.[7]

After the Phipps case, the result cannot be overstated, having a Black ancestor effectively defines one as Black *but* having a white ancestor does not define one as white. In the following amusing anecdote, Jared Ball illustrates this arbitrary hypostatization.[8]

We were in Manhattan and the Black Israelites set up on the corner and I pulled one of them aside. I was just listening to what they were saying and — 'cause their whole rhetoric was antiwhite — and I asked them, I said, "So where do I

6. Interesting personal anecdotes of being reminded, unexpectedly, that race is more than a trope are found in Gates (1992).

7. *Plessy v. Ferguson* set the judicial precedent for the doctrine of separate but equal.

8. Jared's name is from Genesis 5, the biblical chapter listing the generations of Adam (Man/Mankind), a single line of descendants from Adam to Noah. Jared (Yered) is referred to in Genesis 5:15: he was the great-great-great-grandfather of Noah (Yered, Hanoch, Metushela, Lemekh, Noah).

stand?" And then this guy said, "Well, were you from the seed of a black man?" and I said yes and then he said, "Well, you're sliding in safe." And that's exactly how he said it (*laughs*): "*Well, you're sliding in safe*" and we laughed about it and I thought it was kind of funny. So by their definition, I'm Black and by the United States of America's definition you only need, what 0.01 percent whatever a drop.

Philosopher Lewis Gordon (whose grandfather was of Jewish and African heritage) articulates a school of thought shared by Black intellectuals who refuse both the essentialism of Afrocentricity and the political myopia of deconstructionists. He underscores, in a roundtable symposium on race, that "Black people don't have problems — they are perceived as the problem. . . . Blackness as a marker of racial ideology permeates not only the structures of employment and opportunity but also the directions of social scientific *explanations* as well ('race-causal explanations')" (Gordon 1995b, 41). This school does not preclude the significance of class, gender, or any other axes of difference or their intersection; rather, it accentuates the central role race has played in the American social, economic, and political orders separately and in concert.

The tension in the language of "multiplicity" and "plurality" reflects an intellectual crisis — a manifestation of a political rupture, social dislocation, and, arguably, economic disorder. The result of this mood is that those who previously insisted on unity, uniformity, and homogeneity find their authority to interpret under challenge and this, in turn, necessitates new strategies. While poststructuralists in the academy have advanced the notion of "fragmentation," in the public arena of television talk shows, "biraciality" has become the decade's fashionable and marketable identity. In the rush toward representing heterogeneity and complexity, "the academic hegemony of detached, metatheoretical discourse" (Bordo 1990, 142) has overlooked the fact that among american Blacks difference is not a novel concept, as is attested to by writer Lisa Jones, whose Jewish grandparents never accepted her and whose mother was embraced by her husband's family:[9] "Black

9. In this case, the racism of and rejection by Jones's maternal grandparents was, ironically, counterbalanced by her father; LeRoi Jones's public desertion of his wife and daughters was accompanied by anti-Semitic statements, which at the time he made no attempt to excuse.

communities have always been shelter to multiethnic people, perhaps
not an unproblematic shelter, yet a shelter nonetheless. Black folks, I'd
venture, have welcomed difference in their communities more than
most Americans" (Jones 1994, 60).

Struggles over identity, "that being-perceived which exists fundamentally through recognition by other people" (Bourdieu 1991, 224),
are *active* pursuits. The importance of community in this context is
essential, for it is within the community that an individual receives
recognition — this entity has the authority, through its representatives
and as a collective body, to confirm or deny the privileges of membership or to extend or withdraw support.

The receptivity of the american Black community to difference,
which Jones contrasts with white American provincialism, can be emphasized with a critique of liberalism. A brief comment highlights the
sharp contrast between inclusion and multivocality noted in chapter 1.
In the first, inclusion, the other is always the outsider, the one who is
always already defined as different and therefore is responsible for ac-
commodating to the situation in which s/he is entering. Inclusion means
permission to enter, a permission that can always be rescinded. The
space has already been carved out by the powerful participants — members of the dominant group. Again, Lewis Gordon's remarks are ger-
mane to a critique of liberalism and the corollary myth of integration:

Institutions (e.g., universities) boast about "having" blacks, as though one can
have black people through the "possession" of one or two. The representative
dimension of such "possessing" comes to the fore, however, when we think of
them as "representing" blacks who are absent. In a world of having blacks,
there is an evasion of black inclusion itself. (1995b, 44).

Racial Ambiguity

From the outset, a set of detailed questions served to anchor and to
provide an elastic framework within which to structure each particular interview. Two first interviews, with Belinda and Claire, suggested
alternative ways to consider the broader problem of self-reflexivity
and representation. In Gluck and Patai's collection of essays *Women's
Words* (1991), contributors share their concerns about managing the

ways in which control and power subtly shape the relationship between the researcher and the informant.

Belinda was my childhood acquaintance through our parents; Claire was her friend from childhood. Their parents shared a Communist Party background. Although eager to see Belinda after so many years, during the interview I felt peculiarly uncomfortable. Both interviews, each in turn at a busy West Side restaurant, comprised an event that when halfway through — I was not sure how — seemed to contest my authority to focus on the particular topic itself. Here were two articulate women, one very fair-skinned and the other quite brown, insisting on the irrelevance of race in their everyday lives.

My immediate impressions were scribbled down in the backseat of a taxi whose Bengali driver (I have the habit of reading licenses) wound his way through the heavy Friday evening traffic from one end of the city to the other in less than ten minutes (a brazen act of chivalry in response to my concern that I was late for a meeting at the Doral Inn). Despite the fact that the women agreed to be interviewed, an emphatic tone bordering on pontification (one of the adjectives scrawled across my notepad) hinted at a hidden agenda in meeting with me. It *felt as if* they wanted to register, through me in order to reassure themselves, that race and ethnicity were neither necessary nor salient components of their identity.

The dissatisfaction and unease that intruded into my concentration during these two interviews were completely unexpected and did not recur in any of my subsequent interviews. In order to explain why these interviews were marked by discomfort, I need to single them out for particular attention. Both acutely highlight the ethical dilemmas of ethnography and the limitations of current theories of identity.

The dilemmas of interpretation and theoretical inadequacy revealed and reenforced a frustration with having my own assumptions undermined. Here it is necessary to emphasize candidly and clearly that during the interviews and until I actually listened to the tapes and transcribed them, my impression was of *sameness* in their narratives. Instead of hearing the nuanced differences, I was preoccupied by their nodding in agreement, their similar and dismissive tone of voice, and most important, the depoliticized content of their answers. The two women forced me to reconsider how to bring their thoughts into a conversation with my own without superimposing my ideas on them. After all, the purpose of this inquiry was to explore what it means to construct and maintain a sense of identity that links the individual to a community and a history.

In general, the interviews provided an opportunity for the informants to construct and present a skeleton autobiography. In this sense, although their narrative unfolds in response to my questions, I do think the format temporarily empowered my collaborators to be self-reflective on issues that otherwise they took for granted. At the same time, they could confidently authorize a response without having it challenged as inauthentic.

Belinda and Claire insisted that they think of themselves as human beings and refuse to privilege race in their lives. As mentioned earlier, the arrangement of the three of us sitting together as I interviewed each in turn allowed for moments in which one could interject a comment. It was in this intermission that their experiences lent themselves to different perspectives far *less* subtly than they explicitly acknowledged (at least in my presence).

The issue of racial ambiguity is notable in one instance. Belinda is light enough to pass as or be misrecognized as white, although most African Americans would doubt that she was a European American. Her husband is white, not Jewish, and the photo of her daughter shows a visibly white-skinned child, with fairly straight, medium-brown hair — coloring similar to that of my own daughter, Dorit-Chen. I note this because I have always been fascinated by the color of my children — a fascination that increased after I read *Sally Hemings* (1979) years ago.[10] Belinda was emphatic about transcending racism: "I refuse to let it dictate my life" and insistent in her rejection of a race-based outlook on life

It's never been an issue as far as *my* self goes. If it's an issue for somebody else that is their problem. It only becomes your problem if you allow them to let it

10. Russell, Wilson, and Hall write on the phenomena of color variation among siblings and note that "in interview after interview that we conducted with the adult biracial children of Black-White marriages, all maintained that their parents had been very attuned to color issues. Perhaps because the parents had thought carefully about the consequences of race-mixing, they proved better equipped to handle color-related conflicts than many Black parents" (1992, 99).

become your problem. I can honestly say that I think — no I know — *all* my life when I'm with a person I went right to the heart.

When I had asked about her college experience, Belinda, sharply critical of what she considered a voluntary separatist attitude among her Black peers, spoke in tones of studied fervor. Although emphatically reiterating her disdain for their behavior, she calls attention to her experience of actively taking a position against racially based coalitions:

I don't have to accept it so I choose to be with *whomever* I care to be with and if someone can deal with that then fine, you know. If they can't, then they have their own lessons to learn but I cannot, and will not, let it totally, be led around the nose by it or make it a priority of one's thought all the time.

The key phrase here, to "make (race) a priority of one's thought all the time" is interesting because Belinda never specifically addresses whether there is a relation between being "racially ambiguous" and having the freedom to defer race as incidental.

I interviewed two other women who, like Belinda, were fair-skinned enough to move comfortably in white circles without having their "race" questioned. The last person I interviewed, Lindsey Smith, was a very pretty nineteen-year-old whose skin color was a shade lighter than the literary phrase "olive complexion" and who lacked features that visibly marked her as Black. Even in the South, there are socially defined white people with dark black hair and brown eyes so, unless she indicated her racial background among white people, it could be assumed that she was a white Caucasian.[11] It is not unusual that whites will assume a very light-skinned African American to be white, whereas

11. Jewish anthropologist Hortense Powdermaker discovered with surprise how association, rather than skin color, determined perception of race as a social category during her fieldwork in Mississippi. She notes that although the situation seemed to have been undergoing change during the civil rights movement, in the mid-1930s having white skin did not automatically indicate being socially defined as white: "I was mistaken for a Negro by colored and white people. Aware of this whenever we were in a Negro restaurant or hotel, I was amazed that my physical appearance did not count at all. My companion was quite dark but I met Negroes lighter than I" (1966, 135). Historian August Meier (1992), also found that it was easy (and wise) to pass as colored in the South as an efficient solution for trespassing racial boundaries when conducting fieldwork and research in Mississippi.

other Blacks will be suspicious—as Lindsey experienced during her stay at a local college.

When examining the central role racial ambiguity plays in protecting a person from immediate contact with racialism, how does one interpret the declaration that race is insignificant? Does Belinda illustrate an example of a person constructing a persona that draws from and reinforces racial ambiguity as an identity? If so, what does this suggest about ways in which the *idea* of being "a human being" conforms to an invisible white norm? On white identities, Peter McLaren candidly asserts, "Being white is an entitlement . . . to a raceless subjectivity. That is, being white becomes the invisible norm for how dominant culture measures its own civility" (1991, 244).

In contrast to Belinda, Lindsey was very cognizant of the advantage and disadvantage of being light-skinned. On the university campus, Lindsey had encountered unfriendly glances from Black students as they sized each other up for recognition, as this passage poignantly narrates:

[T]he new club down here—there's usually a lot of Black kids sitting in here and I walk by and I just feel like, you know, there's tension. That could be me; it could be me 'cause I never look. I always just look straight ahead and keep walking; I never look, but I do feel that way and that could be something, that could be me. I do feel that, a little bit. And I don't know why that is—I mean I've been told that it's because I have light skin.

There are almost twenty years between Belinda's college experience and Lindsey's. However, both experience in similar ways *the effect* of the pressure of being a Black student on a white campus—which is to coalesce socially with other Blacks as a group. Based on visual observations one assumes that only Black students separate themselves from white students. In contrast, it never appears unusual or a matter for anxiety or speculation that visually the members of most groups of students in informal interaction appear to be the same color and that on a predominantly white campus, most of these groups will—intentionally or not—*not* be integrated. This issue of the politics of campus separatism incidentally came up with Frantz. With his brown skin and dreadlocks, Frantz, is unself-consciously comfortable with "being a mixed person" who moves easily between white and Black worlds. I asked him why he chose to attend Morgan State, a traditionally Black college.

Yeah, because it was close and because it was cheap. But now that I'm here, I really enjoy being in an all Black university. Just very comfortable, you know. You say hi to everyone. Everyone speaks. It's more like familial. When I go onto campus, I enjoy walking across — everyone is "Hi, how you doing," you know. You feel comfortable in class, talking about issues that you wouldn't feel comfortable talking about in other places. Actually, I went to a predominantly white campus for about, almost a year and I found that difficult. There's not that much mixture of people. Black folks staying with themselves and white folks staying with themselves and I don't like to have to make that decision. Who I'm gonna hang out with. It just doesn't present a problem at Morgan. And I like that, you know.

The comfort zone Frantz finds in a Black college echoes Lisa Jones's (1994) comments on the inclusive characteristic found in the Black community. The difference between Lindsey's discomfort with and Belinda's disdain toward the community of Black students (as a collective) is that Lindsey recognizes what Belinda overlooks: the role light skin plays. It is a crucial moment, for only light-skinned people have the option of standing in the middle and literally crossing race lines at ease.

As proposed in chapter 1, an individual can never apprehend him/herself in his/her totality but rather commands a plurality of invented selves that accommodate any situation. This seems almost, and I would argue it is, reminiscent of Pierre Bourdieu's notion of habitus as pre-reflexive, quasi-instinctual, a sense of place but also a sense of the other's place (1991, 235). All the interviewees are aware of a distinction that still places value on light skin — positively or negatively — in the Black community (Russell, Wilson, and Hall 1992).

Compare Belinda and Lindsey in the academic setting to Jared's experience in the navy, where the ranking hierarchy seems to coincide with a color range — the continuum from dark skin and lower rank to light skin and higher rank. Jared's light color elicited attention among his darker shipmates. His personal background is complicated, and he is keenly cognizant of his particularity on the one hand and, on the other hand, the reductionism inherent in and the futility of temporalizing an accurate representation of (him)self to others. The plurality or multifaceted sense of self in the public sphere entails choosing how to position oneself. In order to align himself with his peers on board the ship, Jared had to refashion and project an image compensating for a physical characteristic (phenotype) and its social connotation (some-what tempered by the build of a football player). He mastered a stereo-typed but recognizable persona from the inner city, which was familiar to his peers and which became a competent performance.[12] Taking into consideration the efficacy of gesture, tone, and manner of speech in establishing for others an identity, it is clear that his role-playing was *systematic and (self-)conscious*:

[W]hen I met a person in the Navy and he said, "Where are you from" — that was one of the first (questions) — "where are you from?" If I tried to explain, "Well I was born in D.C. but I pretty much grew up in the suburbs of Columbia, Baltimore where" — by the time I went through the whole thing, not only was he not interested anymore, he had already figured, "He's a weak individual," "He's a punk," or whatever. To the people I met when I just stopped and said, "Well I'm originally from D.C.," which is true but that's just (a *fragment*), then I was looked at a whole different way 'cause I'm a big guy, they'd see me in the weight room. I'm pretty strong; they'd say, "Oh big strong man from D.C., you'd better not mess with him." Plus I'm loud and I argue all the time[13] and, you know, grammar and proper word choice does go out the window when I argue. So a lot of times you might think I was from their same environment and I was treated a lot better then.

The gaze, as Sartre describes well, brings forth and accentuates a self-consciousness from being the object of an other. It is this sense of being objectified that creates discomfort and dis-ease but also demands a response that enables the person under view to reconstitute him/her-self as a subject, an agent — someone in control of how s/he views herself without the influence of being looked at. Lindsey accommo-dates and affirms being Black and Jewish, whereas Belinda rejects this identity. Belinda's rejection is the exercise of an option that disengages from, and therefore disrupts, a sense of participation. Jared's Jewish-ness, in contrast, becomes a positive factor in positioning himself so-

12. Jared is consciously calculated about performing a role for a temporary, limited, and strategic purpose. Indeed, Russell, Wilson, and Hall also comment on how "some light-skinned Black males learn to compensate by exaggerating their masculinity — acting tough and streetwise" (1992, 66).

13. This was an amusing comment because of the stereotype of Jews being loud and argumentative — an image often manipulated by Jewish comedians.

cially and strategically. I had asked him how the fact that he was Jewish would become public and he drew on an example from the navy. In the following quotation, he narrates how volunteering to relieve someone of duty at the Christmas holidays is welcomed but also seen as peculiar. After the initial surprise, Jared is requested to show some proof that he is Jewish and, fortunately, he is able to recite a sentence of a prayer in Hebrew.

Well, in the navy for instance, I think a lot of it would come around the holiday season. Like in the navy you have duties which means you have to stay on the ship no matter what. So people, come Christmas time, they would pay you if necessary—you weren't supposed to pay—"Take my duty for me." "Well, what're you going to do for me?" So I'd say, "I'll do it—how important is Christmas to you?" And they would say, "Well what's your problem?" I'd say, "Well, I'm not Christian, you know, my Hanukkah was early in the month so we have no conflict." And they would say, "Hanukkah!? You're not Jewish!" (*drawn out with incredulity*) and I'd say, "Yes, I *am*" and they would say, "Bullshit, no you're *not!*" and I would say, "*Yes I am!*" and then they would, you know, "Well, say something" and I might say one of the prayers or something and they'd say, "whew!" So that's pretty much how it came about.

Community and Memory [14]

We know that the Jews were prohibited from investigating the future. The Torah and the prayers instruct them in remembrance, however. This stripped the future of its magic, to which all those succumb who turn to

14. My appreciation to Rabbi Steven Saeger, of Beth El Synagogue, Durham, North Carolina, for graciously answering questions about customs, laws, and rabbinical interpretations and to Professor Ken Surin, at Duke University, for appraising the plausibility of my appropriation of the Bible. Although many years have passed, I am also indebted to my teachers at the Reconstructionist SAJ Hebrew High School in New York and to Rabbi Alan Miller. The biblical text I work from is the Hebrew *Tanakh* (an acronym for the three parts of the Bible). For a discussion of the serious differences between the *Tanakh* and the Christian New Testament, see Harold Bloom (1991, 3) and Jack Miles (1995, 414–19). In addition, the main source of information for the material presented here on covenants, circumcision, dogma, and dualism are synthesized from the *Encyclopedia Judaica Yearbook*.

soothsayers for enlightenment. This does not imply, however, that for the Jews the future turned into homogeneous, empty time. For every second of time was the strait gate through which the Messiah might enter. (Benjamin 1968, 264)

The political ramifications of the history of slavery, and of slavery and miscegenation, have meant that race can never be entirely ignored by people of color in general and american Blacks in particular.[15] Pigmentation in the color-conscious United States has resulted in a crucial difference in the experience of Jews and Blacks (N. Friedman 1969). One is visibly marked as different and therefore often reminded of one's difference. For secular Jews, on the other hand, Jewish identity has been an intractable existential and intellectual problem since the Emancipation.[16] Some type of performance — an act and not merely a gesture[17] — is sufficient but not necessary for an individual to maintain a Jewish identity, a sense of belonging to the Jewish community. But the continuity of Jewish identity requires and is fundamentally based on, nurtured by, and reproduced within a community.

The Jewish collective experience is manifested in a covenant between God and a people, and it is this event that conditions the possibility of a Jewish people coming into being (Fackenheim 1970, 255). From William Benjamin and Gershom Scholem to Emil Fackenheim

15. Lewis Gordon's directness is astute: "while whites can act as though there were no such realities as race and racism, any black who chooses to do so acts at his or her peril" (1995b, 43).

16. This is not merely a diaspora issue but has surfaced as a debate among Israeli Jews as well (Levinas 1992).

17. Andre Brink, affirming that Afrikaner dissident Bram Fischer will always be an unforgotten hero, points out from Sartre the distinction between *an act* that is *a commitment* — it obligates — and *a gesture*, which is merely *a performance* for an audience. The political distinction is profound: "An act, implies involvement in the whole chain of cause and effect; it leads to something; it has a direct moral or practical bearing on the situation in which it is performed; and thereby it commits the (wo)man who performs it." The heroic rebel, in other words, is committed to a rebellion not *against* but *toward* something (Brink 1983, 61). I refer the reader to the revolutionary spirit of the prophets Amos and Isaiah, who challenged the opulence of materialism and the corruption of monarchies. See quotation from Israel Knox (quoted in Berson 1971) at the end of this section.

and Emmanuel Levinas, the Bible as document, exegesis, and commandments is recognized as the grid around which Jews as a people are constituted as a collectivity. Fackenheim, a philosopher distinguished for his expertise on Hegel, was ordained as a Reform rabbi in Berlin in 1939. He pivots Jewish identity on God and faith, and this leads him to conclude that Doubt—beginning with the Enlightenment[18] and continuing into contemporary North America—defers a present God to the realm of absent: "The modern expulsion of God from the human world made Jewish existence problematic. . . . The moment the living God became questionable, Jewish existence became questionable. The Jew had to embark on the weary business of self-definition" (Fackenheim 1970, 261).

One is born a Jew, and this definition generates and reproduces a people but is an insufficient guarantee for historical continuity. Fackenheim, pessimistic about the process of secularization and assimilation among American Jews, points to one of the most significant characteristics of the Jewish people:

[I]f a single generalization may be safely made about the contemporary Jew, it is that he still regards Jewish survival as a duty, to be performed whether he likes it or not. He may not have the slightest idea why it should be a duty; he may even consciously reject this duty. Still he feels it in his bones. (Fackenheim 1970, 262)

Among both Blacks and Jews, cultivating and activating memory is one of the critical strategies used to establish and maintain continuity. For Jews this has traditionally been seen as a moral obligation, and some Blacks have recommended using the Jewish approach as a model.[19] For

18. Hans Peter Rickman, however, underlines Spinoza's rejection of Descartes's systematic skepticism (doubt) that undermines any certainty. "A person who knows anything by that very fact knows that he knows" (Spinoza, *Ethics*, part 2, prop. 21; quoted in Hans Peter Rickman 1983, 78).

19. One of the sources for Malcolm X's conception of a Pan-African orientation was the Zionist movement as the political realization of a community with a loose but tenacious sense of collective identity. Malcolm X was not the first African American to realize this as a model for Black unity, but it is an aspect of Malcolm X's thinking that is not usually addressed. In a letter to Jim Booker at the *Amsterdam News*, written from Accra, Ghana, on 10 May 1964, Malcolm X drew an analogy

instance, Frantz Fanon criticized the strategic mistake and false prem-
ises of an identity defined as *only* human because it denies the efficacy of
memory. The crucial difference between empathizing with another's
cause and being directly implicated in it is that those who fit the latter
condition have an obligation to remember. As mentioned in the prelude,
when Texas State Representative Al Edwards sponsored the bill to celebrate Junteenth he reminded his constituents, "the Jews say, if they
ever forget their history, may their tongues cleave to the roof of their
mouths . . . let the same thing happen to us" (quoted in L. Jones 1994,
192).[20] The same political sentiments are articulated by Howard University professor and filmmaker, Haile Gerima. Speaking to the importance of collective memory and returning to, and retaining, a sense of
the historical past, the central theme in his fact-based film on slavery

---

between Pan-Africanism and Zionism: "We can learn much from the strategy used
by the American Jews. They have never migrated physically to Israel, yet their
cultural, philosophical, and psychological ties (migration) to Israel has enhanced
their political and economic and social position right there in America. Pan Africa-
nism will do for people of African descent all over the world, the same that Zionism
has done for Jews all over the world. If we too return to Africa (not physically) but
philosophically, culturally, and psychologically, it will benefit us right there in America, politically, economically, and socially. Just as Jews all over the world help Israel
and Israel in turn helps Jews all over the world, people of African descent all over this
earth must help Africa to become free and strong, and Africa in turn must obligate
itself to help people of African descent all over the earth."

20. In an essay written in early 1967, Alice Walker commented on the civil rights
movement in a style modeled on a passage from the Passover Haggadah: *Dayanu*
("If . . . it would have been enough"). In this context, she notes that "[w]hile the
hippies are 'tripping,' Negroes are going after power, which is so much more important to their survival and their children's survival than LSD and pot. Everyone would
be surprised if the Israelis ignored the Arabs and took up 'tripping' and pot smoking.
In this country we are the Israelis. Everybody who can do so would like to forget
this, of course. But for us to forget it for a minute would be fatal. 'We Shall Overcome' is just a song to most Americans, *but we must do it.* Or die" (Walker 1984,
128). See also Walker's response to Letty Cottin Pogrebin's "Anti-Semitism in the
Women's Movement," which appeared in the June 1982 issue of *Ms.* Walker's essay
provocatively focuses on the implications of "a close, often unspoken bond between
Jewish and black women" and the consequent mutual responsibility and account-
ability between the groups "that grows out of their awareness of oppression and
injustice, an awareness many gentile women simply do not have" (Walker 1984,
347).

from the perspective of the field slaves, *Sankofa* (1993), Gerima stresses that the individual can store collective memory of past generations within him/herself. "Jews for example, after so many years of banishment, they continue to say, 'Next Year' and they are trying to have a life in Israel, People are capable of storing memory in the marrow of their bones" (Woolford 1994, 100).[21]

Elinor's mother was born in Prague, Czechoslovakia, in 1934, and in 1939 her family escaped and went first to Ecuador because they were unable to enter the United States. They lived there for ten years until they were eventually granted American visas and moved to the United States. The phrase "identify with" in the following quote is a significant semantic reminder that "identity" is conceptually distinct from, although it can overlap with, "identification." I suggest a consideration of this phenomenon as parallel to the idea of the cognitive and experiential fact of *being and belonging* in various subject positions, presented in chapter 1. In Elinor's statement, the distinction between the existential question of identity and the practical political issues of identity, recognition, and (re)presentation is salient.

If you had to define what your sense of Jewishness is, how would you define it?

Umm — I guess the struggle. The thing I identify most with[22] in the Jewishness is I guess the Holocaust and the fact that they had to leave and the fact that no matter how far away I might be from Jewish faith itself,[23] if it came down to it and there was another Holocaust, I'd be taken in two seconds. You know: the fact that I'm Black and the fact that I'm Jewish, so I guess that's what I identify with.

21. See also Berlin (1994).

22. A possible definition of Jewish*ness* that accentuates context and, implicitly, political context would be "to identify with" the Jewish collective experience.

23. Note the distinction between religion and peoplehood, where the latter puts the emphasis on a sense of membership/community. Virginia Dominguez's excellent study of peoplehood and contemporary Israeli Jews overlooks the imported Western dichotomy of a division between "religious" (*dati*) and "secular" (*khiloni*). In Hebrew, there really is no word for secular — rather the word used to signify secular (not practicing religion or a nonbeliever) actually refers to a defiler (similar to a holy/profane dichotomy). The appropriation is a problematic solution to accommodate this imported distinction.

These sentiments are echoed in almost identical terms by Chelsea, who is self-conscious about the important role of instilling an identity in her two-year-old son, Avi:

My feeling about identity and Jewishness is historical and cultural. I mean — religion is not really my thing; I don't really believe the Bible. I mean there are some lessons, I guess, to be learned from the Bible but it's not really my identity; it's definitely not based on the religious aspect of (Jewishness). But the religious-ness is so wound up in the culturalness in the historicalness of it that it plays a role. Like holidays; like Passover. I feel like I can bring my whole self into Passover and look at my whole history on both sides. I mean my philosophy was always: well I better accept the fact that I'm Jewish whether I want to or not because if Hitler was here today, he would take me as soon as he would take someone else and I just think it's important to pass these things on to Avi.

In order to compare how Black and Jewish as forms of identity and as conceptual notions coincide or diverge at the personal, subjective level, I followed up my invitation for a definition of Jewishness with one of Blackness. The theme of struggle and oppression that resonates throughout all the interviews is succinctly stated by Elinor here in the context of the tension between Jews and Blacks through which those who stand in the intersection are often forced to navigate.

And how do you define the whole notion of "Blackness"?

Again, it's a struggle in the historical sense and it's the color of my skin.[24] And both sides — it's a struggle in the United States and a struggle that starts way back generation and generation ago. And the fact that, I think it's my great-great-aunt was a slave. And so it's kind of funny 'cause you get it from both sides. And you think about slavery and you think about the Holocaust there are so many similarities between them and I just wish that these communities could come together on that and realize that they both have such rich histories and so much struggle within their histories and they should be using them to their benefit to come together rather than pushing them apart. And I think that that's the biggest problem that I have with being Black and Jewish: the fact that the two sides can't come together.

24. "Whatever experience is, it is not just a *construct* but something that *constructs*" (Robert Scholes, quoted in Fuss 1989, 25). See my discussion on biraciality and interruption in the coda.

Chelsea's mother is Black, and her family are from Georgia; her father is the second generation of Russian Jews who immigrated in 1911. Like Elinor, Chelsea articulated the responsibility to remember history that she feels must be handed down from generation to generation. As the parent of a two-year-old, she feels implicated and personally obligated to recount the history of previous generations because

I'm like the last generation that will have actual contact on the Jewish side with say, like a Holocaust survivor and on the Black side, I'm the last person who will have direct contact with someone who had direct contact with a slave. So I feel like so much could be lost if I just look away or don't even give it much thought. I mean, that's part of the reason I really try to carry on some kind of tradition and in a sense give something to Avi.

In the following passage, she has linked anti-Semitism in Europe and the Holocaust with slavery in the United States.

For me personally — what makes it so important for me to carry out traditions is what my actual great-grandparents went through on both sides; what they went through and what they stood for — it just seems like I can't just turn, turn back and go on "Oh, I'm just a light-skinned person; a light-skinned black person."

Her moving affirmation of assuming an obligation to histories that still unfold encapsulates the essence of a passage from Exodus repeated annually in the reading of the Passover Haggadah:

In every generation, each person must regard himself[25] as if he himself had come out of Egypt, as it is said, "And thou shalt relate it to thy son in that day, saying this is done on account of that which the Lord did unto *me*, when I came forth out of Egypt." (Exodus 13:8)

Although there are numerous biblical covenants, within Jewish tradition the Mosaic covenants (Exodus 19–24) and the covenant of circumcision (*brit milah*), which begins with Abraham (Genesis 17:11–12), are paramount and obligatory.[26] Circumcision is, at once, interpreted and practiced as a ritual, a medical expedient, and a mark of

25. English nouns, unlike Hebrew, have no gender. I have not altered the masculine translation of the Hebrew pronoun, as the English "person" (too) often presumes a male and functions as the equivalent of "*Adam.*"

26. Rabbinical authorities are not unanimous as to which of the two covenants takes precedence in importance.

belonging to a community.[27] Since the days of Paul, the bodily inscription of difference distinguished Jews from Christians (n.b. Jews were not the first to practice circumcision). The erudite and controversial Baruch Spinoza (perhaps, an indication of self-defense) noted that the ritual of circumcision, carried out on the eighth day of the birth of a son, was sufficient to ensure the continuity of the Jewish people.[28]

One might formulate a proposition from Spinoza's forecast (and there is no attempt here to corroborate my interpretation with rabbinical sources): if the body is the preobjective site of perception, and memory is an embodied process, then the mark of difference is *in potential* a personal and visible reminder of Jewishness from which *in actuality* there is no escape. In other words, there is a subtle correlation between identity and subjective experience and literally inscribing a sign of collective identity on the embodied male subject. Circumcision henceforth signifies a tangible link with a history, a tradition, and a people. In combination, therefore, matrilineal descent and the ritual of circumcision are complementary and complimentary strategies for ensuring at least the reproduction of a community of Jews — though not necessarily a Jewish community.[29]

Chelsea made a decision to have her son circumcised in order to

27. As a mark of the collective conscience, circumcision has also been interpreted as an expression of nationalism. In particular, Hadrian's interdiction against circumcision was a chief provocation precipitating the Jewish rebellion led by Bar-Kochba, which was defeated in CE 135. (This revolt signals the final break between Judaism and Christianity. In addition, the Romans' attention to the specificity of Jews, as the Other distinct from the faction following Paul, becomes pronounced.)

28. *Encyclopedia Judaica Yearbook* (vol. 5, 575) quoting Spinoza, *Tractalus Theologico-Politicus* (1670, 3:53). Spinoza's challenge to the interpretive authority of the powerful rabbinical establishment (see esp. vol. 1, ch. 7) in Amsterdam led to the imposition of a *herem*. Often mistranslated as "excommunication," a *herem* is the equivalent of severe ostracism (a boycott), but the potential for its being lifted is never rescinded. Spinoza published in Latin under the name Benedict. The name publicly formalized his rift with the Jewish community; however, he never converted to Christianity. For a more lengthy elaboration of Spinoza's ideas, see the introduction to the translation of the *Tractalus Theologico-Politicus*, vol. 1, by R. H. M. Elwes (Spinoza 1951).

29. An extraordinary example is Leon Trotsky's grandson, an orthodox Jewish Israeli. If the grandfather was a non-Jewish Jew (Deutscher 1968), nevertheless two generations later the Jewish grandson represents a continuity.

ensure that he would have a reminder and a marker to fortify his Jewish identity. This was particularly important for her because her Jewishness was self-cultivated and always under question because her father — not her mother — was Jewish. In addition, neither her father nor her grandfather made an effort to provide her with a Jewish education, an absence she attributes to their own lack of faith or religiosity. Moreover, she emphasizes that with the death of her paternal grandmother, who was a converted Jew, the management of a Jewish household was divested of its guiding hand.

Every year we'd have a seder. I wanted him to have something solid to grasp onto and relate with. That was why I decided to have a brit in the first place as opposed to just a regular circumcision in the hospital. . . . It was just such a big ordeal and I felt I was a horrible mother for doing this to him just so he could have something to hold on to. But now after it's all said and done, I'm happy it happened and, I don't know; I guess I would do it again if I ever had another boy; you can't do for one of them and then not the other.

I am, of course, indulging in possibilities and not addressing what Bourdieu terms *the reality of practices* (1990, 67). I asked each of the three men I interviewed about their circumcision. David Lincoln was adopted when he was three by an interracial couple (Jewish mother and Black father) through the Louise Wise Services[30] and only then was circumcised. Frantz's circumcision was not only late, but was not memorable as a particularly Jewish experience:

(*Laughs with a tinge of embarrassment.*) [I]t's kind of interesting. I wasn't circumcised originally, but when I was seven — six or seven — I got some kind of infection or some kind of problem

That late?

Yeah, painful experience.

Jared's story, however, is the perfect exemplification of *the reality of practices*. His response to my question surprised us both, and offering a more detailed context to his answer is relevant.

30. See chapter 2 for information on the Louise Wise Services adoption agency.

Jared was bar-mitzvahed; his mother, a self-described "staunch atheist," never considered herself white.

She believed in Judaism as a culture and she believes in the history of the people and she was *proud* to be Jewish but as far as believing in God, on that side of everything she didn't really (believe). She always thought that it was important to teach me about the culture and everything but as far as religion, she didn't — she did say, "read the Bible," 'cause it was a great story; she said the best story every written.

Although Jared's own attitudes toward religion are similar to his mother's, his Black identity overshadows, but does not eclipse, a Jewish identity, where identity refers to a self-conscious representation of self: "When I was in the navy, I put no religious preference. Because I don't — I do feel somewhat guilty. I was bar-mitzvahed and my mother's Jewish which by law makes me Jewish."

In the navy he encountered anti-Semitism blatantly for the first time and came into more regular contact with racial prejudice. In the following passage, he tells about Columbia, Maryland, with its high percentage of biracial children and his interaction with a racially diverse environment. He also speaks here about growing conscious about the meaning of being a Jew, in contrast to previously taking it for granted:

This is up until (*laughs slightly*) really, I mean I didn't really get hit over the head with the problems of this world until I joined the navy, till I was seventeen. I mean I really had no idea about anything and I didn't care. So you know, if my mom wanted to call me Jewish, that was fine with me — there wasn't much of the blatant racism, you know. I mean there were people who, you know, (said) "don't Jew me."

(*I made a facial expression of incomprehension.*)

You know, like "lend me a dollar don't be Jewish."

Did you ever say anything?

I would sometimes; usually I didn't say anything cause I don't think I understood what was happening and I was like "Wait a minute," . . . um . . . see, I didn't get called, flat out called a "nigger," until I was in tenth grade. So my entire life till then was, you know, Dr. King had already taken care of those problems.

The first year Jared was on board ship, there was a Jewish Chaplain whom his mother had contacted when he joined the navy. Jared made a point of stressing the anonymity that can exist even though five thousand people are in fairly close quarters. That year, a seder was held in the captain's private quarters. Here we might refer back to Sartre's point that the "Jew among whites can disappear."

I mean the ship had — you know when you go out to sea there's 5,500 people on board, on the aircraft carrier that I was on, so there could be people that live right next to you that you would never converse with. I don't know for a fact that people hid it (being Jewish), but I did find it kind of hard to believe that whenever there was a Jewish function — 'cause my mom (*laughs and then says*) I can't believe she did this to me — she called the ship and got in contact with the rabbi — he was like a lieutenant, an officer, and I'm at the bottom of the enlisted rank, and he called me into his office and tells me that my mother had called — it was just embarrassing. She wanted me to have somebody that I could talk to. But she was trying to be helpful. So the one Jewish function I got invited to, there were maybe six or seven people and three or four of them were high-ranking officers including the captain who were just there for political reasons. Just like the president goes and cuts the tape at some function, that's what they do, you know. So — and I don't remember, I don't think I knew any other Jewish people on board.

Without hesitating, Jared responded to my question of the existence of anti-Semitism in the navy and, in the same association articulated so well by Fanon,[31] he links racism and anti-Semitism.

I'm sure, I mean I have no doubt that was the case. 'Cause we had arguments over time slots for the enlisted lounge which is where, a lot of the major functions you know, for the crew (took place). So I remember there were arguments over time slots between the Black Baptists, the Muslims got pushed around a lot . . . everybody got pushed around, based on what, I think, the chaplain wanted. And the chaplain being Christian and white, I would *not* be surprised at all if he just pushed everything off to the side and said, "Jews you get your five minutes over here, and Muslims you get your other five minutes" — so that wouldn't surprise me at all. And just the fact that there was so much racism period, I'm sure there was anti-Semitism.

31. See chapter 1.

With so many Jewish elements integrated in his life, and despite the secular Jewish cultural/political atmosphere in which he grew up, when Jared said he had not been circumcised, I was taken aback because I had simply assumed that he had been.

Would you circumcise your sons?

I wasn't circumcised. (*slight laugh*)

You were not circumcised?

So I probably won't worry about that either. Unless it was from the purely
   medical standpoint 'cause I do hear it is healthier so that would probably be

But not as a mark of Jewishness?

Uh uh (no).

And your mother didn't circumcise you?

Uh uh (no).

Did she ever tell you why? I mean, did you ever ask?

I don't think I ever asked—no I don't think I did ask. I don't think it ever
   came up.

Six months later, I sent the unedited transcript of our interview for his review, and Jared called me with a few revisions. On the subject of circumcision he said, "this is embarrassing, but I am circumcised. My mother wanted me to have a cultural tie." Clearly, the mark of being Jewish remains notable even in the absence of belief; consequently, Jared's unawareness was a lesson about modesty that was remarkable for the naive candor and incredible for the gap between the ritual and the impression it had *not* made. I asked "but how could you not know, not notice differences?—I mean, you're all men in the shower!" Jared laughed and answered that no one stared, so there was nothing he could compare himself to. "All the pictures I had seen up 'til then were from sex education class with diseased organs." The humor here is mitigated somewhat by the reality that the mark of circumcision per se no longer represents a visible sign of Jewish (male) difference.

At the end of our interview, and again in the conversation a few months later, Jared expressed the fact that my questions had been interesting to him but more than that, he felt that they gave him an opportunity to reflect on issues that were not new but that he had never previously focused on. Jared demonstrated his impression of the interview's significance in other ways: he shared the transcript not only with his mother but also with friends, who were fascinated. It subsequently provided engaged conversation about the meaning of biraciality, what it is to be Jewish, and the significance of being raised by a single parent of the opposite socially defined racial category.

I would like to insist on the following: as Roy Wagner (1981) effectively argues in relation to the invention (and notion) of culture, in calling attention to something one simultaneously makes it visible and (re)invents it. Thus the very fact that the *Encyclopedia Judaica Yearbook* makes incidental reference to Spinoza's comment and I, in turn, incorporate it to argue that one cannot go forward without knowing where one has been,[32] permits a proposition. When interracial people who are Jewish by descent insist on being recognized as both Jewish and Black, it presents a different challenge to considering the problem of "assimilation."

David Schoem (1989), an anthropologist who has conducted work on the impact of supplementary Jewish education (after-school programs) on Jewish children, argues — not incorrectly — that if structurally neither Jews nor the Jewish community are disappearing, *qualitatively* the lack of substance to Jewishness is an indication of increasing inauthenticity.[33] He found total lack of interest on the part of most of the children attending the after-school program — an attitude best summed up in the dismissive statement of one child, "what do you care if Moses crossed the Sea or something? I don't care!" (Schoem 1989). For most american Blacks with a sense of history (and particularly, like Chelsea, if their family is from the U.S. South) this statement is unthink-

32. In his well-known song "Buffalo Soldier," Bob Marley reproaches those without memory: "If you knew your history, you would know where you were coming from and you wouldn't have to ask me" (Marley 1975).

33. This might be considered and contextualized with respect to Barry Kosmin's report on the nondenominational Jews who identify themselves as "Just Jewish." See chapter 3 for a brief summation of preliminary conclusions of researchers at the North American Jewish Data Bank.

able. Even without a specific interest in being an educated or practicing Jew, the significance of liberation from slavery is unquestionable. When Schoem underscores the threat of anti-Semitism as having greater input than authenticity, identity, and community, I can appropriate his point to highlight the potentiality that for those who are interracial, the common past of oppression and persecution is a necessary and sufficient factor in publicly announcing one's Jewishness.

In the following passage, Frantz testifies to the manner in which a direct link between Jews and Blacks is established in the context of participation in the celebration (which entails reading the Haggadah — the narration of slavery to liberation). He describes the temporal gap of identifying with events in the past and how this gap is intensified by contemporary politics of race, which in turn impact on his identification with Jews who self-reference themselves as white Americans. Major holidays, including Passover, were celebrated at Frantz's grandmother's house:

[M]y grandmother was always saying, "Now don't forget the Jewish side was also slaves as well," you know. She never really let me forget that. That's the one thing she always harped on.

So do you think of the parallels between African American history and Jewish history?

Definitely. It's like the hard part for me now is that seems — the Jewish slavery part seems so far off and I feel removed from it, you know what I mean, so when I think about it, I kind of feel the pain of slavery — I can feel that in me and I understand it, but it's not as strong or as immediate a feeling as Black people. Especially with the Jewish people I've come across in my lifetime, it's hard to see that kind of connection.

The Holocaust is closer in time than slavery in Egypt, and Frantz is careful to explain why it is easier to feel a closer identification with the Black experience without, however, feeling distant from the Jewish catastrophe. But to reproduce a sense of identity and affiliation one must feel invested, although, recalling Haile Gerima's comment on the capacity of an individual to store generations of memory, this may sometimes be a passive reservoir that is mobilized in times of crisis. The following lengthy passage is reproduced in order to retain and convey the coherent unity of Frantz's response.

But what's your personal investment in this? Is there any?

My personal investment; well, with Black people I like, I still maintain our heritage you know. Just to remember and be able to feel it and I don't think that could ever be taken away. So I don't worry about it as strongly. With Jewish people, I think that they focus on that as well — maintaining their heritage and their culture; they teach it. So I don't see them letting that disappear.

But you — Frantz Fanon Walker?

Do I have a problem?

What is your investment in continuity, in keeping — in passing on

A strong one. With anything I just think it's very necessary to pass on your ways to your children, you know. Like I would name my children for people in my family — all of them. Just to have that line. To know where you're coming from I feel is very important — like I wish I knew so much more. 'Cause it does determine who you are. It really does. Little things make it obvious, like your parents saying you know, "you remind me so much of your grandfather or your Uncle this or Uncle that." I think that's necessary to maintain. Especially when it's trying to be taken away all the time. I think both groups do a pretty good job of that.

David is thirty-six and father of one son. He was married to a non-practicing Christian African American and although they attended several meetings with a Reform rabbi, she did not convert. The marriage terminated with considerable ill will and since then David has joined a Jewish single parents' club as well as a support group for Black men. As a father, David decided to provide his son with a Jewish education in order to inculcate a Jewish identity. This eventually may pose a dilemma if his son ever seeks formal recognition as a Jew, although some Reform and Reconstructionist rabbis do recognize paternal descent *on condition that there is a genuine effort to maintain a Jewish identity and affiliation.* It should be noted that the introduction of paternal descent by the Reform Movement caused a major debate with the Union of American Hebrew Congregations and still does not have widespread approval or acceptance even among many secular, non-affiliated Jews and is completely rejected by the Orthodox and Conservative Rabbinate.

In line with his determination to incorporate elements of a religious and cultural Jewish identity, David had his son circumcised in a ritual ceremony carried out in the hospital. Part of his divorce settlement included having custody of the child for Jewish holidays, and David and his son usually attend synagogue on those occasions. The importance of an institutional setting, in this case a synagogue, cannot be underestimated, even for people who never attend services. It is the site for coming together and it is for this reason that although Judaism does not endorse the notion of intermediaries between God and humans, a minyan—or collective of at least ten people[34]—is required before the Torah can be read. Regular synagogue attendance, once a year or once a week, is a practical means of building up a sense of belonging. David points to certain features, such as Hebrew, that are characteristic of Judaism as a religious, cultural, and political entity and integrated into his son's early experience without yet having to be made explicit.

And, how does he feel about being in the synagogue?

There's a playroom on every floor, there's a gym, so he gets to play with other children that go to synagogue. He likes it as a place for Jewish people to go, a temple where there's a different language spoken.

David lights candles with his son on the Friday evenings they are together, thus instituting a consciousness of Shabbat as different from other days of the week. In addition, David has conscientiously built up a circle of friends and acquaintances with children the same age as his son, and they regularly get together for different holiday celebrations. In fact, many of the Jewish celebrations, such as Hanukkah, Simhat Torah, Purim, and Passover, are particularly amenable to children's active participation. I asked David about some of the activities he has undertaken to reinforce a sense of Jewishness in his son. He responds that he celebrates "mostly Jewish holidays, Hanukkah, Rosh Hashanah, Yom Kippur, probably more now than I did when I was a child because I have a son, and since he's not in the Hebrew school yet, it's probably more important."

Being a parent requires, for most people, an actualization of prin-

---

34. Traditionally a minyan is comprised of ten men who have passed their bar mitzvah, which occurs at age thirteen.

ciples that one may have as a single person yet not felt bound to enact. In order for parents to reproduce those ideas and pass them on to their child, some act — a commitment — has to be undertaken. *Doing* and thus establishing norms and models is inherently the purpose of socialization.

Jewish tradition does not discourage prayer in private — indeed Orthodox Jews pray alone each morning when they rise — however the stipulation of a minyan ensures that reading from the Torah (as a Book *of the People*) and death burials are never conducted outside the presence of a group. Quite explicitly, then, the institutionalization of prescribed forms of communion reinforce and reproduce both a group identity and confirm the particularity of the individual as a member of a community. It is no coincidence that naming the child takes place during circumcision, the celebrated moment in which the child is welcomed into the Jewish people. The importance of genealogy is then affirmed for a child, who is always referred to as "so-and-so, son of . . ." or "daughter of . . ."

The theme of *doing* something in order to give content to a sense of identity is linked to being a participant in a community in order to ensure its continuity. Writing about the *idea* of the Black community whose *reality* is crime, poverty, and class divisions, law professor Regina Austin, advocates a politics of identification that goes beyond the nostalgia of memory:

> To be a part of a real black community requires that one go Home every once in a while and interact with the folks. To keep up one's membership in such a community requires that one do something on-site. A politics of identification is not a way around this. It just suggests what one might do when one gets there. (1995, 158–59)

For Blacks and for Jews one is always a member of the community — there is always a community to which to come back "Home." However, to give meaning to this membership and substance to the identity that is inherited with membership has been far more problematic for Jews.[35] In part these difficulties illustrate further the arbitrary criteria of

---

35. To "inherit" is to be the recipient of a legacy and thus a link in a chain of continuity, although one can be a member but lack a self-conscious identity.

"race" as a mobilizing factor that has been advocated and employed as a politics of reaction to racism. Austin's prescription stands in complete contrast to the views articulated by one Jewish activist, Robert Paul Wolff, during the "Young Radicals" symposium held in 1962 under the auspices of the journal *Dissent*: "Jewishness is not a matter of *doing* something, but merely of *being* something. It is therefore understandable that one might wonder just what it was to *be* a Jew ("Young Radicals" 1962, 155). And yet to be a Jew is more than an ontological status — a state of being — as suggested by Wolff. Lenora Berson defers to Israel Knox, famed socialist

who captured in words the elusive and strange creature — the non-believing Jew who remained a Jew: "To accept things as they are, the world as it is (with tragedy at its very heart), as already redeemed, is to cease being a Jew, is to be guilty of the gravest transgression against the prophetic heritage. To be a Jew it doesn't matter if you pray or observe dietary laws, it does matter if you cherish messianic expectancy." (Berson 1971, 140)

The Drama of Identity

The use of theatrical metaphors, such as dramatization, performance, and cues, in an ethnographic text suggests that the individual mimetically enacts a character. Working within a phenomenological paradigm, Bruce Wilshire, a professor of theater, analyzes the adoption of theatrical metaphors in sociology (which applies as well to anthropology).

The role-playing metaphor is exceedingly slippery and dangerous because almost inevitably when we deliberately transfer the notion of role playing to offstage life, we carry with us, smuggled in, the notion of fictionality of the actor's portrayal. (Wilshire 1982, xvi)

Considering identities as dramatization, in which performance and style are crucial and conscious components, calls attention to a tension between the spoken and the spectacular (in other words, speech, and the lived body performance). The cues interviewees employ register the context within which a persona is projected: the tension between interpretive content (what people say about the meaning of "to be Black and Jewish") and what the individual is doing in the interview scene (how people talk about it).

People gave their time to meet with me on the implicit understanding that I would be faithful to their commentaries. For this reason, it seems crucial to avoid privileging theories over voices, and here is where the anthropological contribution, with its focus on real people, remains distinct even with the adoption of an interdisciplinary approach. In accordance with new lines of inquiry opened up by the feminist practice of oral history,[36] I remain sensitive to the need to address the gaps, incongruencies, and areas of convergence between theory and concrete individual's experiences.

There should not be an assumption that the narratives I solicited, and then refashioned for an audience of readers, reveal truth or present an unequivocal translation of people's memories, feelings, or ideas. In brief, I found that there are no predetermined answers to what comprises the identities a single individual may construct for him/herself. A provisional conclusion impressed itself after each interview: each of the narrators had a sense of themselves not as closed totalities — as critics of the singular concept "identity" define it — but as people fully cognizant of *embodying* heterogeneity, occupying multiple subject positions in a society where "race" has metamorphosed into a social fact (Durkheim 1982).[37]

Lindsey, like the other interviewees, is not always sympathetic to

36. I'm using Gluck and Patai's definition of oral history as it "refers to the whole enterprise: recording, transcribing, editing, and making public the resulting product" (1991, 4). Oral history as a methodology has drawn its insights from anthropology and sociology, psychology and literary theory, speech communication, and linguistics, as well as from the New Social History. *Women's Words* is a collection that both reflects and reflects on the specific contributions of feminist scholarship to the methodology and practice of oral history. In particular, this has been a "concern with connection and collaboration" (1991, 5n.5). In other words, the power dynamics that mark the relationship between the narrator and her story and the interviewer who uses the text for her own arguments are not taken for granted but interrogated from the initial encounter all the way through to the marketed product. The feminist practice of oral history gives the commitment to writing about and for women top priority and as such examines questions that arise from the experience of women and that had traditionally been eclipsed by male-centered interests. Methodologically, feminist practices required rethinking ways of listening and questioning, interpreting, and translating in order to move away from information gathering to the interactive process.

37. I refer to Durkheim's notion of social fact as intangibles that are external constraints on the individual.

curiosity about her background, and this is illustrated by the following anecdote,

> Everywhere I go somebody says, "what are you?" Everyday; happened yester-
> day. Happened the day before and I say, "what do I look like?" (*laughs at her*
> *rhetorical tone*) 'cause I think it's very clear. If you look at me it's clear as can
> be. I am Jewish and I'm Black. That's what it is. And then people first guess
> Puerto Rican or Spanish or Mexican. And then sometimes, Indian. I look
> Arab. But then when I tell them they say, "oh of course."

So what do you tell them?

I tell 'em, Jewish and Black.

On the other hand, Lindsey shares with other interracial people a sense of common experience that legitimates and, therefore validates, curiosity about people with similar mixed heritage. I asked her whether she questions or is questioned by people who are also interracial. Lindsey's description of being the Object of interest, and of being interested in an other, seems textually uncertain; this hesitancy reflects, however, the difficulty in articulating an experience that is not personally unique, but which is also not usually recognized as a general phenomenon:

> [W]ell that actually happened two nights ago. Someone who was — what was
> he? I think he was half-white and half-Black. Actually, I asked him. And I know
> that after being asked all the time, just like I'm being asked (it can be annoying),
> so I kinda asked — sort of like — "I'm wondering what nationality you are,
> what's your background" and he says, (*miming an emphatic tone*) "You know I
> hate when people ask me that." And I said, "I know, so do I," and he said, "Um,
> I'm Black." And I said, "You are" (*using the rhetorical tone*). And um, he said,
> "Well, I'm Irish too." And so that was a little strange and then he asked, "Well
> what are you?" and I said, "Weren't you wondering what I was as well?" and he
> says, "Well yeah" so that he knew that, right off the bat; and he said, "You're
> probably Jewish and Black."

To state *what* one is — a factual (re)presentation that includes declaring one's relation to a reference group — may elicit a reaction that infuses and reinforces an identity with a previously inconsequential significance. This was best evidenced when I asked Jared to describe a moment in which the fact (i.e., the actuality of a genealogy) of his being Jewish and Black became public. In the example I presented earlier from his experience in the navy, he spoke of the reaction to his volunteering for duty at Christmas: "[T]hey would say, '. . . You're not Jewish!' (*drawn out with incredulity*) and I'd say, 'Yes, I *am*' and they would say, 'Bullshit! no you're *not*!' and I would say, '*Yes I am!*' "

I want to pause here and consider the issue of difference from an alternative perspective that is respectful of both unity and plurality. I refer to Jewish interpretations of the Creation — order and unity were founded on separation and a recognition of, and respect for, difference. The biblical narrative of Creation, in the Torah, suggests a paradigm through which to imagine that (in their separate realms) material objects and people compliment and complement each other (in their respective domains), and therefore the constant possibility for a more egalitarian order exists. This is a difference based both on diversity and variety but without structures of domination. The model conceptually accommodates ideas of scissiparity while at the same time preserving an idea of integrity of the whole as a collective, a totality. As a proposition, it is analogous to multivocality. In other words, this model of multiplicity, rather than articulated as plurality or inclusion, permits speaking of identity without reducing it to a fixed and singular referent. This system contrasts with the legacy of a Cartesian framework, which is grounded in dualist ontologies, and, paradoxically, undergirds theories that seek to disrupt the strict segregation of the particular, the body, and emotion from the universal, the mind, and reason (Hartsock 1990). We need to replace theories based on "either/or" with, using Stuart Hall's phrase, theories grounded by the "logic of coupling" (1992, 29).

In other words, the artificiality of the language of theory and the politics that condition its emergence began to irritate rather than inspire me. In this context, the terminologically convenient "identity" does function as a *constructed* category that invites contestation, and there is much to be gained intellectually and politically from destabilizing the category of "identity" as self-evident (like body, culture, experience, etc.).

However, I am also inclined to appreciate the limitations of theory that is disengaged from the politics and practice of everyday life. Nancy Hartsock's interrogation of the disabling potential — indeed the fundamentally disempowering characteristic — of postmodern theories is valuable:[38]

Why is it that just at the moment when so many of us who have been silenced begin to demand the right to name ourselves, to act as subjects rather than objects of history, just then the concept of subjecthood becomes problematic? (Hartsock 1990, 163)

For people — label them "subjects" or "concrete material beings" — whose genealogical roots preclude the possibility of uniformity (i.e., homogeneity), except as a conscious decision, identity is "always already"[39] understood as multiplicity. This identity is pluralized though not fragmented, socially constructed but not invented.[40] The point is that (in terms of social definitions) the biracial and multiracial people I interviewed are conscious of embodying difference and take for granted that they are "subjectivities which (are) both multiple and specific" (Hartsock 1990, 163). It is this knowledge that informs their sense of self (identity). As expressed by Bruce Wilshire,

It is vexing to realize that the term *identity* has no single sense. When coupled with the term *self*, as in identity of *self*, each of the terms exacerbates the difficulties in the other. *Identity* can pertain to atemporal entities like numbers, to temporal ones, like persons. . . . Pertaining to a temporal being that is a person it means, presumably, that the being is identical with itself through time and change. (1982, 143)

38. In an essay that interrogates the implications of racial ambiguity among people of interracial background, I have argued that the repudiation of race as a term of difference does not address the political strategies that follow the question: Where do we go once we have acknowledged that "the Negro was invented by whites?" (Azoulay 1996). A more direct criticism of the gap that can sometimes develop between theory and practice is recorded in the unforgettable (and to some infamous) words of the community organizer and sociologist, theorist and strategist Saul Alinsky: "The sociology department is the kind of institution that spends $100,000 on research projects to find the location of houses of prostitution which a taxi driver could tell you for nothing" (quoted in Berson 1971, 141; Glazer 1969).

39. Diane Fuss argues that the phrase "always already" implicates deconstructionist theory as grounded on an anti-essentialist essentialism (1989, 15 ff.).

40. My discussion is limited to first-generation "interracial" people, but I reiterate that race is a historical construction.

Wilshire insists on differentiating identity of person/self from personality. Personalities, Wilshire argues, are generally stable and fairly consistent over time. I tend to agree with this interpretation because anyone who has visited the newborn section in a hospital can testify to the fact that in each crib is a being with a distinct personality that remains recognizable as they mature over time. Drawing on my own experience with three children, from the moment each was born — and I think even during each pregnancy — each had a distinct personality. Although studies have shown a correlation between the environment of the womb and the evolving baby, it is sufficient here to note that personality, as presented through Wilshire's perspective, can be understood as an essential core unique and particular to a specific person. Personality here might be coterminous with the pre-Bourdieu meaning of "disposition"; for example, the trait of tending toward a cheerful disposition or one that is melancholic is reinforced or mollified through socialization.[41]

In contrast, identities are always being negotiated, shifting, and in process. Recognition of this dynamic state does not mean that one must accept the notion of "fractured identities" popular among postmodernists and criticized best by Susan Bordo as the "epistemological fantasy of becoming multiplicity" (1990, 145). More appropriately, perhaps is Trinh T. Minh-ha's notion of "I" as *infinite layers* (1989, 90–91).

Although my interviews definitely evidenced the open ended, plural, malleable character of identities, they also document a sense of stability and continuity that does not negate, but instead compliments and complements, conceptualizing the plurality of a human being as an unfolding project. Diane Fuss, in a move parallel to Nancy Hartsock, does an excellent job of sabotaging the opposition that has been imposed between the concepts of essentialism and constructionism. Emphasizing that the concrete material being — a person — is obscured in both singular universalizing categories and in the plurality of heterogeneity, Fuss argues that pluralizing categories (e.g., "women" instead of "woman") does not discontinue the semantic unity implied by essentialism. She

41. Bourdieu's operative definition of "disposition" refers to a mode of reality construction (Bourdieu 1990, 338).

posits that plurality displaces but does not disrupt essentialism, consequently the danger of universalizing heterogeneity or multiple identities
and establishing a new norm.

In this context, I suggest that Aijaz Ahmad's criticism of the idea of
hybridity[42] and its proponents are very relevant. Ahmad argues that

42. Outside the scope of the discussion undertaken in this book, but waiting for
sober interrogation, is the ease with which the term "hybridity" (the roots of "mulatto" can be traced to the Spanish *mulo* [mule], a hybrid; that "mulatto" can be used
in a nondeprecating way affirms a positive reexamination of "hybridity") has been
legitimized and (re)entered the discourse of identity via Homi Bhaba (MacLaren
1994, 203–4). This project has been superbly initiated by Robert J. C. Young in his
excellent book *Colonial Desire: Hybridity in Theory, Culture and Race* (1995). In
the context of my work here, some reference to its offensive history should be
mentioned. In 1839, not a decade after Nat Turner's revolt, George Morton, a
central player in promoting scientific ethnology, published *Crania Americana*, the
results of years of collecting and comparing skulls and a work that brought national
prominence to and legitimacy for his promotion of polygeny (Smedley 1993, 236;
Gould 1993, 96). His studies of craniometry (quantitative studies of the skull) established him as the founder of the first school of American anthropology (Smedley
1993, 237). Morton worked closely with an Egyptologist, George R. Gliddon, and
his student, Dr. Josiah C. Nott of Mobile, Alabama, whose studies of the mulatto
reinforced his belief that the mixed-race person was "a genuine hybrid, weaker and
less fertile than either parent stock" (Fredrickson 1971, 75). He was obsessed with
Blacks and called his project "the nigger business or niggerology" (Fredrickson
1971, 78; Gould 1993, 112).

These three proponents of racism were significantly empowered by the support
they received from Louis Agassiz, a Swiss biologist who emigrated to the United
States in 1846 to accept a position with Harvard. Agassiz "helped Josiah C. Nott to
formulate a concept of hybridity applicable to racial intermixture, as well as the
crossbreeding of animal species" (Karcher 1975, 428). In a letter to his mother, he
wrote of his physical revulsion and recoil from the idea that the races were a single
species: "it is impossible for me to repress the feeling that they are not of the same
blood as us. In seeing their black faces with their thick lips and grimacing teeth, the
wool on their head, their bent knees, their elongated hands, their large curved nails,
and especially the livid color of the palm of their hands. . . . What unhappiness for
the white race—to have tied to their existence so closely with that of negroes in
certain countries!" (quoted in Gould 1993, 95). Stephen Jay Gould writes, "The
standard *Life and Letters*, compiled by Agassiz's wife, omits these lines in presenting
an expurgated version of this famous letter. Other historians have paraphrased them
or passed them by. I recovered this passage from the original manuscript in Harvard's Houghton Library and have translated it, verbatim, for the first time as far as I
know" (1993, 95).

the idea of hybridity—which presents itself as a critique of essentialism, partakes of a carnivalesque collapse and play of identities, and comes under a great many names—takes essentially two forms; cultural hybridity and what one may call philosophical and even political hybridity. (1995, 13)

He notes that obviously this idea is a truism. The problem is that the figure of "the migrant (postcolonial) intellectual residing in the metropolis, comes to signify a universal condition of hybridity and is said to be the Subject of a Truth that individuals living within their national cultures do not possess" (1995, 13).

The metaphors of boundaries and borderlands, frontiers and hinterlands have anchored themselves securely in the discourse of identity, at least among intellectuals working in the West. Boundaries—political and social—are no longer hermetically sealed, and therefore are porous:[43] "From the boundary perspective, identity is more like a performance in process than a postulate, premise or originary principle" (Conquergood 1991, 185). As an abstract proposition, we may consider a distinction between identities that are constructed and unfold in the presence of, or imposed by, others and self-identification, or what can be termed self-reference, where an individual specifically claims membership in a given group, privileging at a particular moment an always present dimension of identity. This still coheres with Taylor's discussion of the politics of recognition but leads more easily toward Trinh Minh-ha's concept of identity as infinite layers and whose complexity is obscured by the typography of I/i.

The differences made *between* entities comprehended as absolute presences—hence the notions of *pure origin* and *true* self—are an outgrowth of a dualistic system of thought peculiar to the Occident. . . . They should be distinguished from the differences grasped *both between* and *within* entities, each of these being understood as multiple presence. (1989, 93–94)

The slippery distinction marks the following passages from Frantz and Jared respectively:

43. This metaphor is problematic precisely because although it celebrates the phenomenon of regional political unification (e.g., Europe) it ignores the tenacity of balkanization. The theories that have been built from this metaphor are not innocent and can eclipse the personal investment of their architects. This dynamic is explored by Ali Behad (1993).

You know, if somebody says, "What are you?" then I'll say "Black and Jewish." And then you know, maybe but usually not, maybe someone will say, "Oh, you know that's interesting" or "You have two strikes against you." That type of thing. It doesn't really come up that often. (*laughs*) Its not an issue you know. When I'm walking down the street I don't feel Jewish. I feel Black. So I don't think its very much of an issue. Very rarely.

Jared first explains that his mother accentuated the multidimensional aspects of Jewishness — historical and cultural, not merely the religious facets. Knowing that all members of the armed forces wear dog tags that include religion (information necessary for deaths and burials), I asked Jared what religious preference he listed in the navy, but he had listed none. His racial identity, reinforced by others' perceptions of him, did not negate but did mitigate against a strong sense of belonging to a generalized collective Jewish community:

I do feel somewhat guilty, I was bar-mitzvahed and my mother's Jewish which by law makes me Jewish, but I have a huge problem with organized religion as a whole anyway — which some might say is an excuse. . . . Well I think part of it is being biracial has something to do with it. I don't think that if you saw me walking down the street you'd guess I was Jewish. Puerto Rican I've been called.[44] You know (speculation of being) Black or whatever, or a question-mark, people will always wonder — but Jewish, no.

For Claire the issue of being Jewish by law (descent) is incidental although not dismissed entirely. The written text exhibits a hesitant moment, which is absent from the tone in which she spoke, and should, therefore, not be overinterpreted as a vacillation in attitude:

As far as being Jewish, I never really — I mean I think of myself culturally — well, I don't know if culturally is the word — not religious at all. My family isn't

44. The issue of visibility, and representation, in terms of an imaginary image of what a Jew "looks" like is a constant theme whenever the discussion of Jews who are not white takes place. In the interviews, I found that mention of "looking Puerto Rican" or Hispanic surfaced continually. Although there is no place here to elaborate on this theme, an interrogation of ideas of color and ethnicity and their association with something Latin(o) in the Black community would be enlightening, particularly in relation to the national imagination.

religious. So I don't think of myself as Jewish a lot. And I think that has a lot to do with how you're perceived. Maybe if I looked more mixed.[45]

The concluding reference to impression and reception will be discussed further, in the context of and in relation to skin color and appearance, but here it is useful to underline the point Claire raises regarding the dialectic of being recognized by others and how one internalizes this into a form of "self-recognition." Turning to Frantz and Jared again, the former emphasizes the visibility of race at the expense of the invisibility of being Jewish and yet, parenthetically, he links racism and anti-Semitism.

Plenty of times I've had plenty of hostility toward me because of being Black you know — people yelling "nigger" and had fights, you know. But I think that's typical pretty much for every Black male. The Jewish part — no, because people don't know. You know, if I go into a bar or school or whatever, it's not like people say, "that dirty Jew." (*laughs*)

Jared's experience, and note the similarity to Frantz, illustrates the subtle politicization of an attitude that can easily be converted into a specific standpoint position:

Then there were Black people who didn't care, and there were white people who didn't care. You know, they looked at me not necessarily as a lost case, but "he's so odd anyway this is just one more thing to add to the list" and then there were of course the white people who would say "Jesus he's already half nigger and now he's Jewish too — I mean this guy's all messed up," you know.

I asked Claire about her usage of the words "white" and "Jewish." Her response would intrigue me as a means to clarify how respondents identify themselves when challenged by the language of "half-white" or "Jewish."

I tend to say, I probably say "Jewish" more than I say "white" just because I happen to associate — I think I'd rather associate — with Jews. I mean I think there're a lot of different ethnic groups among whites and I'd rather, I'd probably rather be clear that it was Jewish.

45. Claire is not light-skinned and could not be mistaken for not being a member of "the African diaspora."

At this point, Claire seemed more ambivalent about the way she described herself. Nonetheless, the conditional adverbs seemed motivated more by the fact that it was not an issue to which she had given much thought. Here she responded to the question of self-description with a certain measure of hesitancy (starting and then interrupting herself with "I don't know"), but the hesitancy reflects in a tone that was both off-handed and casual,

I think sometimes I call myself—I don't know what I call, I don't call myself half and half. If I identify myself—yea, I do "other" and I may specify or I may leave it blank depending on the mood (*laughs*) and—

If you specify, how do you specify?

Black and white.

Have you ever put Black and Jewish?

Probably not. Probably not.

Later I returned to the question of self-identity and asked whether she felt that the linguistic racial hierarchy of "thinking in terms of Black and white" was founded on an image of mathematical fractions that was challenged by laws of descent in Judaism and by the one-drop rule in America. I was fishing for evidence of Stuart Hall's notion of "the logic of coupling," which so aptly described my own sense of identity. This time Claire was firm: "as far as I am concerned, I am half and half—not all one or the other." "or one *and* the other or," I asked. "No, I am not—I am half *and* half," she replied.

Actually, the reserved manner of Claire's responses were in line with a posture she had maintained from the outset of the interview that contrasted with the resolute style I observed in the office. In the first statement she says, "I don't call myself half and half," and moments later she seems to disclaim her comment with "I am half and half." On the one hand, the vague indecisiveness, can be attributed to the serious consideration she gave to answering my questions. Therefore, it would be inaccurate to conclude that the certainty with which Claire asserted biraciality contradicted either the tone or content of what she previously articulated with less intensity. Furthermore, how one calls oneself—naming—in the public sphere does not need to correspond to how one thinks of oneself as a particular individual with a history and a future (in other words, the subtle distinction between self-identification and self-identity).

On the other hand, this appraisal, that Claire's remarks should not be evaluated as inconsistent, is emphasized by the context of her final remarks to me. Toward the end of the interview, Claire did comment on times when she did, in fact, lay claim to and declare the fact that she was Jewish. Although we had concluded the interview with Belinda, the three of us continued to converse informally, and I asked if I could turn the tape recorder back on. Belinda prided herself on being tolerant of ignorance and felt that her background empowered her to impress on people the *in*significance of race, saying

I find I am constantly in a position of teaching people on a one-to-one basis because as we discussed in the office before, there are those people who have never — I've encountered people who have never been outside of their own close-knit community.

In contrast to Belinda, I have a low level of tolerance for other people's curiosity when it feels as if prejudice rather than ignorance is guiding their inquisitiveness. Consequently, one of the questions I asked all the people I interviewed was whether they sometimes revealed their family background in order to shock people out of their stereotypes. Often before I would even ask, the respondent would bring up her/his own anecdote. Belinda and Claire, however, were my second (and third) interviews.

I asked for comments on the strategy of surprise as a tactic for contesting stereotypes and explained that Elinor, the young woman I had interviewed earlier in the day, expressed glee and amusement at undermining prejudices:

I will just give people complexes like you wouldn't believe: "Well you know I'm Jewish, I'm extremely offended by that joke" (*laughs*) and things like that and they'll come "I'm sorry."

And the shock on their face?

I guess the way I like to use it is I like to shock people. I like to shock people and I've always liked to shock people at anything I did and I like to stir up controversy. And I am myself a controversy. I'm not a controversy to myself but I'm a controversy to others. And I don't mind it and I have fun with it.

Belinda disparaged this approach as "a prime example of energy wasting" whereas Claire approved it as a learning process. Claire stressed that sometimes the only way to jolt people out of their prejudices and force them to confront their ignorance is through the tactic of surprise:

I absolutely agree with that. I do that for that reason and also, okay—I would say that I do that sometimes not only so people know that not only are whites Jewish, but to make people (know) they can have more in common with people than they would ever imagine.

Claire's responses indicate that regardless of the conceptual approach one takes, in both cases (identity as a reaction or assertion and identity as voluntary and consensual) identities can register an act of resistance or they can comply with the pressures of a given social, political, or economic context. Consciously occupying a number of politically infused social categories that are considered unique in the public sphere can be tedious.

One experience shared by most of the interviewees is the moment when the issue of Jewish involvement in the slave trade surfaces. As a contentious point of contemporary debate between some sectors of the Jewish and Black communities, the manner in which Blacks who are Jewish and interracial respond to the anti-Semitic overtones of the issue are interesting. Jared's reaction is to turn the question back on to the other person:

Honestly there were just days when I didn't feel like having to defend every side of—I mean it is somewhat difficult to have to defend so many different kinds of people. People bring up "well Jews had a lot to do with the slave trade." I mean that may be true but there were a lot of Jews who fought hard in the Civil Rights Movement—"so what do you want me to do," I would ask them. "So what do you want me to say? I consider myself to be conscious of the Black community and conscious of the evil ways of the society but what do you want me to do?"

Did you say that you were Jewish?

Yeah. I mean once everything came out, I would just send it all out. And sometimes, if they caught me in the right mood, sometimes somebody would say something and ask me about my mother and I would just give them my whole life history. The son of Russian Jews and militant Black man, I mean you know, whatever you want.

Sometimes, however, speaking from the authority of being Black and Jewish is invigorating, as Elinor relates from a moment at Lincoln University:

Well, I was in class one day. it was an African American history course and we were talking about some topic or another that the teacher was talking about and the guy behind me, Malik, and I used to send notes back and forth to each other constantly and one day he wrote a note saying, its all the Jews' fault. And I wrote a note back to him telling him I was Jewish and he asked me well *how* are you Jewish? (*laughs slightly, almost derisively*) And I explained it to him and he said, "Oh, okay" and then I really think I got him to start looking at things a lot differently.

The identities of Black/Jewish on which I focus do not exhaust the possibilities for self-definition. Instead, they are a specific outcome or product of a system of political inequalities and societal differentiation. The common denominator for all the people I spoke with, with the possible exception of Belinda, was a consciousness of being Black (visible) and Jewish (invisible) and of that combination being perceived as unique and different. Chelsea's statement is representative:

Have you found yourself feeling as if you were the mediator?

Yeah. (*pause*) I feel that way a lot of times when it's not even dealing with Black and Jewish; 'cause I think my position and my dual background helps me to see things in other ways that a lot of other people can't see and I'll always feel like I am often trying to show people how I see things. I think I'm just more sensitive to issues of racism and identity and stereotyping.

More important, although the *content* of Jewish identity was amorphous—a phenomenon characteristic of secular Jews in general and particularly for children of interreligious marriages, regardless of race—each of the interviewees did make a point of having his or her background known and recognized, illustrating the statement "To exist socially means also to be perceived, and perceived as distinct" (Bourdieu 1991, 224). It is this understanding of self that also informs an always accessible, sometimes unself-conscious, feeling of being a mediator, as Frantz testifies:

As someone who's in the middle, do you feel there's not been enough effort to use people like yourself? As mediators?

I've never really thought about it; I'm sure there hasn't been enough effort made. I kind of instinctively use myself as a mediator though. I kind of take the other side to whoever I'm talking with, you know. If I'm talking with a Jewish person, I'll say well you have to understand this or that, if I'm talking with a Black person—I usually come right out and say I'm both Black and Jewish and I agree with the issues on both sides. And I always disagree with anyone using any kind of racism.

I think the challenge here lies in the implications of being self-conscious that one is a Jew, which is subjective, in contrast to having an interest in being Jewish, which in turn requires *doing* something even if it is only a mental act. But in both cases, being Jewish is as political as being Black although — in the United States — the first *seems* less immediate while the second *is* inescapable.

Anthropologist Manning Nash, writing against the social psychology approach to ethnicity that harbors the notion of primordial ties, underlines the point that the Law and the Covenant (as a contract between God and a people) combine to make Jews a separate people. "The Law," he contends, "constitutes the category of Jews, observance makes a person a Jew, and being a Jew is being set apart from a mere biological existence on the one hand, and from others who are not Jews on the other" (Nash 1989, 78). The metaphor of boundaries, therefore, may detract from, rather than enhance, a discussion on Jews, Jewishness, and the system of signification that emanates from the Law and constitutes a Jewish people, for "it is the practicalities of life in a non-Jewish world of secular national states that raise the issue of who is a Jew, rather than the abstract argument about the boundaries of the category" (Nash 1989, 68).

Neither Frantz nor Jared is particularly interested in actively pursuing a Jewish lifestyle and, like the other people I spoke with, they make distinctions among religion, culture, and ethnicity that are simultaneously clear and ambivalent. Jared's mother, an atheist, nevertheless created the conditions in which he might develop a sense of Jewishness as well as Blackness. He was circumcised and trained for his bar mitzvah, and when he entered the navy, his mother informed the ship's rabbi. Frantz, on the other hand, received most of his Jewish sense of self from his grandmother, with whom he and his mother celebrated the major holidays at a gathering that included his (white-skinned) more affluent Jewish cousins. He did not have a bar mitzvah, and his circumcision was not a religious ritual but rather an emergency medical procedure. He notes, nevertheless,

Instinctively I would just say Jewish because that's what I am and I don't know, I consider my mother white but first Jewish. I don't know, that's just the way I've looked at her. I don't think other people go that far into it you know. But I always say that she's Jewish first. That I'm Jewish first.

Most of the people I interviewed testify that Black identity coexists with a critical awareness that the social definition of Blackness, including and because of its politicized meaning, always incorporates a supplementary dimension, regardless of whether it is explicitly addressed. Frantz's statement encapsulates this:

Are there moments in which you felt — and you kinda said this — but being interracial makes you unique in a special way?

I always feel like that. I can feel, I can like feel other people's fears and their likes and dislikes, you know. And that gives you enough in any situation — there's always the problem that people can't relate to each other you know. That Jewish people can't relate to Black people. Asian (Moslem) people can't relate to Hindus or whatever. And I don't have that problem. So — sometimes I think everybody should be so lucky to have (the interracial experience).

Although Belinda insisted on a personal philosophy built on the idea that "bodies are merely vehicles to get the spirit around," like other american Blacks she has had to contend with racism. As a light-skinned Black woman she encountered the antagonism of Black students at college when she refused to join the Black Students Union and the impudent hostility of white bank customers who resented dealing with a bank manager who was a Black woman. Here I agree completely with Gwendolyn Etter-Lewis's criticism on the inadequacy of "existing norms of self in narrative texts (that) have failed to account for black female life experiences" and her more general observation that "[i]n essence, race is not a hidden quality that surfaces only in connection with external events, it is an essential component of existence imposed by a prejudiced society upon the lives of black Americans" (Etter-Lewis 1991, 44). Thus, despite the reluctance of Claire and resistance of Belinda to think of racial identities as primary, the saliency of race *as a social fact* serves as a brake against completely transcending it and only identifying in the general, universalizing rubric.

Although the distinction I have proposed sets up a very narrow line, identity as consensual or compliant should not be seen *in opposition* to self-reference, as voluntary and deliberate. The language of analytic constructs (identity/self-reference) permits me to make a purely conceptual difference here in order to accentuate that self-referentiality presumes greater flexibility in which to orchestrate conceptions of self. This may be illustrated by Belinda's drawing a comparison with Claire over her experience as light-skinned and often misrecognized: "This differs from Claire in that people always thought that I was something, either something exotic or they — I mean I've always been sort of — if someone thought they must assign something they'd come out with all different types of mixes and things." Belinda, in fact, takes the "chameleon approach to mediating an identity." In other words, those who do not feel indignant about the ability to inadvertently pass also have the most to gain from identifying actively not as Black, but as multiracial (Rosner 1993, 139; Russell, Wilson, and Hall 1992, 73). Claire's experience has been that of a Black woman who is too dark to be recognized as "mixed-race."

In a sharp-witted essay entitled "Is Biracial Enough? (Or What's This about a Multiracial Category on the Census: a Conversation)," writer Lisa Jones dismisses the "census movement"[46] as a campaign for assimilation in which "race is not seen as a political/economic construct, a battleground where Americans vie for power and turf but a question of color, a stick-on, peel-off label" (Jones 1994, 57). Skin color as a visible marker — the shells protecting Belinda's spirits — makes a crucial difference in one's reception by and response to others. Whereas Belinda

---

46. The campaign to add the category "multiracial" to the next U.S. census.

consistently insists that racial labels are irrelevant and Claire agrees, Claire is also able to counter, "call it multiracial or biracial or whatever-racial but I do think it is important that you have a category."

The experience acquired from being positioned in an empowering or disabling site, determines, in my opinion, the extent of mobility and thus leverage to negotiate identities. A similar stance is implied in Ahmad's critique of Homi Bhabha for dispensing "with the idea that a sense of place, of belonging, of some stable commitment to one's class or gender or nation (*or race: kga*) may be useful for defining one's politics" (Ahmad 1995, 14). Shrewdly he accentuates the problem that

Most individuals are really not free to fashion themselves anew with each passing day, nor do communities arise out of and fade into thin air of the infinitely contingent. . . . Post coloniality is also, like most things, a matter of class. (1995, 16)

It is obvious that the representation of these interviews results from my authority to rename or shape the perspectives of the narrators. One can refer to Kevin Dwyer, who comments on ways anthropologists mold material to fit their own understandings: these questions deliberately reiterate that my interpretation may conflict with the intention of the informant (Dwyer 1987, xvii). My own inclinations tend toward viewing the world through the lens of politics, although I made a conscious effort to temper this when I began my interviews. Not entirely unexpected, therefore, theorization of racial identities, as consequence and reverberation of my own prioritization of politics was challenged when three of my interviewees seemed to me to be resistant to politicizing their voices. In this context, I have had to address whether it is appropriate to define and stress as *absence*, or *lack*, a sense of race consciousness among those who insist that they do not identify or act in ways that might be construed as racialized.

As one who thinks of this as an apolitical position that denies the coherency of race in a society founded on racial stratification, I have had to consider a different possibility. This meant distilling from the interviewees' responses those comments that do evidence a politics of race and then rethinking them from their perspective.

The politics of an intentionally apolitical stance were well illustrated when I questioned Belinda about the political debates our parents shared. Her father purchased the first album of Malcolm X's speeches, but our memories do not coincide. Where I remember her father's supportive stance toward Black nationalism, she insists on the centrality of Martin Luther King Jr.

> I can honestly say that I think — no I know — *all* my life when I'm with a person I went right to the heart. And they (parents) were very big on the teachings of Martin Luther King and —

> *And Malcolm X, I remember.*

> Well, *I* remember Martin Luther King, *okay*, and what I remember most is that you judge a person by the content of their character and not the color of their skin.

Here it is important to call attention to both Belinda's admission that she had disengaged from any involvement with politics and Claire's enthusiastic endorsement.

> (*Claire interjects heatedly, with fervor.*) Everything was always so serious, everything, everything was political, everything was always so serious, so serious, and you just wished your parents would gossip about TV or something like that, you know." (*followed by self-conscious laughter*)

> *Belinda:* That was the biggest thing — Claire and I are like minds with this; when you're growing up in a household where everything is a debate you just have a big hunger for quiet — its like you want to say, "Will you just lighten up? We know there are problems in the world."

These pronouncements yielded a proposition to work from: perhaps a presentation of identities that *are* constructed as political are *not* inherently, or even necessarily, juxtaposed to constructions that initially appear as "not racial." Without distorting the responses to my questions, proceeding from this proposition avoids assuming that what appears as an apolitical identity is not in itself a political position. Both Belinda's and Claire's parents had been members of the Communist Party and in both cases, the home environment was one charged with political discussions. Their apparent *disengagement* from politics was a withdrawal from a *preoccupation* with politics. It manifested itself in an insistence on finding activities to do that were "merely" social as well as taking only a cursory interest in current events. In a way, even the institutions in which both women worked (banking and commercial publishing company respectively) provided environments that discouraged political debates. As with the range of strategies of resistance (on a continuum with acts of armed struggle at one end and obsequious conduct at the other end), Belinda's and Claire's apolitical positions represent a politics of withdrawal, *not* a withdrawal from politics.

Experience

The question of approach is a methodological one and concerns selectivity. Mapping out an idea or topic that heretofore, in everyday life, was either a marginal or a nonissue for interviewees raises a question that few anthropologists have begun to address: When is a topic invented by the researcher? In this regard, Elvi Whittaker has aptly commented, "Awaiting consideration are matters such as the anthropology of description and the anthropology of observation. . . . We need to ask: to what conditions must cultures and persons conform in order to be observable or describable?" (Whittaker 1990, 227; Carrithers 1990).

The idea of what it means, and if it has significance, of being Black, Jewish, and interracial was not invented by me — if anything, I am the invention or product just as are the people with whom I met. Furthermore, this *idea* is not an abstract concept but an *experienced* phenomenon. All of my collaborators, in one way or another, have had occasion to think about their heritage and how they felt linked, personally, to this heritage, as well as how their identity was "conceived as part of a group" (McKay, quoted in Etter-Lewis 1991, 53). As Bourdieu has amply demonstrated, an idea will be more persuasive and pervasive if there are corresponding indications that make it recognizable: "the theory effect . . . is all the more powerful and above all durable when the processes of objectification and of rendering explicit are rooted in reality, and hence the divisions in thought correspond more precisely to real divisions" (Bourdieu 1991, 135). Parenthetically, I'd like to state that rather than being an "invented topic," it breaks the peculiar silence around an intimate aspect of Jewish and Black interrelations and makes it visible. In part, then, this project is a response to the exclamations of incredulity — "What, you're *Jew-ish*!" — that all of us have experienced.

Social beings are concrete material beings whose sociality and self-hood are constituted through the process of experience. Differences, therefore, are also constituted through experience and the production of different types of knowledge. The position of a person (i.e., the site in which subjects are constituted) shapes and in turn is shaped by the knowledge s/he produces, what Donna Haraway terms "situated knowledges." It is the foundation and resource upon which one acts whether in the form of resistance or resignation. Identity, thus, as an analytic concept implies relationality. A paradigmatic illustration of this is found in the Book of Exodus, which offers an early model for revolution and liberation.

The relation between God and the Israelites is founded with the Covenant at Mount Sinai. This event, in turn, marks the invention of a people who will differentiate themselves on the one hand by the Cove-nant and the Laws and, on the other hand, with the mark of circumci-sion inscribed on the body of its male members, although the line is carried forward only by mothers. The point is that "alterity" exists only when identity operates as a relational concept (or signifier), and "iden-tity" can only be a meaningful signifier when linked to the notion of differentiation. Identity is to alterity, I think, as two sides of the same paper. Viewed this way, differentiation and alterity are not a presump-tion of opposition or conflict. Identity and alterity do not exist indepen-dently or autonomously from each other.

One can abstract from experience an explanation of, and rationale for, an aspect of "being" — ontologically and metaphorically — in a subject position that is particular and unique to the individual (Allen Grimshaw, quoted in Fuss 1989, 25). If "beingness" here suggestively resonates with "identity," then caution is required against assuming inherent, fixed qualities. A subject position — what Sandra Harding astutely elaborates as a standpoint position — motivates and propels forward a semiotic and historical moment of "being" this or that at at given time and place. Lewis Gordon, whose work on explicating racism leans heavily on Sartre, represents the self — the I — as "empty and unre-flective; being without content" (Gordon 1995a, 19).

Identities, following Gordon's logic, infuse and give content to the self, although this process seems to approximate an image of a receptacle rather than a canvas. In assigning a name to this temporal and spatial entity *and* project (as process), meaning is created. In other words, naming as a ritual and not merely a linguistic sign, establishes both a point of departure and a reference point. Jared's response to the question of the significance of racial labels underscores my point:

I think that I would like to be able to, finally for once, be able to, find one word or one quick phrase that encompasses me entirely, but — and I think it's important for people to have a sense of belonging to a community or to a group but; so yeah. I think, I guess that, it's important and I probably would put multiracial.

Naming, in this example, empowers individuals or groups to recognize their positions. Aijaz Ahmad's criticism of "migrant intellectuals" reaffirms that one needs to grasp, in the Levinasian sense,[47] the location from which a subjectivity is constituted and in which identities are constructed, and this requires naming "the ground we're coming from" (Rich, quoted in Fuss 1989, 52). Finally, although naming insists on recognition it neither forecloses possibilities of dissolution and reconstitution nor privileges plurality at the expense of particularity.

Although in the classical era spatial metaphors were pivotal to descriptions of "experiencing" the world, in the contemporary period "experience" is understood through metaphors of sight — to perceive, to apprehend, to reflect, and, finally, to know (Mudimbe 1993a; Hymes 1974a, 21–22; Hodgen 1964). The processual unfolding of these sensory expressions is what is meant by "experience" (J. Scott 1992). Concretely, language is inadequate to the task of representing in words the reality that is apprehended through the senses. When we speak of experience as a foundation to identity, we align and link words that are contested and yet without which a coherent conversation is difficult.

Joan Scott disputes the use of experience as uncontested evidence and worries that historians view the concept as an ontological foundation of a group's identity, politics, and history. She instructs them to

47. Emmanuel Levinas discusses the correlation of knowing and being in which knowledge, a mode of thought that involves our material existence in a physical world, is directly related to perception and, as such, refers back to an act of grasping (1992, 85).

interrogate the self-evident assumptions embedded in the notion "experience" (Scott 1992, 30). There is merit to her argument on condition that we keep in mind that the particular is not easily generalized to the universal. It is the distinction that makes individuals unique: their particular experiences are comprehended against, and in the context of, the socialization in the family and the school and through the transmission of values.

The process of socialization experienced by members of a community, independently and collectively, enables them to share a sense of familiarity and divergence when they compare experiences. Whether by choice or chance, individuals are members of more than one social group, and therefore can take part in and share a collective identity among different groups. When people generalize their experience to confirm sameness or difference, they do not lose their individual and particular sense of identity informed by their specific experiences.

In an experimental ethnography, Kevin Dwyer attempted to transcend his "dissatisfaction with academic anthropology" (1987, xvii). Traditionally, anthropology has centered on examining and exploring various aspects of communities and peoples who are very different. The quest for knowledge and curiosity that stimulates the very desire for understanding is always political and thus always involves power:

[T]he anthropologist singles out 'events' and poses questions; the informant answers, embellishes, digresses, evades. The anthropologist, in part for reasons and in a matter reflecting his own society's concerns, is pushed to impose form upon his own experience, and his questions provide a skeleton designed to provoke the informant to respond; the informant's responses add flesh to this frame and dress it, often in unexpected ways. The events and the dialogues do not hide this inequality but, instead, help to display it: as we look at the events in a text, we can begin to question how the anthropologist defines his experience; from the questions he asks, we gain some insight into the kind of understanding he seeks. (Dwyer 1987, xvii)

Dwyer considers the anthropologist as an outsider, an experientially different position from that of an insider. A member of the community, with a view from within, is (usually) in a better position to bring form into visibility. Thus, it is as a daughter among the Awlad 'Ali that Lila Abu-Lughod gains access to and is able to "grasp more immediately just how the social world worked and how its members understood it" (Abu-Lughod 1986, 22). It is as a member, not merely an observer, that Abu-Lughod is strategically positioned to take notice of and subsequently attend to the ways in which poetry is used to express radically different sentiments from those expressed in the same situations using nonpoetic language.

In my research, the subject matter and the people with whom I sought interviews provided a framework in which I am simultaneously participating and reflecting. Frequently, our experiences were compared and contrasted during the telling and listening. Bruce Wilshire concisely articulates this process.

To see what one actually is is to see this as only an instance of the possibility projected by the fiction — and it is to see the possibility as only one among many. Persons knowing persons is a special case of a general epistemological claim that cannot be overstressed: we grasp what actually is only after we have imagined what it might have been. We see what a thing is only after we have imagined how there could be any possible thing of that sort. (Wilshire 1982, 5)

Joan Scott has discussed historians' efforts at pluralizing their conceptualization of history as a field of study and a discipline, and methodologically in terms of what constitutes evidence. She argues that it is a mistake to receive "experience as uncontestable evidence and an originary point of explanation" without situating it as an object of inquiry. Experience, in her view, is subjective and as an origin of knowledge and identities, it should not be seen as self-evident but rather as a product and an outcome reflective of a particular discursive formation.

This approach, accentuating constructionism, produces the impersonal language of subjects and positioning that is problematic and threatens, I think, an elision of the concrete material being that is the particular person. Hence the challenge in the idea that "it is not individuals who have experience but subjects who are constituted through experience" (Scott 1992, 25–26). Masked behind this dispassionate approach is a grammar that quietly illustrates the disappearance of the particular being, a named person with a life history that makes her/him unique and marks the individual as different from another being. Furthermore, the language of subjects, suggestive of "simple epiphenomena of structure" detracts attention away from agency — the strategies that individuals produce and subjectively adjust to situations (Bourdieu 1990, 9, 11). Lévi-Strauss's remarks seem particularly relevant, especially in the context of misevaluations of his intellectual objectives and political directions.

[O]ne may wonder if the catastrophes that have struck the West may also find their origin there. . . . Because it has given people the idea that society is to be ruled by abstract thought, when instead it is formed of habits and customs; by crushing these in the mortar of reason, one pulverizes ways of life founded on a long tradition, reducing individuals to the state of interchangeable and anonymous atoms. True freedom can be based only on a concrete foundation and is made up of a balance among small adherence, little solidarities. Pitted against these are theoretical ideas proclaimed as rational. When they have achieved their goals, there is nothing left for them but to destroy each other. Today we are observing the result." (Lévi-Strauss 1991, 117–18)[48]

In general, theorizing about experience, identity, and cultural fluidity needs to be tempered by a conceptual framework that persistently interrogates the space of theoretical procedures and the conditions of theory's claims. For instance, David Scott challenges the way theory is taken for granted as a "narrative that was authored (and authorized) the hegemonic career of the West." In this context, he questions the move to undermine the notion of *culture*: "this recognizably 'anti-essentialist' characterization of 'culture' as mobile, as unbounded, as hybrid and so on, is itself open to question: for *whom* is 'culture' unbounded — the anthropologist or the native?" (1992, 375–76). And again, Lewis Gordon's insightful interjection is appealing: why should Blacks give up race just because it has been decided that race is constructed? On this specific point, I do agree with those who argue that Black people should be cautious of and interrogate the approach taken by "Negro deconstruc-

48. Lévi-Strauss — for whom systems of representation were important — critiqued the nineteenth-century anthropologist Edward Burnett Tylor for assuming that elements in a culture might be compared without the use of history and argued that "abstract reconstructions do not teach about how and why people invent, acquire, modify or borrow new institutions" (Lévi-Strauss 1973, 7). Lévi-Strauss overturns the biological models by adopting metaphors from mathematics and physics. For an excellent exploration of his challenge to racism, ethnocentrism, and the notion of progress, see Almeida (1990).

tionists" (Baraka 1994, 21), who advocate: "The attempted disconnection of literature from real life To render beauty and intelligence neuter and abstract. To make truth mysterious and an individual perception; and society metaphor and metaphysical" (Baraka 1994, 21).

Jared's interview highlights a theme common to all my interviews: language and the social fact of race are always at odds with each other as evidenced in specific situated experiences.

There are times when I use different things to describe[49] myself; if I'm talking to a group of Black people about you know, Black problems or history or whatever, I probably'd call myself "Black," but in this kind of discussion "biracial" *because* I do—I can't honestly say that I feel 100 percent Black. Ah—simply because I'm not.

Jared's anecdote about "sliding in safe in the seed of a Black man" marvelously demonstrates the ridiculousness of the presumption that a perspective rooted in Blackness is automatically essentialist. Instead, it illustrates the self-conscious awareness that one is born into a society that ascribes blackness—one is not born black. Jared aligns himself more closely with an Afrocentric approach, but he is adamant about not negating or ignoring the Jewish dimension of his heritage. Note the following two passages:

(I) I do think it is disrespectful to her mother for Halle Berry to want to deny her whiteness or her—white mother anyway. And I don't think its completely fair for her to say that—that she is Black—well, maybe; I don't know (*sigh*) I think it's good to see her making strides and including the Black community. I think it's good that the Black community includes *her*; and Jasmine Guy and others.

(II) *Can you see yourself at any point completely pulling yourself back from Jewishness?*

No because I would just think that that was complete and that's sort of what I was saying about Halle Berry. I think that would be *completely* disrespectful to my mother—if for nothing else, 'cause I don't think I owe the Jewish community anything, and I don't feel that—so it's not that—it would be

---

49. "Describe" and "Naming" may—in the usage to which the terms are put by Jared—be theorized as overlapping conceptual modes of reflecting on self.

purely as a disrespect to her mother and her sister and her brother. 'Cause they have all three been tremendous for me so I could *never* just say, well all white people are the devil and Jews should burn in hell or whatever; I could *never never*, no uh!uh! I may have some militant views and thoughts like that, (*but*) it just would be impossible. And I think anybody who could do that is wrong.

Like other interviewees whose mother is Jewish but also visibly white and treated as white, he is perceptive to the issue of how one treads the racial line without disrespecting one's mother and therefore an aspect of one's self (yes — mother as part of self is intended here). These are political attitudes that lead to political choices.

I create the opportunity to consider in greater depth than usual their own reflections on identity and continuity. This consideration of self is important but *the primary significance* of these interviews is the impression that multiplicity as unique is so much a part of who and what we are that it is also very much taken for granted by ourselves. The sense of self-confidence displayed and articulated in the interviews emerges as reflective of naturalizing, by taking for granted, an ontology of social being-ness, constitutive of and incorporating variation and variety.

In some of my interviews, there is evidence that the arbitrary intervention I made into their lives created a moment in which they paused to reflect on a dimension of their self-identity that ordinarily was both self-evident and insignificant. My questions sometimes elicited the answer, "I never thought about it before," yet the response would always evidence, unself-consciously perhaps, that consideration of the issues had, in fact, taken place. Chelsea called me a few weeks after our meeting to ask whether I had found any Black Jewish psychologists; Jared asked for more copies of his transcript in order to share them with friends and relatives; David contacted me to make revisions of some of his remarks and commented that seeing his words in print gave him the opportunity to rethink some of his ideas.

Social theorist Douglass Kellner regards the popularity of the discourse of identity as a phenomenon that became particularly salient in the 1960s and has remained topical ever since. Kellner notes that forms of identity are now characterized by a great deal of elasticity even though they are still shaped within a circumscribed set of social roles and norms (Kellner 1992, 41). He likens this flexibility to a game of "disposable identities" analogous to putting on and taking off clothing (153).

Two interviews suggested that identity, as an analytical construct, might also be considered paradigmatically as a persona, assembled and slipped into in the presence of another person. If coherent and salient ethnic or racial identities require the influence of external stimuli, does the recession of external pressure inhibit or diminish their salience? In other words, if racial or ethnic aspects of a person's identities surface and are accentuated and verbalized more forcefully at times of prejudice or discrimination, then perhaps *the absence* of prejudice tempers or even obscures the immediate relevance of a racially informed identity, which would explain why *being Jewish* for most of my interviewees has the semblance of a contextual identity. *The particularity of an identity of being Black* or "mixed" cannot be discussed in the language of "more or less important or significant" than the identity of Jewishness. The differentiation is grounded on a misleading foundation and a result of thinking in opposites instead of mutual generation and support (Trinh Minh-Ha 1989, 67). What may often appear as inconsistency in the responses of an individual interview reflects what Naomi Zack (herself interracial and Jewish, although she prefers thinking in terms of micro-diversity) appropriately insists on in the Introduction to her *American Mixed Race: The Culture of Microdiversity*:

If this is confusing, no one is in a position to apologize for it and no one has the right to override the racial experiences of others, in the interests of "clarity." The confusion is not the result of intellectual error but a consequence of the contradictions inherent in the social and historical reality of race. (1995, xviii)

CODA:

AN ETHNOGRAPHY OF DESCRIPTION OR

PRESCRIPTION?

I would like to insist that the effort made here is to anthropologize philosophy and not the opposite. This crucial distinction anticipates, and in part explains, being situated intellectually not on the margins of the field of cultural anthropology, but in the in-between space where disciplinary boundaries are under contest.

The originality of this text lies in its specific topic, which opens the door for investigations on the manner in which, in the United States, the possibility of a Jewish and Black identity has been negated, denied, or suppressed on the one hand and cultivated, nurtured, or maintained on the other. The issue is delicate and raises important epistemological questions. I follow Pierre Bourdieu on this point (*can a native be a good anthropologist?*), noting that his ethnographic sites have been those in which he was an indigene. Can a Jewish Black woman be a good student of an ethnography of being Black/being Jewish? On this point, the reader is referred to Bourdieu's statement in *Homo Academicus*

[W]e have been tempted to adopt the title *A Book for Burning*, which Li Zhi, a renegade mandarin, gave to one of those self-consuming works of his which revealed the rules of the mandarins' game. We do so, not in order to challenge those who, despite their readiness to denounce all in inquisitions, will condemn to the stake any work perceived as a sacrilegious outrage against their own beliefs, but simply to state the contradiction which is inherent in divulging tribal secrets and which is only so painful because even the partial publication of our most intimate details is also a kind of public confession. (Bourdieu 1988, 5; Mudimbe 1993b, 153)

This book has proposed an *idea* of identity — being (socially defined as) Black and Jewish (by a law of descent) — whose specificity seems to be peculiar to the context of the United States. As an object of knowledge which originates in and is explored from a subjective bias, this project relies on an effort, regulated by a disciplined self-reflexivity, to be faithful to objective criteria without compromising political urgency. Questions of identity are both personal and communal, although they are always shifting and witness the intervention of history, economics, and politics. This dynamic cannot be overlooked in an ethnography that brings being*ness* of Black *and* Jewish, in the United States, into a visible arena for investigation. Therefore, the significance of Michel Foucault's concept of discursive systems has been a decisive influence on my methodology.

Discursive systems are constructed primarily through themes and images dispersed and echoed in different contexts and texts and not merely through causal linkages (Foucault 1972). This point is demonstrated by V. Y. Mudimbe, who insists on the necessity of overcoming the tendency to think of works as the original products of their authors (Mudimbe 1988, 1994; Montag 1993). Throughout the time that I have reflected on and addressed this topic, I have been attentive to the thin line between description and prescription (Bourdieu 1991). (Re)presenting a social group is to bring categories of perception and construction together and, possibly, to cause them to overlap:

> Even the most strictly constative scientific description is always open to the possibility of functioning in a prescriptive way, capable of contributing to its own verification by exercising a theory effect through which it helps to bring about that which it declares. (Bourdieu 1991, 134)

Engaging in description (ethnography) is, undoubtedly and as Bourdieu carefully but explicitly contends, a very political act; one in which academic scholarship is always implicated.[1]

Let me reiterate my central theme: the idea of an identity named in these pages as Black and Jewish — explicitly limited by and linked to intermarriage through the logic of coupling[2] — is thinkable as a collec-

---

1. See Bourdieu's discussion of the elevated style of language that authorizes the obfuscation, and therefore neutralization, of Heidegger's affiliation with Nazi politics: "the definition which exludes any overt reference to politics in philosophy has been so profoundly internalized by professors of philosophy that they have managed to forget that Heidegger's philosophy is political from beginning to end" (1991, 158).

2. The discerning reader will notice that the ethnography presented here has obscured a parallel but often silenced discourse of religion and the conflict inter-

tive being-in-the-world *only* and *on condition that* they are brought into contact with preexisting American ideas about race. By calling disinterest into question and by bracketing "weighted" words, Foucault's concept of "discursive formations" encourages an examination of an entire field in which knowledge is produced and a given discourse is possible *on the basis of specific conditions of possibility* (Foucault 1972). In the attempt to pioneer an investigation, drawing from a range of sources seemed the best strategy from which to make visible how the production of a knowledge of difference is naturalized and how certain intellectual ideas are appropriated into a way of *seeing* and *talking* about differences — in other words, a system of self-evident truths (Bourdieu 1991, 100). In order to think unconventionally, I have turned to some texts which are familiar but which I have put to a different use.

Reconsider Scripture as texts that invite, indeed compel, interpretation followed by practical application. Everything in the Torah, the foundation for rabbinical commentary, admits to the *invention* of the Jewish people — long before Benedict Anderson (1991) and the infusion of the language of social construction.[3] More than a master charter, the Torah is not simply or merely a mythical genesis but very definitely (re)presents processes of becoming *and* incorporating change. To (re)produce a people — as a collective subject — requires a vigilant, conscious, and conscientious retelling in performance;[4] reference points as symbolic landmarks.[5] For this reason, the founding events and the

---

religious unions cause when there are children. This eclipse instantiates an unresolved problem reflected by the tension of language — from the outset, there has been an empirical reality that corresponds too neatly with a suspicious theoretical presupposition. In sum, the text begins with and proceeds from a notion of interracial that presupposes interreligious *instead of* calling religious concerns into question. If this was not unanticipated, it was also unavoidable. Future studies may approach this topic differently and compare "monoracial" and "biracial" inter*religious* marriages and the identities of the children. Depending on the scholar's perspective, interests, and foci, the salience of the specific issue of race — which anchored this project — will be more or less pronounced.

3. One may recall Leach's (1983) structural analysis that nicely demonstrates that Moses had to have a sister — without this detail, this paradigm of liberation would not have been possible (Leach and Aycock 1983).

4. For an excellent and reliable discussion, see Virginia Dominguez (1989).

5. In a gross simplification, I refer here to three cycles, each of which have significance for religious rituals but which are so rooted in a cultural and ecological

covenants have been recalled and given periodic prominence in my discussion.

Within the evolving notion of a collective Jewish community, the law of maternal descent was logical: regardless of war, conquest, or forced migration there can be no question that a particular baby is born from a particular woman. It is a law that, in principle, ensures the reproduction of a community in spite of rape (at worst) and marrying out (at best). In part, this permits the romantic notion of the ingathering of the exiles from the four corners of the world. It is in the ascension of Jews to Israel and the resultant demographic diversity in a rainbow of colors (from the tall blonds of northern Europe to the black-skinned Ethiopians) to which Jews in the diaspora who live in countries where race has been a predominant political issue (e.g., England, South Africa, the United States) have pointed in order to accentuate the meaninglessness of race to Jewish identity.[6]

Rather than being a new invention, my linkage between interracial, Black, and Jewish was anticipated by the mass migration of Jews from Europe to the United States and the historical process in which, as a social group, Jews were progressively accepted as white (a process that included internalization of this identity), and therefore this tripartite identity precedes struggles over contemporary notions of "multiracial" and "multicultural."

I deliberately do not speak of B/*black* Jews: it is a choice that refuses the adjective a space in this discussion — physical attributes have no meaning in any definition of Jewishness. It is the *American* public discourse that makes reference (both inherent and explicit) to Black people inescapable (Morrison 1993). And it is this fetishization that infects the way Jews begin to self-identify as white. In the discourse of *multi-isms*, race thinking is the necessary precondition to marking *Black and Jewish*

---

context that they are amenable to, and therefore significant for, secular observance. The nonreligious aspect of Jewish peoplehood as a collective identity marked by a tradition, a culture, and a language becomes explicit in the Middle East, where the terrain and climate cohere with (and thus manifest the logic of) the cycles. The month of Tishrei, in the fall, marks the start of the calendar year; the agricultural cycle begins in the spring and is thus associated with Passover; finally, the holiday of Shavout, which celebrates reception of the Torah, also signals the start of summer.

6. There is no attempt here to connect or fuse this discussion with the existential and political questions concerning the State of Israel in regional politics.

as unusual or unique (negating the diversity among Jews and among Blacks as a result of diaspora and dispersion); "multiracial" (presupposing, falsely, Jewish as an extension of whiteness) or "multicultural" (presupposing, inaccurately, Blackness as a cultural phenomenon).

Where Jewish is grammatically an adjective, it is nevertheless *also* present as a noun — *to be* Jewish is to be born a Jew or to convert and become Jewish.[7] In rare cases, one may lose the privilege of being recognized as a Jew — as in the 1963 case of Brother Daniel[8] — a born Jew who converted to Catholicism.[9] Here the issue of tying one's fate to a people superseded matrilineal lines of descent. Note carefully, however: the issue is *recognition*. Brother Daniel is not recognized as a member of the Jewish people because he tied his fate elsewhere, but he nevertheless remains a Jew. This is a theological dilemma witnessing also an

7. The fact that proselytizing is discouraged makes conversion a difficult procedure, which includes rigorous study culminating in a commitment to adhere to the Laws. My thanks to V. Y. Mudimbe for pointing out to me that in the Romance languages, the word for a Jew, the noun, does not share the same etymological root as the adjective. In Hebrew the noun and the adjective are the same and genealogically stem from the Kingdom of Judea. Although this seemed provocatively curious, I leave it to the linguists to interrogate how far one may push this distinction from both a linguistic and then a political perspective.

8. My most sincere thanks to Roger Loyd, director of the Duke Divinity School Library, for his critical assistance in finding references on Brother Daniel.

9. All countries that permit immigration have regulations and laws for attaining citizenship. In Israel, a state established after the Holocaust as a haven for all Jews wishing "to return" and an immediate refuge for Jews persecuted in their countries of residence, the case of Brother Daniel (Oswald Rufeisen), a Carmelite monk, sets a legal precedent. Brother Daniel was entitled to apply for citizenship as a Catholic sent by his order to live and work in Israel, as did other Catholics such as Professor Marcel Dubois, a Franciscan on the faculty of Hebrew University of Jerusalem. Brother Daniel, however, sought entry to and recognition in Israel *as a Jew.* The Law of Return provides for immediate citizenship for anyone with a Jewish grandfather. Brother Daniel could enter as anyone else, but his conversion and subsequent adherence to Catholicism were interpreted as an act of dissociation from the Jewish people. The secular High Court of Israel, in a vote of 4-1, refused Brother Daniel's request for citizenship under the Law of Return. It is the disconnection and subsequent allegiance to the Church, at his own initiative, that formalize the rupture. The religious and the secular definition of "who is a Jew" seemed, in this case, to differ, with a stricter meaning applied by the secular authorities (Frimer 1964; Jocz 1963; Lichtenstein 1963; Wyschogrod 1964). See also Rufeisen (1981).

ethical[10] and pragmatic political policy—it never becomes an ontological question. If this interpretation is plausible, the adjective "Jewish" may be considered, therefore, as merely incidental.

In April 1995, the Archbishop of Paris, Cardinal Jean-Marie Lustiger, a Jew who converted to Catholicism, currently rumoured to be a possible candidate for the papacy, arrived in Israel at the invitation of Tel Aviv University. Lustiger converted in 1940 at the age of fourteen while attending a Catholic school to which his parents sent him at the beginning of the war. His mother, who died in Auschwitz, and other family relatives were murdered by the Nazis. Lustiger insists that "I have always seen myself as Jewish, even if that is not the Rabbi's opinion. I was born Jewish and will stay Jewish." In an interview on Israeli television, he argued that "I am as Jewish as all the other members of my family who were butchered in Auschwitz or in other camps."

Fortuitously, his lecture to the symposium on "The Silence of God," conflicted with the Holocaust Commemoration ceremonies and therefore the extension of an invitation, usually accorded to visiting officials, was avoided. In the interim, however, a national debate ensued that does not reflect a religious dispute or a political argument along party lines. In fact, the Chief Rabbi, Israel Meir Lau—himself a Holocaust survivor—spoke for many staunch secularists when he said, "he betrayed his people and his faith during the most difficult and darkest of periods." Rabbi Lau's castigation, "The Path of spiritual destruction which Lustiger represents, leads, like physical destruction to the final solution of the Jewish problem," seems an audible echo of the sentiments of Dov Ber Borochov, the Jewish-Russian Marxist Zionist, "Death and suicide are the most radical solution to the Jewish problem. If there were no Jews, there would be no problem" (Borochov 1937, 85). The issue was not apostasy. Instead, Brother Daniel and Cardinal Lustiger did the unthinkable: in the words of Dr. Yosef Burg, a former Minister of the Interior and currently the chairman of the Yad Vashem

10. The ethical dimension reflects sentiments of betrayal and treachery: to align oneself with Christianity in general, and the Catholic Church in particular, is to ignore at best, and disregard, at worst, theological anti-Semitism that fostered, encouraged, and justified violence against Jews—because they were Jews—culminating in the Holocaust, and not excluding the resounding silence of Pope Pius XII (Gilman 1986, 1985; Miles 1995).

international council, "Someone who has converted to Christianity has crossed the lines and doesn't belong to the Jewish people."

In retrospect, the reader may ask why the equal weight of nouns suggested by the title of this book, is *un-balanced* in the text, which leads toward privileging a focus on Jewish identities.

The answer is simple.

My ambition has been to insist on this particular object of knowledge in order to disrupt a complacency that is political *and* a politics that is silenced. The complacency is best told in the following, personal anecdote. Shortly after meeting me and hearing about my background and research, a friend and colleague from the university, Andre Robinson, discovered that his aunt's maternal grandmother had been a Jewish woman who passed as a Negro in New Orleans in order to be the wife of a Black minister. The aunt, now in her seventies, has apparently always felt an affinity with Jews and this discovery validates her intuitions. The matrilineal line is broken by Andre's father, so he cannot claim membership in the Jewish community, but the reversal of passing in the nineteenth century remains intriguing. Unfortunately, no further information about the woman, her parents, or siblings is immediately available (although it evokes curiosity and invites serious investigation).

A year later, Andre is in conversation with a colleague from the Department of Cultural Anthropology, a Jewish woman from a large Midwestern city. She is realizing that in the South her Jewishness marks her as different from the white community; or, at least, she has a *cognitive sense* of being made to feel different. Contra Sartre, she is a Jew among whites, but she is not invisible. The woman and I are not acquainted, although she does know that in addition to being Black, I am Jewish and Israeli. In their conversation about Jewishness and whiteness, Andre remarks on the example of Katya, to which she replies, "Oh, but that's different."

"What's different about it?" he asks.

"You know."

"Know what?" he asks, rhetorically and with deliberate obtuseness. "She's as Jewish as you, and besides she's Israeli." To Jews in the diaspora, there is still a certain mystique about *aliya* — immigration.[11]

---

11. Quite literally, *aliya* means to go/rise up. One goes up to Israel, and one goes up to Jerusalem. Every other geographical movement is just to go or to go down.

Here Israeli citizenship and fluency in Hebrew (and then to this is added three Israeli-born children) intentionally privileges me — by "pulling rank" — over the Jewish woman who is white-skinned and American by several generations.

Each time a variation of this anecdote occurs, it presents itself as an inappropriate revelation *because of* the intervention of race thinking and *race* as a social fact in the United States (Roditi 1967). Throughout this book, Blackness as an identity has received less attention because it seemed increasingly necessary to demystify the false assumption that there is a symmetry between being Jewish and being white. The *idea* of being interracial, is conditioned by laws and social custom that were instituted and institutionalized as part of a race-rooted political order and economy. The idea is Euro American — it has no place in Jewish discourse:

Deep within the word "American" is its association with race. . . . American means white, and Africanist people struggle to make the term applicable to themselves with ethnicity and hyphen after hyphen after hyphen. (Morrison 1993, 47)

Andre Gluckman's discussion of Socrates and the meanings and implications of interruption and contestation as threatening seem pertinent and applicable to the issue of biraciality and being Black, Jewish, and interracial. Consider the following: the question of "how change comes about" presupposes a belief that change is possible. Gluckman questions the reasoning that permits rationalization and asks: when do reasonable explanations become unreason? Reason, the contention goes, is used by people in power but can be undermined by the freedom to interrupt. Interruption, therefore, is threatening because it involves loss of control, introducing and intensifying anxiety, for the direction of an interruption is unpredictable.[12] In other words, freedom — as acts of questioning and dissent — is operative as a challenge to arguments based on reason, for the definition of what is reasonable is always suspect when determined by those in a position of authority or power (Gluckman 1980).

Moving from this abstract philosophical proposition to a concrete example, I suggest that the children of intermarriage between any two

---

12. See chapter 1 for a brief explanation of my use of "anxiety."

given groups of people who are socially, politically, or legally differenti-
ated will be, as Joel Williamson points out for "white-skinned"-looking
slaves on the plantation, a contradiction and refutation of projected
norms of that society.

Contestation depends on the preservation of difference: "Is every
contestation eventually buried by what it challenges and what it has
transformed through its struggle?" To pose the question in this manner
is to anticipate a privileging of Reason through implication. Thus "plus
ça change plus c'est la même chose" is an adage that habituates its
listeners to acquiescing to the suppression of interruption. This, ultimately, represents the triumph of a will to knowledge and a will to
power, for it is an appeal to Reason in order to argue against, refute,
and silence contestation. The one who questions is silenced by authority and risks destruction as happens to Socrates. Gluckman contends, I
think correctly, that the very existence of s/he who challenges constitutes a threat to order — *not* because the outcome is known but precisely because of the potentiality of the unknown. It is this potential
that is then appealing and, in turn, threatening.

It follows, then, that contestation cannot take place if conformity
were to be the outcome each time. This argument can now be extended
to consider recognition of "multiracial" as an ambiguous but potential
foundation for preserving and transcending difference in contrast to
apprehending difference as threatening. From this point, it is possible
to argue that those of us who cannot easily be classified (or shelved)
into a category (and who resist the attempt) are intimidating not because of (or at least, not *merely* because of) *who* we are but rather
(primarily) of *what* we are (perceived to be). Addressing biraciality in
these terms is a problem: does the question "*What* we are?" imply a
return to the issue of ontological status that Hannah Arendt defers to
theologians and calls a question of nature (i.e., what does beingness
signify and how does it acquire meaning)?[13]

To argue that being biracial/multi-anything is to be endowed with
a special nature (essentialism at its worst), then adding the question
of *who* (the concrete material presence) in her/his particularity and
uniqueness, leads directly into an entanglement with impossible seman-

13. See chapter 1.

tic — and thus political — confusion. This may, however, be immediately and radically modified: eliminating the notion of "nature" and "essentialism" and replacing it with the understanding that "the principle of difference is an ontological principle, while the creation of Other is a social process" (Kazmi 1994, 73). Just as language is a means of communication made possible and coherent through shared meaning, the limits of translation are best illustrated by the "*feel*," which is different for monolingual and bi/multilingual people. Even though "biracial" *is* an arbitrary idea, it remains significantly meaningful because of a given social and political milieu — just as being fluent in more than one language inheres a sensitivity to multiple meanings not readily accessible to those who lack this competence. Bracket the *Who*, and the particularity of *being* biracial as a unique experience is, in fact, paradoxically essentialized but nevertheless calls to attention the false juxtaposition of essentialism and constructionism: "it might be necessary to begin questioning the *constructionist* assumption that nature and fixity go together (naturally) just as sociality and change go together (naturally)" (Fuss 1989, 6).

To be Jewish and Black and interracial — is to occupy a three-tier standpoint position that is inherently political but neither an essentialist idea nor a constructionist social category; it is a standpoint position from which to challenge racialist nationalism and misguided prejudice, eloquently expressed by Robin Washington, the managing editor of the *Bay State Banner* (a Bostonian Black newspaper) whose mother is a German-English Jew and whose father is a Chicago-raised american Black:

> I usually introduce myself as Robin Washington, I'm black and a Jew. I want to put my identity in your face; I want you to deal immediately with who I am. (Miron 1994, 9)

The point is, *on its own* biracial is an arbitrary concept, a term without meaning. But *within the context* of a society that understands it as exotic, unusual, forbidden, or viewed with disdain, then biraciality becomes some-thing people *see* as part of who they are. Adrienne Rich's conceptualization of the particularity of the body — as a standpoint from which individual experience is a construct *and* a continual reservoir of knowledge and self-recognition speaks directly to this issue:

When I write "the body," I see nothing in particular. To write "my body" plunges me into lived experience, particularity: I see scars, disfigurements, discolorations, damages, losses as well as what pleases me. . . . To say "the body" lifts me away from what has given me a primary perspective. To say "my body" reduces the temptation to grandiose assertions. (quoted in Fuss 1989, 52)

In sum, to be biracial — a cognitive and physical process of *being* in the world — in, and as a result of, a race conscious society, is *to be* an interruption, *to represent* a contestation, and *to undermine* the authority of classification.

Although Arendt's view on Black politics and the Jewish bourgeoisie were, respectively, problematic and justifiably controversial,[14] her response to friend and intellectual comrade Gershom Scholem concisely articulates my own sentiments: "what confuses you is that my arguments and my way of thinking are unpredictable (*nicht vorgesehen*). Or in other words that I am independent" (quoted in Syrkin 1963, 345).

14. See L. Gordon (1995a, 88–89); Heilbut (1983); Podhoretz (1963).

REFERENCES

Abu-Lughod, Lila. 1986. *Veiled Sentiments: Honor and Poetry in a Bedouin Society*. Berkeley: University of California Press.

———. 1991. "Writing Against Culture." In *Recapturing Anthropology: Working in the Present*, edited by Richard G. Fox, 137–90. Santa Fe, N.M.: School of American Research Press.

Ahmad, Aijaz. 1995. "The Politics of Literary Postcoloniality." *Race & Class* 36 (3): 1–20.

Alcoff, Linda. 1988. "Cultural Feminism Versus Post-Structuralism: The Identity Crisis in Feminist Theory." *Signs* 13 (3): 405–36.

———. 1991/2. "The Problem of Speaking for Others." *Cultural Critique*: 5–32.

———. 1995. "Mestizo Identity." In *American Mixed Race: The Culture of Microdiversity*, edited by Naomi Zack, 257–78. Lanham, Maryland: Rowman & Littlefield.

Alinsky, Saul D. 1972. *Rules for Radicals: A Pragmatic Primer for Realistic Radicals*. New York: Vintage.

Almeida, Mauro W. Barbosa. 1990. "Symmetry and Entropy: Mathematical Metaphors in the Work of Levi-Strauss." *Current Anthropology* 31 (4): 367–85.

Anderson, Benedict. 1991. *Imagined Communities: Reflections on the Origin and Spread of Nationalism*. London: Verso.

Appadurai, Arjun. 1991. "Global Ethnoscapes: Notes and Queries for a Transnational Anthropology." In *Recapturing Anthropology: Working in the Present*, edited by Richard G. Fox, 93–114. Santa Fe, N.M.: School of American Research Press.

Appiah, Kwame Anthony. 1985. "The Uncompleted Argument: Du Bois and the Illusion of Race." *Critical Inquiry*, no. 12 (autumn): 21–37.

———. 1992. *In My Father's House: Africa in the Philosophy of Culture*. New York: Oxford University Press.

Arendt, Hannah. 1958. *The Origins of Totalitarianism*. Cleveland, Ohio: World Publishing Company.

———. 1963. *Eichmann in Jerusalem: A Report on the Banality of Evil*. New York: Penguin.

———. , ed. 1968. Introduction to *Illuminations*, by Walter Benjamin. New York: Harcourt, Brace & World.

———. 1989. *The Human Condition*. Chicago: The University of Chicago Press.

Aronowitz, Stanley. 1992. *The Politics of Identity: Class, Culture, Social Movements*. New York: Routledge.

Arvey, Verna. 1984. *In One Lifetime*. Fayetteville: University of Arkansas Press.

Austin, Regina. 1995. " 'The Black Community,' Its Lawbreakers, and a Politics of Identification." In *After Identity: A Reader in Law and Culture*, edited by Dan Danielsen and Karen Engle, 143–64. New York: Routledge.

Azoulay, Katya Gibel. 1996. "Outside Our Parent's House: Race, Culture and Identity." *Research in African Literature* 27 (1): 129–42.

Baldwin, James. 1970. "Negroes Are Anti-Semitic Because They're Anti-White." In *Black Anti-Semitism and Jewish Racism*, 3–12. New York: Schocken.

———. 1988. "Blacks and Jews." *Black Scholar* 19 (6): 3–15.

Baldwin, James, and Margaret Mead. 1971. *A Rap on Race*. New York: Dell.

Banton, Michael. 1977. *The Idea of Race*. Boulder, Colo.: Westview.

Baraka, Amiri. 1994. "Malcolm as Ideology." In *Malcolm X In Our Own Image*, edited by Joe Wood, 18–35. New York: Doubleday.

Barkan, Elazar. 1992. *The Retreat of Scientific Racism: Changing Concepts of Race in Britain and the United States between the World Wars*. Cambridge: Cambridge University Press.

Barthes, Roland. 1986. Conclusion: Semiological Research to *Elements of Semiology*, translated by Annette Lavers and Colin Smith, 95–98. New York: Hill and Wang.

Bastide, Roger. 1969. "Color, Racism and Christianity." In *Color and Race*, edited by John Hope Franklin, 34–49. Boston: Beacon.

Bauman, Zygmunt. 1992. *Intimations of Postmodernity*. London: Routledge.

Behdad, Ali. 1993. "Travelling to Teach: Postcolonial Critics in the American Academy." In *Race, Identity and Representation in Education*, edited by Cameron McCarthy and Warren Crichlow, 40–49. New York: Routledge.

Benhabib, Seyla. 1992. *Situating the Self: Gender, Community and Postmodernism in Contemporary Ethics*. New York: Routledge.

Benjamin, Walter. 1968. *Illuminations*. New York: Harcourt, Brace & World.

Berger, John. 1972. *Ways of Seeing*. London: Penguin.

Berlin, Ira. 1994. "Emancipation and Its Meaning in American Life." *Reconstruction* 2 (3): 41–44.

Berman, Ruth. 1990. "Aristotle's Dualism to Materialist Dialectics: Feminist Transformation of Science and Society." In *Gender/Body/Knowledge: Feminist Reconstructions of Being and Knowing*, edited by Alison M. Jagger and Susan Bordo, 224–52. New Brunswick, N.J.: Rutgers University Press.

Berson, Lenora E. 1971. *The Negroes and the Jews*. New York: Random House.

Bloom, Harold. 1991. *The Book of J*. New York: Vintage.

Boas, Franz. 1921. "The Problem of the American Negro." *Yale Review* 10: 393–95.

———. 1962. *Anthropology and Modern Life*. New York: W. W. Norton.

Bond, Horace Mann. 1965. "Negro Attitudes towards Jews." *Jewish Social Studies* 27, no. 1 (January): 3–9.

Bordo, Susan. 1990. "Feminism, Postmodernism, and Gender-Scepticism."

In *Feminism/Postmodernism*, edited by Linda J. Nicholson, 133–56. New York: Routledge.

Borochov, Dov Ber. 1937. *Nationalism and the Class Struggle: A Marxian Approach to the Jewish Problem*. New York: Poalei Zion Zeirei Zion of America.

Bourdieu, Pierre. 1977. *Outline of a Theory of Practice*. New York: Cambridge University Press.

——. 1984. *Distinction: A Social Critique of the Judgement of Taste*. Cambridge: Harvard University Press.

——. 1988. *Homo Academicus*. Cambridge: Polity.

——. 1990. *In Other Words: Essays towards a Reflexive Sociology*. Stanford: Stanford University Press.

——. 1991. *Language and Symbolic Power*. Edited by John B. Thompson. Cambridge: Harvard University Press.

Bourguignon, Erika. 1991. "Hortense Powdermaker, the Teacher." *Journal of Anthropological Research* 47 (4): 417–28.

Bracey, John, and August Meier. 1993. "Towards a Research Agenda on Blacks and Jews in United States History." *Journal of American Ethnic History*: 60–67.

Bradley, Jennifer. 1995. "Hillary's Nightmare: The Woman Who Loves Phil Gramm." *The New Republic* 3 April, 16–19.

Branch, Taylor. 1989. "The Uncivil War: Blacks and Jews." *Esquire*, May.

Brink, Andre. 1983. *Mapmakers: Writing in a State of Siege*. London: Faber and Faber.

Brodsky, Garry. 1993. "A Way of Being a Jew; a Way of Being a Person." In *Jewish Identity*, edited by David Theo Goldberg and Michael Krausz, 245–63. Philadelphia: Temple University Press.

Brotz, Howard. 1964. *The Black Jews of Harlem: Negro Nationalism and the Dilemmas of Negro Leadership*. New York: The Free Press.

——. 1965. "The Negro-Jewish Community and the Contemporary Race Crisis." *Jewish Social Studies* 27, no. 1 (January): 10–17.

Brown, Phil. 1989–90. "Black-White Interracial Marriages: A Historical Analysis." *The Journal of Intergroup Relations* 16 (3 & 4): 26–36.

Burg, B. R. 1986. "The Rhetoric of Miscegenation: Thomas Jefferson, Sally Hemmings and Their Historians." *Phylon* 47 (2): 128–38.

Cahnman, Werner J. 1967. "The Interracial Jewish Children." *Reconstructionist* 33 (8): 7–12.

Camper, Carol, ed. 1994. *Miscegenation Blues: Voices of Mixed Race Women*. Toronto: Sister Vision.

Carmichael, Stokely, and Charles V. Hamilton. 1967. *Black Power: The Politics of Black Liberation in America*. New York: Vintage.

Carrithers, Michael. 1998. "Is Anthropology Art or Science?" *Current Anthropology* 31, no. 3 (June): 263–82.

Carson Jr., Clayborne. 1981. *In Struggle: SNCC and the Black Awakening of the 1960s.* Cambridge: Harvard University Press.

———. 1984. "Blacks and Jews in the Civil Rights Movement." In *Jews in Black Perspectives*, edited by Joseph R. Washington, 113–31. Cranbury, N.J.: Associated University Press.

Cerroni-Long, E. L. 1987. "Benign Neglect? Anthropology and the Study of Blacks in the United States." *Journal of Black Studies* 17, no. 4 (June): 438–59.

Chase-Riboud, Barbara. 1994. *The President's Daughter.* New York: Crown Publishers.

———. 1979. *Sally Hemings.* New York: Viking Press.

Cleage, Albert B. 1968. *The Black Messiah.* New York: Sheed & Ward.

Clifford, James. 1983. "On Ethnographic Authority." *Representations* 1 (2): 118–46.

Clifford, James, and George E. Marcus, eds. 1986. *Writing Culture: The Poetics and Politics of Ethnography.* Berkeley and Los Angeles: University of California Press.

Clinton, J. Jarrett. 1993. "From the Agency for Health Care Policy and Research." *Journal of the American Medical Association* 270 (18), 10 November: 2158.

Cohen, Steve. 1988. *American Assimilation or Jewish Revival.* Bloomington: Indiana University Press.

COI (Conference on Intermarriage). 1964. *Intermarriage and the Future of the American Jew: Proceedings of a Conference.* Long Beach, California: Commission on Synagogue Relations and Federation of Jewish Philanthropies.

Collins, Patricia Hill. 1986. "Learning from the Outsider Within: The Sociological Significance of Black Feminist Thought." *Social Problems* 33 (6): S14–S33.

Conquergood, Dwight. 1991. "Rethinking Ethnography: Towards a Critical Politics." *Communication Monographs*, no. 58 (June): 179–94.

Cooper, Anna Julia. (1892) 1988. *A Voice from the South.* New York: Oxford University Press.

Courtney, Brian A. 1995. "Freedom from Choice: Being Biracial Has Meant Denying Half of My Identity." *Newsweek*, 13 February, 16.

Cross Jr., William E. 1991. *Shades of Black: Diversity in African-American Identity.* Philadelpia: Temple University Press.

Cruse, Harold. 1967. *The Crisis of the Negro Intellectual.* New York: William Morrow.

Dabney, Virginius. 1981. *The Jefferson Scandals: A Rebuttal.* New York: Dodd, Mead.

Dahlberg, Gunnar. 1942. *Race, Reason & Rubbish: A Primer of Race Biology.* Translated by Lancelot Hogben. New York: Columbia University Press.

Danielsen, Dan, and Karen Engle, eds. 1995. *After Identity: A Reader in Law and Culture.* New York: Routledge.

Davidson, Arnold I. 1990. "Introduction to Musil and Levinas." *Critical Inquiry*, no. 17 (autumn): 35–45.

Davis, Allison, and Burleigh B. Gardner. 1965. *Deep South: A Social Anthropological Study of Caste and Class.* Chicago: The University of Chicago Press.

Davis, F. James. 1991. *Who Is Black? One Nation's Definition.* University Park, Pennsylvania: The Pennsylvania State University Press.

Dawidowicz, Lucy. 1975. *The War Against the Jews 1933 –1945.* New York: Holt, Rinehart and Winston.

De Beauvoir, Simone. 1982. *The Second Sex.* Middlesex, Eng.: Penguin.

De Certeau, Michel. 1988. *The Practice of Everyday Life.* Berkeley and Los Angeles: University of California Press.

De Lauretis, Teresa. 1994. "The Essence of the Triangle or, Taking the Risk of Essentialism Seriously: Feminist Theory in Italy, the U.S., and Britain." In *The Essential Difference*, edited by Naomi Schor and Elizabeth Weed, 1–39. Bloomington: Indiana University Press.

De Saradan, Jean Pierre Olivier. 1992. "Occultism and the Ethnographic 'I'." *Critique of Anthropology* 12 (1): 5–26.

Derricote, Toi. 1993. "At an Artist Colony." In *Daily Fare: Essays from the Multicultural Experience*, edited by Kathleen Aguero, 34–46. Athens, Ga.: University of Georgia Press.

Deutscher, Isaac. 1968. *The Non-Jew and Other Essays.* New York: Oxford University Press.

Devor, Holly. 1989. *Gender Blending: Confronting the Limits of Duality.* Bloomington: Indiana University Press.

Diner, Hasia. 1977. *In the Almost Promised Land: American Jews and Blacks 1915–1935.* Westport, Conn.: Greenwood.

Dolgin, Janet L. 1977. *Jewish Identity and the JDL.* Princeton, N.J.: Princeton University Press.

Dominguez, Virginia. 1989. *People as Subject, People as Object: Selfhood and Peoplehood in Contemporary Israel.* Madison: University of Wisconsin Press.

Douglas, Mary. 1970. *Purity and Danger: An Analysis of Concepts of Pollution and Taboo.* New York: Praeger.

Du Bois, W. E. B. 1971. *The Thought and Writings of W. E. B. Du Bois: The Seventh Son.* Edited by Julius Lester. New York: Random House.

Duker, Abraham G. 1965. "On Negro-Jewish Relations: A Contribution to a Discussion." *Jewish Social Studies* 27, no. 1 (January): 18–29.

Durkheim, Emile. 1982. *The Rules of Sociological Method.* New York: Free Press.

Duster, Alfreda M., ed. 1970. *Crusade for Justice: The Autobiography of Ida B. Wells.* Chicago: University of Chicago Press.

Dwyer, Kevin. 1987. *Moroccan Dialogues: Anthropology in Question.* Prospect Heights, Ill.: Waveland.

Dyson, Michael Eric. 1993. *Reflecting Black: African-American Cultural Criticism*. Minneapolis: University of Minnesota Press.

Edelman, Jonah Martin. 1992. Foreword to *The Measure of Our Success: A Letter to My Children and Yours*, ix–xiii. Boston: Beacon.

Edgcomb, Gabrielle Simon. 1993. *From Swastika to Jim Crow: Refugee Scholars at Black Colleges*. Melbourne, Fla.: Krieger.

Encyclopaedia Judaica Yearbook. 1973. Jerusalem: Encyclopaedia Judaica.

Etter-Lewis, Gwendolyn. 1991. "Black Women's Life Stories: Reclaiming Self in Narrative Texts." In *Women's Words: The Feminist Practice of Oral History*, edited by Sherna Berger Gluck and Daphne Patai, 43–58. New York: Routledge.

Fackenheim, Emil L. 1970. "Jewish Existence and the Living God: The Religious Duty of Survival." In *Arguments and Doctrines: A Reader of Jewish Thinking in the Aftermath of the Holocaust*, edited by Arthur A. Cohen, 252–66. New York: Harper & Row.

Falk, Candace. 1984. *Love, Anarchy and Emma Goldman*. New York: Holt, Rinehart and Winston.

Fanon, Frantz. 1967. *Black Skin, White Masks*. New York: Grove.

Ferber, Abby L. 1995. "Exploring the Social Construction of Race." In *American Mixed Race: The Culture of Microdiversity*, edited by Naomi Zack, 155–67. Lanham, Maryland: Rowman & Littlefield.

Fields, Barbara Jean. 1990. "Slavery, Race and Ideology in the United States of America." *New Left Review*, no. 18: 95–118.

Fields, Mamie Garvin, and Karen Fields. 1983. *Lemon Swamp and Other Places: A Carolina Memoir*. New York: Free Press.

Flax, Jane. 1990. "Postmodernism and Gender Relations in Feminist Theory." In *Feminism/Postmodernism*, edited by Linda J. Nicholson, 39–62. New York: Routledge.

Foucault, Michel. 1972. *The Archaeology of Knowledge*. New York: Tavistock.

Frankenberg, Ruth. 1993. *White Women, Race Matters: The Social Construction of Whiteness*. Minneapolis: University of Minnesota Press.

Franklin, John Hope. 1988. *From Slavery to Freedom*. 6th ed. New York: McGraw-Hill.

Fraser, Gertrude. 1991. "Race, Class, and Difference in Hortense Powdermaker's *After Freedom: A Cultural Study in the Deep South*." *Journal of Anthropological Research* 47, no. 4 (winter): 402–15.

Fraser, Nancy. 1994. "Rethinking the Public Sphere: A Contribution to the Critique of Actually Existing Democracy." In *Between Borders: Pedagogy and the Politics of Cultural Studies*, edited by Henry A. Giroux and Peter McLaren, 74–98. New York: Routledge.

Frazier, E. Franklin. 1957a. *Black Bourgeoisie*. Glencoe, Ill.: Free Press.

———. 1957b. *The Negro in the United States*. New York: Macmillan.

Fredrickson, George M. 1971. "Toward a Social Interpretation of the Development of American Racism." In *Key Issues in the Afro-American Experience*, edited by Nathan I. Huggins, M. Kilson, and D. M. Fox, 240–54. New York: Harcourt Brace Jovanovich.

——. 1972. *The Black Image in the White Mind: The Debate on Afro-American Character and Destiny, 1817–1914*. New York: Harper Torchbooks.

——. 1988a. *The Arrogance of Race: Historical Perspectives on Slavery, Racism and Social Inequality*. Middletown, Conn.: Weslyan University Press.

——. 1988b. "The Black Image in the White Mind: A New Perspective." In *Historical Judgments Reconsidered: Selected Howard University Lectures in Honor of Rayford W. Logan*, edited by Genna Rae McNeil and Michael R. Winston, 99–109. Washington, D.C.: Howard University Press.

Friedman, Jonathon. 1992. "The Past in the Future: History and the Politics of Identity." *American Anthropologist* 94 (4): 837–59.

Friedman, Norman L. 1969. "The Problem of the 'Runaway Jewish Intellectuals': Social Definition and Sociological Perspective." *Jewish Social Studies* 31, no. 1 (January): 3–19.

Frimer, Norman E. 1964. "The Jewish Fraternity." *Letter. Judaism* 13, no. 1 (winter): 102–7.

Funderburg, Lise. 1994. *Black, White, Other: Biracial Americans Talk about Race and Identity*. New York: W. Morrow.

Fuss, Diana. 1989. *Essentially Speaking: Feminism, Nature & Difference*. New York: Routledge.

Gates Jr., Henry Louis. 1992. *Loose Canons: Notes on the Cultural Wars*. New York: Oxford University Press.

Gatewood, Willard B. 1990. *Aristocrats of Color: The Black Elite, 1880–1920*. Bloomington: Indiana University Press.

Geertz, Clifford. 1973. *The Interpretation of Cultures*. New York: Basic Books.

——. 1983. "'From the Native's Point of View': On the Nature of Anthropological Understanding." In *Local Knowledge*, 55–70. New York: Basic Books.

Gelfand, Lou. 1993. "Section: If You Ran the Paper." *Star Tribune*, 13 June, 21. Accessed through Nexis.

Gergen, Kenneth J. 1969. "The Significance of Skin Color in Human Relations." In *Color and Race*, edited by John Hope Franklin, 112–28. Boston: Beacon.

Gibel, Inge Lederer. 1965. "The Negro-Jewish Scene: A Personal View." *Judaism* 14 (1): 12–21.

——. 1968. "The Possible Dream." *Reconstructionist* 34, no. 11 (11 October): 16–23.

——. 1985. "Intermarriage: A Very Jewish Question." *Response* 14 (4): 53–65.

———. 1987. "Anti-Semitism and Its Role in International Politics." In *Women of Faith in Dialogue*, edited by Virginia Ramey Mollenkott, 152–64. New York: Crossroad.

Gilman, Sander L. 1985. *Difference and Pathology: Stereotypes of Sexuality, Race and Madness*. Ithaca: Cornell University Press.

———. 1986. *Jewish Self-Hatred: Anti-Semitism and the Hidden Language of the Jews*. Baltimore: Johns Hopkins University Press.

———. 1991. *The Jew's Body*. New York: Routledge.

———. 1993. *The Case of Sigmund Freud: Medicine and Identity at the Fin de Siecle*. Baltimore: Johns Hopkins University Press.

———. 1994. "Dangerous Liaisons: Black Jews, Jewish Blacks and the Vagaries of Racial Definition." *Transition*, no. 54: 41–52.

Gilroy, Paul. 1993. *The Black Atlantic: Modernity and Double Consciousness*. Cambridge: Harvard University Press.

Giovanni, Nikki. 1994. *Racism 101*. New York: William Morrow.

Glazer, Nathan. 1969. "The New Left and Jews." *Jewish Journal of Sociology* 11, no. 2 (December): 121–31.

———. 1961. *The Social Basis of American Communism*. New York: Harcourt, Brace & World.

Glick, Leonard B. 1982. "Types Distinct from Our Own: Franz Boas on Jewish Identity and Assimilation." *American Anthropologist*, no. 84: 545–65.

Gluck, Sherna Berger, and Daphne Patai, eds. 1991. *Women's Words: The Feminist Practice of Oral History*. New York: Routledge.

Gluckmann, Andre. 1980. *The Master Thinkers*. New York: Harper & Row.

Goldberg, David Theo, ed. 1990. *Anatomy of Racism*. Minneapolis: University of Minneapolis.

———. 1995. "Made in the USA: Racial Mixing 'N Matching." In *American Mixed Race: The Culture of Microdiversity*, edited by Naomi Zack, 237–55. Lanham, Maryland: Rowman & Littlefield.

Goldberg, David Theo, and Michael Krausz, eds. 1993. *Jewish Identity*. Philadelphia: Temple University Press.

Goldberg, J. J. 1992. "America's Vanishing Jews." *Jerusalem Report*, 5 November, 28–32.

Goldfield, Michael. 1991. "The Color of Politics in the United States: White Supremacy as the Main Explanation for the Peculiarities of American Politics from Colonial Times to the Present." In *The Bounds of Race: Perspectives on Hegemony and Resistance*, edited by Dominick LaCapra, 104–33. Ithaca: Cornell University Press.

Goldman, Anne E. 1993. "Is That What She Said? The Politics of Collaborative Autobiography." *Cultural Critique* 25: 177–204.

Goldman, Ari L. 1992. "Blacks and Jews Join Hands for a Brighter Future: Audience Prays for Healing and Understanding at Emotional Gathering at the Apollo." *The New York Times*, 18 December, B1.

Goldstein, Sidney. 1990. "A 1990 National Jewish Population Study: Why and How." In *North American Jewish Data Bank*. New York: Council of Jewish Federations, 1990 rpt. series, 4.

Gordimer, Nadine. 1987. *A Sport of Nature*. London: Jonathan Cape.

Gordon, Albert I. 1964a. *Intermarriage: Interreligious, Interethnic, Interracial.* Boston: Beacon.

——. 1964b. "Negro-Jewish Marriages: Three Interviews." *Judaism* 13, no. 2: 164–84.

Gordon, Lewis R. 1995a. *Bad Faith and Antiblack Racism*. New Jersey: Humanities Press.

——. 1995b. "Race and Racism." *Social Text*, no. 42.

Gornick, Vivian. 1977. *The Romance of American Communism*. New York: Basic Books.

Gossen, Gary H. 1993. "The Other in Chamula Tzotzil Cosmology and History: Reflections of a Kansan in Chiapas." *Cultural Anthropology* 8, no. 4 (November): 443–75.

Gould, Stephen Jay. 1993. "American Polygeny and Craniometry Before Darwin: Blacks and Indians as Separate, Inferior Species." In *The 'Racial' Economy of Science: Toward a Democratic Future*, edited by Sandra Harding, 84–115. Bloomington: Indiana University Press.

Greenberg, Melinda. 1994. "Exhibiting Unity: Ethiopian Jewry Group Takes Its Artifact Show on the Road to Show That Blacks and Jews Don't Have to Be Disparate." *Baltimore Jewish Times*, October, 24.

Grimshaw, Allen D., ed. 1990a. *Conflict Talk: Sociolinguistic Investigations of Arguments in Conversations*. Cambridge: Cambridge University Press.

——. 1990b. Introduction to *Conflict Talk: Sociolinguistic Investigations of Arguments in Conversations*, 1–20. Cambridge: Cambridge University Press.

Grossberg, Lawrence. 1993. "Cultural Studies and/in New Worlds." *Critical Studies in Mass Communications*, no. 10: 1–22.

Grosz, Elizabeth. 1993. "Bodies and Knowledges: Feminism and the Crisis of Reason." In *Feminist Epistemologies*, edited by Linda Alcoff and Elizabeth Potter. New York: Routledge.

Guild, June Purcell. 1936. *Black Laws of Virginia: A Summary of the Legislative Acts of Virginia Concerning Negroes from Earliest Times to the Present*. New York: Negro Universities Press.

Haizlip, Shirlee Taylor. 1994. *A Family Memoir in Black and White*. New York: Touchstone/Simon & Schuster.

Halevi, Yossi Klein. 1992. "The Struggle of the Kesim." *The Jerusalem Report*, 22 October, 19–20.

——. 1996. "Lost Tribe: Ethiopian Jews Five Years After the Exodus." *The Jerusalem Report*, 30 May, 14–19.

Hall, Stuart. 1987. "Minimal Selves." *ICA Documents*, no. 6: 44–46.

————. 1992. "What Is This 'Black' in Black Popular Culture." In *Black Popular Culture*, edited by Gina Dent and Michele Wallace. Seattle: Bay Press.

Handelman, Susan. 1991. *Fragments of Redemption: Jewish Thoughts and Literary Theory in Benjamin, Scholem and Levinas*. Bloomington: Indiana University Press.

Handlin, Oscar. 1965. "Cultural Pluralism in the United States." In *Minority Problem*, edited by Arnold M. Rose and Caroline B. Rose, 7–16. New York: Harper & Row.

Harding, Sandra, ed. 1993a. *The 'Racial' Economy of Science: Toward a Democratic Future*. Bloomington: Indiana University Press.

————. 1993b. "Rethinking Standpoint Epistemology: 'What is Strong Objectivity'?" In *Feminist Epistemologies*, edited by Linda Alcoff and Elizabeth Potter. New York: Routledge.

Harris, J. William. 1993. "Etiquette, Lynching and Racial Boundaries in Southern History: A Mississippi Example." Typescript.

Harris, Marvin. 1968. *The Rise of Anthropological Theory: A History of Theories of Culture*. New York: Thomas Y. Crowell.

Hartsock, Nancy. 1990. "Foucault on Power: A Theory for Women?" In *Feminism/Postmodernism*, edited by Linda J. Nicholson, 157–75. New York: Routledge.

Harvey, David. 1990. *The Condition of Postmodernity: An Enquiry into the Origins of Cultural Change*. Cambridge, Mass.: Basil Blackwell.

Heilbut, Anthony. 1983. *Exiled in Paradise: German Refugee Artists and Intellectuals in America from the 1930s to the Present*. Boston: Beacon.

Henry, Marilyn. 1995. "UJA Bringing Intermarried Mission Here." *Jerusalem Post*, 13 August, 12.

Herskovits, Melville. 1937. "The Significance of the Study of Acculturation for Anthropology." *American Anthropologist* 39, no. 2: 259–64.

Higginbotham, A. Leon, Jr. 1988. "Racism in American Legal History." In *Historical Judgments Reconsidered: Selected Howard University Lectures in Honor of Rayford W. Logan*, edited by Genna Rae McNeil and Michael R. Winston, 111–25. Washington, D.C.: Howard University Press.

Hill, Robert A. 1984. "Jews and the Enigma of the Pan-African Congress of 1919." In *Jews in Black Perspectives*, edited by Joseph R. Washington, 55–82. Cranbury, N.J.: Associated University Press.

Himmelfarb, Milton. 1966. "How We Are." In *The Commentary Reader*, edited by Norman Podhoretz, 399–410. New York: Atheneum.

Hodgen, Margaret T. 1964. *Early Anthropology in the Sixteenth and Seventeenth Centuries*. Philadelphia: University of Pennsylvania Press.

Hollinger, David A. 1975. "Ethnic Diversity, Cosmopolitanism and the Emergence of the American Liberal Intelligentsia." *American Quarterly* 27, no. 2 (May): 133–51.

hooks, bell. 1990. *Yearning: Race, Gender and Cultural Politics*. Boston: South End Press.

————. 1994. *Outlaw Culture: Resisting Representation.* New York: Routledge.

Horowitz, Irving Louis. 1974. *Israeli Ecstasies/Jewish Agonies.* New York: Oxford University Press.

Houk, James. 1993. "The Terminological Shift from "Afro-American" to "African-American": Is the Field of Afro-American Anthropology Being Redefined?" *Human Organization* 52, no. 3 (fall): 325–28.

Huggins, Nathan I. 1971a. "Afro-American History: Myths, Heroes, Reality." In *Key Issues in the Afro-American Experience*, edited by Nathan I. Huggins, M. Kilson, and D. M. Fox, 5–19. New York: Harcourt Brace Jovanovich.

————. 1971b. *Harlem Renaissance.* New York: Oxford University Press.

Hymes, Dell H., ed. 1974a. "Introduction: The Use and Abuse of Anthropology: Critical, Political and Personal." In *Reinventing Anthropology*, 3–79. New York: Random House.

————, ed. 1974b. *Reinventing Anthropology.* New York: Random House.

Isaacs, Harold R. 1969. "Group Identity and Political Change: The Role of Color and Physical Characteristics." In *Color and Race*, edited by John Hope Franklin, 75–97. Boston: Beacon.

Jackson, Walter, 1986. "Melville Herskovits and the Search for Afro-American Culture." In *Malinowski, Rivers, Benedict and Others: Essays on Culture and Personality*, edited by George W. Stocking Jr. Madison: University of Wisconsin Press.

"Jewish Values in the Post-Holocaust Future: A Symposium." 1967. *Judaism* 16, no. 3 (summer): 269–99.

Jewsiewicki, B., and V. Y. Mudimbe. 1993. "Africans' Memories and Contemporary History of Africa." *History and Theory*, no. 32 (December): 1–11.

Jocz, Jacob. 1963. "Test of Tolerance." *Christianity Today* 7, no. 13, 29 March: 6–9.

Johnson, Deborah J. 1992. "Racial Preference and Biculturality in Biracial Preschoolers." *Merrill-Palmer* 38, no. 2 (April): 233–44.

Jones, Hettie. 1990. *How I Became Hettie Jones.* New York: Penguin.

Jones, Lisa. 1994. *Bulletproof Diva: Tales of Race Sex and Hair.* New York: Doubleday.

Jones, Jacquie. 1995. "Race and Racism: A Symposium." *Social Text*, no. 42.

Jospe, Alfred. 1964. "Intermarriage . . . the Crucial College Years." In *Intermarriage and the Future of the American Jew: Proceedings of a Conference.* Long Beach, Calif.: Commission on Synagogue Relations and Federation of Jewish Philanthropies.

Kahn, Shlomo. 1970. "Israeli, Hebrew, Jew: The Semantic Problem." *Judaism* 19, no. 1 (winter): 9–13.

Karcher, Carolyn L. 1975. "Melville's 'The Gees': A Forgotten Satire on Scientific Racism." *American Quarterly* 27, no. 4 (October): 421–42.

Katz, Jacob. 1983. "Misreadings of Anti-Semitism." *Commentary* 30, July, 30.

Kaufman, Michael T., and Felicia R. Lee. 1992. "Blacks and Jews on the Relationship: What's Special, What's Myth?" *The New York Times*, 20 December, 40.

Kaufman, Jonathan. 1988. *Broken Alliance: The Turbulent Times Between Blacks and Jews in America*. New York: Scribner.

Kazmi, Yedulla. 1994. "Thinking Multiculturalism: Conversation or Genealogy and Its Implication for Education." *Philosophy & Social Criticism* 20 (3): 65–87.

Kellner, Douglass. 1992. "Popular Culture and the Construction of Postmodern Identities." In *Modernity and Identity*, edited by Scott Lash and Jonathon Friedman, 141–77. Oxford: Basil Blackwell.

Kennedy, Randall L. 1989. "Racial Critiques of Legal Academia." *Harvard Law Review* 102: 1745–1819.

Kochman, Thomas. 1981. *Black and White Styles in Conflict*. Chicago: University of Chicago Press.

Kondo, Dorinne K. 1990. *Crafting Selves: Power, Gender, and Discourses of Identity in a Japanese Workplace*. Chicago: University of Chicago Press.

Kosmin, Barry A. 1986. Review of *Jewish Data Banks: The Historical Background*. New York: *Council of Jewish Federations*, no. 1.

———. 1988. "Contemporary American Jewry: Implications for Planning." *Occasional Papers*, no. 4 (July).

———. 1989. "Intermarriage, Divorce and Remarriage Among American Jews 1982–87." *Family Research Series*, no. 1 (August).

———. 1994. "Report: Jewish Population in 1993." In *American Jewish Yearbook*, by Barry Kosmin and Jeffrey Scheckner, 207. Philadelphia: American Jewish Committee.

Kosmin, Barry A., Sidney Goldstein, Joseph Waksberg, Nava Lerer, Ariella Keysar, and Jeffrey Scheckner. 1991. *Highlights of the CJF 1990 National Jewish Population Survey*. New York: Council of Jewish Federations.

Kosmin, Barry, Paul Ritterband, and Jeffrey Scheckner. 1988. "Counting Jewish Populations: Methods and Problems." In *North American Jewish Data Bank*. New York: Council of Jewish Federations, rpt. series, 3. Reprinted from the *American Jewish Yearbook*, 1988, vol. 88.

Kovel, Joel. 1970. *White Racism: A Psychohistory*. New York: Pantheon.

Kuper, Adam. 1988. *The Invention of Primitive Society: Transformations of an Illusion*. London: Routledge.

Labovitz, Sherman. 1987. *Attitudes toward Blacks among Jews: Historical Antecedents and Current Concerns*. San Francisco: R & E Research Associates.

Lamm, Zvi. 1990. "The New Left and Jewish Identity." *Dispersion and Unity*, no. 10: 54–65.

Laqueur, Walter. 1972. *A History of Zionism*. New York: Holt, Rinehart and Winston.

Launey, Robert. 1988. "Africa by the Lake: Remembering Melville J. Herskovits (1895–1963)." *Arts & Sciences* (spring): 6–9.

"Law of Return Excludes Brother Daniel (Israeli High Court Refuses Citizenship for Wartime Convert to Catholicism)." 1962. Editorial. *Christian Century* 79, no. 51 (19 December): 1553.

Lawrence, Cecile Ann. 1995. "Racelessness." In *American Mixed Race: The Culture of Microdiversity*, edited by Naomi Zack, 25–37. Lanham, Md.: Rowman & Littlefield.

Lazarre, Jane. 1996. *Beyond the Whiteness of Whiteness: Memoir of a White Mother of Black Sons*. Durham: Duke University Press.

Leach, Edmund, and D. Alan Aycock. 1983. *Structuralist Interpretations of Biblical Myths*. New York: Cambridge University Press.

Lederer-Gibel, Inge. 1984. "Israel's Radical Chic Helps the Radical Right: Writing Off the Sephardim." *Christianity & Crisis* 44, 15 October, 367–73.

Lerner, Michael, and Cornel West. 1996. *Jews & Blacks: A Dialogue on Race, Religion and Culture in America*. New York: Plume.

Lester, Julius. 1988a. "Academic Freedom and the Black Intellectual." *The Black Scholar* 19 (6): 16–27.

———. 1988b. *Lovesong: Becoming a Jew*. New York: H. Holt.

———. 1992. "A Report on Black Anti-Semitism." *Jewish Currents* (May): 8–10.

Lévi-Strauss, Claude. 1966. "History and Dialectic." In *The Savage Mind*. Chicago: University of Chicago Press.

———. 1973. *Triste Tropiques*. Translated by John and Doreen Weightman. New York: Atheneum.

———. 1978. *The Origin of Table Manners*. New York: Harper & Row.

Lévi-Strauss, Claude, and Didier Eribon. 1991. *Conversations with Claude Lévi-Strauss*. Translated by Paula Wissing. Chicago: University of Chicago Press.

Levinas, Emmanuel. 1992. "Ethics as First Philosophy." In *The Levinas Reader*, 75–87. Oxford: Blackwell.

Levine, Lawrence W. 1993. "The Historical Odyssey of Nathan Irvin Huggins." *Radical History Review* 55 (winter): 113–32.

Lewis, David Levering. 1988. "Parallels and Divergences: Assimilationist Strategies of Afro-American and Jewish Elites from 1910 to the Early 1930s." In *Historical Judgments Reconsidered: Selected Howard University Lectures in Honor of Rayford W. Logan*, edited by Genna Rae McNeil and Michael R. Winston, 137–70. Washington, D.C.: Howard University Press.

Lichtenstein, Aharon. 1963. "Brother Daniel and the Jewish Fraternity." *Judaism* 12, no. 3 (summer): 260.

Lieberman, Samuel, and Morton Weinfeld. 1977. "Demographic Trends and Jewish Survival." *Midstream* (November).

Liebow, Elliot. 1967. *Tally's Corner: A Study of Negro Streetcorner Men*. Boston: Little, Brown.

Lincoln, Eric. C. 1965. "The Black Muslims." In *Minority Problems*, edited by Arnold M. Rose and Caroline B. Rose, 281–89. New York: Harper & Row.

———. 1970. Foreword to *Bittersweet Encounter: The Afro-American and the American Jew*, vii–xvii. Westport, Conn.: Negro Universities Press.

Lindemann, Albert S. 1991. *The Jew Accused: Three Anti-Semitic Affairs (Dreyfus, Beilis, Frank) 1894–1915*. Cambridge: Cambridge University Press.

Littman, Debby. 1973. "Jewish Militancy." In *Jewish Radicalism: A Selected Anthology*, edited by Jack Nusan Porter and Peter Drier, 288–95. New York: Grove.

Locke, Hubert. 1994. *The Black Anti-Semitism Controversy*. Susquehanna Publishing Co.

Lowenthal, Zvi. 1973. "Right On Judaism . . . J.D.L.'s Meir Kahane Speaks Out — An Interview." In *Jewish Radicalism: A Selected Anthology*, edited by Jack Nusan Porter and Peter Drier, 277–87. New York: Grove.

Mandel, David. 1973. "A Radical Zionist's Critique of the Jewish Defence League." In *Jewish Radicalism: A Selected Anthology*, edited by Jack Nusan Porter and Peter Drier, 296–300. New York: Grove.

Marable, Manning, and Leith Mullings. 1994. "The Divided Mind of Black America: Race, Ideology and Politics in the Post Civil Rights Era." *Race & Class* 36, (1): 61–72.

Marcel, Gabriel. *The Existential Background of Human Dignity*. Cambridge: Harvard University Press, 1963.

Marcus, George E., and Michael M. J. Fischer. 1986. *Anthropology as Cultural Critique: An Experiment in the Human Sciences*. Chicago: University of Chicago Press.

Marcus, Jacob Rader. 1961. *Early American Jewry*. 2 vols. Philadelphia: Jewish Publication Society.

Marley, Bob. 1983. "Buffalo Soldier." Song. Island Production Records, 0-99883.

Marshall, Gloria A. 1993. "Racial Classifications: Popular and Scientific." In *The "Racial" Economy of Science: Toward a Democratic Future*, edited by Sandra Harding, 116–27. Bloomington: Indiana University Press.

Martyn, Bryon Curti. 1979. "Racism in the U.S.: A History of the Anti-Miscegenation Legislation and Litigation." Ph.D. diss., University of Southern California.

Mascia-Lees, Frances, et al. 1989. "The Postmodern Turn in Anthropology: Cautions from a Feminist Perspective." *Signs* 15 (1): 7–33.

McLaren, Peter. 1991. "Decentering Culture: Postmodernism, Resistance and Critical Pedagogy." In *Current Perspectives on the Culture of Schools*, edited by N. B. Wyner. Boston: Brookline.

———. 1994. "Multiculturalism and the Postmodern Critique: Toward a Pedagogy of Resistance and Transformation." In *Between Borders: Pedagogy and the Politics of Cultural Studies*, edited by Henry A. Giroux and Peter McLaren, 192–222. New York: Routledge.

Megill, Allan, ed. 1994. *Rethinking Objectivity*. Durham: Duke University Press.

Meier, August. 1992. *A White Scholar and the Black Community 1945–1965: Essays and Reflections*. Amherst: University of Massachusetts Press.

Melnick, Jeffrey. 1994. "Black & Jew Blues." *Transition* 62: 106–21.

Mencke, John G. 1979. "Mulattoes and Race Mixture: American Attitudes and Images 1865–1918." Ph.D. diss., University of North Carolina at Chapel Hill.

Merleau-Ponty, Maurice. 1973. "Dialogue and the Perception of the Other." In *The Prose of the World*, 131–46. Evanston: Northwestern University Press.

Messer, Ellen. 1986. "Franz Boas and Kaufman Kohler: Anthropology and Reform Judaism." *Jewish Social Studies* 48 (2): 127–40.

Miles, Jack. 1995. *God: A Biography*. New York: Albert A. Knopf.

Mintz, Sidney W., and Richard Price. 1976. *The Birth of African-American Culture: An Anthropological Perspective*. Boston: Beacon.

Miron, Susan. 1994. "Being Black and Jewish in America: Brandeis Symposium Explores a Double Identity." *The Forward*, 22 April.

Mohanty, Chandra. 1994. "On Race and Voice: Challenges for Liberal Education in the 1990s." In *Between Borders: Pedagogy and the Politics of Cultural Studies*, edited by Henry A. Giroux and Peter MacLaren, 145–66. New York: Routledge.

Montag, Warren. 1993. "Spinoza and Althusser against Hermeneutics: Interpretation or Intervention?" In *The Althusserian Legacy*, edited by E. Ann Kaplan and Michael Sprinkler, 51–58. London: Verso.

Montefiore, Alan. 1993. "Structures of Personal Identity and Cultural Identity." In *Jewish Identity*, edited by David Theo Goldberg and Michael Krausz, 212–42. Philadelphia: Temple University Press.

Moore, Henrietta L. 1994. *A Passion for Difference: Essays in Anthropology and Gender*. Bloomington: Indiana University Press.

Morrison, Toni. 1993. *Playing in the Dark: Whiteness and the Literary Imagination*. New York: Vintage.

Moss, Sydney P., and Carolyn Moss. 1987. "The Jefferson Miscegenation Legend in British Travel Books." *Journal of the Early Republic*, no. 7 (fall): 253–74.

Moytoyoshi, Michelle M. 1990. "The Experience of Mixed-Race People: Some Thoughts and Theories." *Journal of Ethnic Studies* 18, no. 2: 77–95.

Mudimbe, Valentin Y. 1988. *The Invention of Africa: Gnosis, Philosophy and the Order of Knowledge*. Bloomington: Indiana University Press.

——. 1991. *Parables and Fables: Exegesis, Textuality and Politics in Central Africa*. Madison: University of Wisconsin Press.

——. 1993a. "The Power of the Greek Paradigm." *South Atlantic Quarterly* 92, no. 2 (spring): 361–85.

——. 1993b. "Reading and Teaching Pierre Bourdieu." *Transition*, no. 61: 144–60.

——. 1994. *The Idea of Africa*. Bloomington: Indiana University Press.

Murray, Pauli. 1984. *Proud Shoes: The Story of an American Family.* New York: Harper & Row.

Myrdal, Gunnar. 1944. *An American Dilemma: The Negro Problem and Modern Democracy.* New York: Harper & Brothers.

Nash, Manning. 1989. *The Cauldron of Ethnicity in the Modern World.* Chicago: University of Chicago Press.

"The Negro and the Warsaw Ghetto." 1952. *Jewish Life,* May, 14–15.

Novak, Michael. 1972. *The Rise of the Unmeltable Ethnics.* New York: Macmillan.

Odenheimer, Micha. 1992. "Somalia: Burned in Memory." *Jerusalem Report,* 22 October, 50.

Omi, Michael, and Howard Winant. 1986. *Racial Formation in the United States from the 1960s to the 1980s.* New York: Routledge.

Outlaw, Lucius. 1990. "Toward a Critical Theory of 'Race.'" In *Anatomy of Racism,* edited by David Theo Goldberg, 58–82. Minneapolis: University of Minnesota Press.

———. 1992. "On W.E.B. Du Bois' 'The Conservation of Races.'" *SAPINA* 4 (1): 13–28.

Oz VeShalom Publications. 1984. *Religious Zionism: Challenges and Choices.* Jerusalem, Israel: Oz VeShalom.

Palmer, Bryan D. 1990. *Descent Into Discourse: The Reification of Language and the Writing of Social History.* Philadelphia: Temple University Press.

Palmer, Paul C. 1965. "Miscegenation as an Issue in the Arkansas Constitutional Convention of 1868." *Arkansas Historical Quarterly* 24, (2): 99–126.

Philips, John Edward. 1990. "The African Heritage of White America." In *Africanisms in American Culture,* edited by Joseph E. Holloway, 225–39. Indiana: Indiana University Press.

Phillips, William M. 1991. *An Unillustrious Alliance: The African American and Jewish American Communities.* Westport, Conn.: Greenwood Press.

Pinar, William F. 1993. "Notes on Understanding Curriculum as a Racial Text." In *Race, Identity and Representation in Education,* edited by Cameron McCarthy and Warren Crichlow, 60–70. New York: Routledge.

Piper, Adrian. 1992. "Passing for White/Passing for Black." *Transition,* no. 58: 4–32.

Podhoretz, Norman. 1963. "Hannah Arendt on Eichmann: A Study in the Perversity of Brilliance." *Commentary* 36, no. 3 (September): 201–8.

———. 1966. "My Negro Problem — And Ours." In *The Commentary Reader,* edited by Norman Podhoretz, 376–87. New York: Atheneum.

Porter, Jack Nusan. 1971. "Black-Jewish Relations: Some Notes on Cross-Cultural and Historical Research." *International Review of Sociology* 1, no. 2 (September): 157–65.

Porter, Jack Nusan, and Peter Drier, eds. 1973. *Jewish Radicalism: A Selected Anthology.* New York: Grove.

Powdermaker, Hortense. 1966. *Stranger and Friend: The Way of an Anthropologist*. New York: W. W. Norton.

Rickman, Hans Peter. 1983. *The Adventure of Reason: The Uses of Philosophy in Sociology*. Westport, Conn.: Greenwood.

Ricouer, Paul. 1974. *The Conflict of Interpretations: Essays in Hermeneutics*. Edited by Don Ihde. Evanston: Northwestern University Press.

Rigby, Peter. 1991. "Appendix: Response to 'Anthropology and Marxist Discourse.'" In *Parables and Fables: Exegesis, Textuality and Politics in Central Africa*, by V. Y. Mudimbe, 197–203. Madison: University of Wisconsin Press.

———. 1992. *Cattle, Capitalism and Class: Ilparakuyo Maasai Transformations*. Philadelphia: Temple University Press.

Robinson, Andre A. (Director), and Pegge Abrams (Producer). 1994. *Symposium on Racial Identity: Power, Deception and the Myth of Race in America*. Durham: SCOLA, Satellite Communication for Learning.

Roditi, Edouard. 1967. "Recent Jewish Writing in France." *Judaism* 16, no. 4 (fall): 485–89.

Rodriguez, Richard. 1989. "An American Writer." In *The Invention of Ethnicity*, edited by Werner Sollors, 3–13. New York: Oxford University Press.

Root, Maria P., ed. 1992. *Racially Mixed People in America*. Newburg Park, Calif.: Sage Publishers.

Rosaldo, Renato. 1989. *Culture & Truth: The Remaking of Social Analysis*. Boston: Beacon Press.

Rose, Arnold M., and Caroline B. Rose, eds. 1965. *Minority Problems*. New York: Harper & Row.

Rose, Tricia, et al. 1995. "Race and Racism." *Social Text*, no. 42: 1–52.

Rosenberg, Harold. 1970. "Does the Jew Exist? Sartre's Morality Play About Anti-Semitism." In *Arguments and Doctrines: A Reader of Jewish Thinking in the Aftermath of the Holocaust*, edited by Arthur A. Cohen, 3–23. New York: Harper & Row.

Rosenberg, M. J. 1973. "To Uncle Tom and Other Jews." In *Jewish Radicalism: A Selected Anthology*, edited by Jack Nusan Porter and Peter Drier, 5–10. New York: Grove.

Rosenberg, Stuart E. 1985. *The New Jewish Identity in America*. New York: Hippocrene.

Rosenthal, Ehrich. 1965. "Jewish Intermarriage in the United States." In *Minority Problems*, edited by Arnold Rose and Caroline B. Rose, 278–80. New York: Harper & Row.

Rosin, Hanna. 1994. "Boxed In: America's Newest Racial Minority." *The New Republic*, 3 January, 12, 14.

Rosner, Ari Senghor. 1993. "Choosing Sides: How Black/White Biracial Amherst College Students Mediate a Racial Identity." B.A. Honor's thesis, Amherst College.

Ross, Robert W. 1980. *So It Was True: The American Protestant Press and the Nazi Persecution of the Jews*. Minneapolis: University of Minnesota Press.

Rufeisen, Daniel. 1981. "Une lettre du Père Daniel sur la mission." *Proche Orient Chrétien* 31: 216–18.

Russell, Kathy, Midge Wilson, and Ronald Hall. 1992. *The Color Complex: The Politics of Skin Color among African Americans*. New York: Doubleday.

Sacks, Karen Brodkin. 1992. "How Did Jews Become White Folk?" Paper presented at the ninety-first annual meeting of the American Anthropological Association.

———. 1994. "How Did Jews Become White Folk?" In *Race*, edited by Steven Gregory and Roger Sanjek, 78–102. New Brunswick, N.J.: Rutger's University Press.

Said, Edward W. 1979. *Orientalism*. New York: Random House.

Saks, Eva. 1988. "Representing Miscegenation Law." *Raritan* 8, no. 2 (fall): 39–69.

San Juan. E., Jr. 1992. *Racial Formations/Critical Transformations*. Atlantic Highlands, N.J.: Humanities Press.

Sandler, Kathe, (Director). 1992. *A Question of Color*. PBS.

Sangren, Steven P. 1988. "Rhetoric and the Authority of Ethnography: 'Postmodernism' and the Social Reproduction of Texts." *Current Anthropology*, 29, (3): 405–35.

Sartre, Jean Paul. 1949. *No Exit and Three Other Plays*. New York: Vintage.

———. 1963. *Black Orpheus*. Translated by S. W. Allen. Paris: Editions Gallimard.

———. 1965. *Anti-Semite and Jew*. New York: Schocken.

———. 1966. "Being-For-Others." In *Being and Nothingness*, 301–556. New York: Washington Square Press.

Saunders, Charles. 1970. "Assessing Race Relations Research." *The Black Scholar* 1, no. 5 (March): 17–25.

Scales-Trent, Judy. 1995. *Notes of a White Black Woman: Race, Color, Community*. University Park, Pa.: Pennsylvania State University Press.

Schappes, Morris N. 1952. *A Documentary History of the Jews in the United States*. New York: Citadel.

Schoem, David. 1989. *Ethnic Survival in America: An Ethnography of a Jewish Afternoon School*. Atlanta, Ga.: Scholars.

———. 1991. *Inside Separate Worlds: Life Stories of Young Blacks, Jews and Latinos*. Ann Arbor: University of Michigan Press.

Schor, Naomi, and Elizabeth Weed, eds. 1994. *The Essential Difference*. Bloomington: Indiana University Press.

Schwartz, Pat. 1987. "The Writer at the Walls of Jericho: Nadine Gordimer Talks about the Word under Seige." *Weekly Mail*, 12 June, 22.

Scott, David. 1992. "Criticism and Culture: Theory and Post-Colonial Claims on Anthropological Disciplinarity." *Critique of Anthropology* 12, (4): 371–94.

Scott, Joan. 1992. " "Experience"." In *Feminists Theorize the Political*, edited by Judith Butler and Joan W. Scott. New York: Routledge.

Shohat, Ella. 1988. "Sepharadim in Israel: Zionism from the Standpoint of Its Jewish Victims." *Social Text*, no. 19/20 (fall): 1–35.

——. 1989. *Israeli Cinema: East/West and the Politics of Representation.* Austin: University of Texas Press.

Shreeve, James. 1994. "Terms of Estrangement." *Discover* 15, no. 11 (November): 56–63.

Shumsky, Neil Larry. 1975. "Zangwill's *The Melting Pot*: Ethnic Tensions on Stage." *American Quarterly* 27, no. 1 (March): 29–41.

Sinclair, Abiola. 1990. "2 Live Crew Revisited." *Amsterdam News*, 18 August, 30.

Singer, David G. 1978. "An Uneasy Alliance: Jews and Blacks in the United States, 1945–1953." *Contemporary Jewry* 4 (2): 35–50.

Sleeper, James, and Alan Mintz. 1971. *The New Jews.* New York: Vintage.

Smedley, Audrey. 1993. *Race in North America: Origin and Evolution of a Worldview.* Boulder, Colo.: Westview Press.

Smitherman, Geneva. 1991. "What Is Africa to Me? Language, Ideology and African American." *American Speech* 66, no. 2 (September): 115–32.

Sowell, Thomas. 1981. *Ethnic America: A History.* New York: Basic Books.

Spaights, Ernest, and Derek Kenner. 1983. "Black Jewish Conflict: A Black Perspective." *Social Development Issues* 7, no. 2: 22–30.

Spencer, Jon Michael, ed. 1991. *The Emergency of Black and the Emergence of Black. Black Sacred Music: A Journal of Theomusicology* 5, no. 1 (spring).

Spinoza, Baruch. 1951. *The Chief Works of Benedict de Spinoza: A Theologico-Political Treatise and A Political Treatise.* Vol. 1. Edited by R.H.M. Elwes. New York: Dover.

Squire-Hakey, Mariella. 1995. "Yankee Imperialism and Imperialist Nostalgia: A View From the Inside." In *American Mixed Race: The Culture of Microdiversity*, edited by Naomi Zack, 221–28. Lanham, Md.: Rowman & Littlefield.

St. Clair Drake, John Gibbs. 1980. "Anthropology and the Black Experience." *Black Scholar* 11, no. 7 (September/October): 2–31.

——. 1984. "African Diaspora and Jewish Diaspora: Convergence and Divergence." In *Jews in Black Perspectives*, edited by Joseph R. Washington, 19–41. Cranbury, N.J.: Associated University Press.

Stahl, Abraham. 1992. "The Offspring of Interethnic Marriages: Relations of Children with Paternal and Maternal Grandparents." *Ethnic and Racial Studies* 15(2): 266–84.

Stepan, Nancy Leys. 1993. "Race and Gender: The Role of Analogy in Science." In *The 'Racial' Economy of Science: Toward a Democratic Future*, edited by Sandra Harding, 359–76. Bloomington: Indiana University Press.

Stepan, Nancy Leys, and Sander L. Gilman. 1993. "Appropriating the Idioms of Science: The Rejection of Scientific Racism." In *The 'Racial' Economy of Science: Toward a Democratic Future*, edited by Sandra Harding, 1970–93. Bloomington: Indiana University Press.

Stocking, George W. 1968. *Race, Culture and Evolution: Essays in the History of Anthropology*. New York: The Free Press.

———, ed. 1986. *Malinowski, Rivers, Benedict and Others: Essays on Culture and Personality, History of Anthropology*. Madison: University of Wisconsin Press.

Swirski, Shlomo. 1981. *Orientals and Ashkenazim in Israel*. Haifa: Makhbarot leMehkar u'leVikoret.

———. 1984. "Oriental Jews in Israel." *Dissent* 31, no. 1 (winter).

Swirski, Shlomo, and Menahem Shushan. 1985. *Development Towns toward a Different Tomorrow*. Haifa: Yated.

"A Symposium: Jewishness and Younger Intellectuals." 1961. *Commentary* 31, no. 4 (April): 306–59.

Syrkin, Marie. 1963. "Hannah Arendt: The Clothes of the Empress." *Dissent* 10, no. 4 (autumn): 344–52.

Szwed, John F. 1974. "An American Anthropological Dilemma: The Politics of Afro-American Culture." In *Reinventing Anthropology*, edited by Dell Hymes, 153–81. New York: Vantage.

Takaki, Ronald T. 1993. "Aesculapius Was a White Man: Race and the Cult of True Womanhood." In *The 'Racial' Economy of Science: Toward a Democratic Future*, edited by Sandra Harding, 201–09. Bloomington: Indiana University Press.

Tate, Greg. 1994. "Last Black Picture Show." *Village Voice*, 19 April, 22.

Taylor, Charles. 1992. *Multiculturalism and "the Politics of Recognition."* Princeton: Princeton University Press.

Theunissen, Michael. 1984. *The Other: Studies in the Social Ontology of Husserl, Heidegger, Sartre and Buber*. Translated by Christopher Macann. Cambridge, Mass.: MIT Press.

Thomas, Brook, ed. 1997. *Plessy v. Ferguson: A Brief History with Documents*. Boston: Bedford.

Thomas, Laurence. 1993a. "Characterizing the Evil of American Slavery and the Holocaust." In *Jewish Identity*, edited by David Theo Goldberg and Michael Krausz, 153–76. Philadelphia: Temple University Press.

———. 1993b. *Vessels of Evil: American Slavery and the Holocaust*. Philadelphia: Temple University Press.

Todorov, Tzvetan. 1984. "Columbus and the Indians." In *The Conquest of America*, 34–50. New York: Harper.

Trinh T. Minh-ha. 1989. *Woman, Native, Other: Writing Postcoloniality and Feminism*. Bloomington: Indiana University Press.

Trouillot, Michel-Rolph. 1991a. "Anthropology and the Savage Slot: The Poetics and Politics of Otherness." In *Recapturing Anthropology: Working in the Present*, edited by Richard G. Fox, 17–44. Sante Fe, N.M.: School of American Research Press.

———. 1991b. "From Planters' Journal to Academia: The Haitian Revolution as Unthinkable History." *Journal of Caribbean History* 25 (1 & 2): 81–99.

Tsukashima, Ronald T. 1978. *The Social and Psychological Correlates of Black Anti-Semitism*. San Franscisco: R & E Research Associates.

Turner, Charles B. 1963. "The Black Man's Burden: The White Liberal." *Dissent* 10, 3 (spring): 215–19.

Wagner, Roy. 1981. *The Invention of Culture*. Rev. ed. Chicago: University of Chicago Press.

Waldman, Steven. 1991. "A Perfect Combination of Chutzpah and Soul." *Washington Post*, 18 August. Accessed through Nexis.

Walker, Alice. 1984. *In Search of Our Mothers' Gardens: Womanist Prose*. San Diego: Harcourt Brace Jovanovich.

Walzer, Michael. 1990. "What Does It Mean to Be an 'American'?" *Social Research* 57 (3): 591–613.

Warfield, Justin E. 1993. *My Field Trip to Planet 9*. Quest Records, PRO-A-6103.

Washington, Joseph R. 1964. *Black Religion: The Negro and Christianity in the United States*. Boston: Beacon.

———. 1970. *Marriage in Black and White*. Boston: Beacon.

———. ed. 1984. *Jews in Black Perspectives*. Cranbury, N.J.: Associated University Press.

Waskow, Arthur I. 1973. "Judaism and Revolution Today: Malkhut Zadon M'herah T'aker." In *Jewish Radicalism: A Selective Anthology*, edited by Jack Nusan Porter and Peter Drier, 11–28. New York: Grove.

Weisbord, Robert G., and Richard Kazarian. 1985. *Israel in the Black American Perspective*. Westport, Conn.: Greenwood.

Weisbord, Robert G., and Arthur Stein. 1970. *Bittersweet Encounter: The Afro-American and the American Jew*. Westport, Conn.: Negro Universities Press.

West, Cornel. 1993a. *Keeping Faith: Philosophy and Race in America*. New York: Routledge.

———. 1993b. *Prophetic Reflections: Notes on Race and Power in America*. Monroe, Maine: Common Courage.

West, Cornel. 1993c. *Race Matters*. Boston: Beacon.

"What Color Is Black: Science, Politics and Racial Identity." 1994. *Newsweek*, 13 February, 62–72.

Whittaker, Elvi. 1990. "Comment." *Current Anthropology* 31, no. 3 (June): 277–78.

Whitten, Norman E., Jr.,, and John F. Szwed, eds. 1970. *Afro-American Anthropology: Contemporary Perspectives*. New York: Free Press.

Williams, Gregory Howard. 1995. *Life on the Color Line: The True Story of a White Boy Who Discovered He Was Black*. New York: Plume.

Williams, Teresa Kay. 1995. "The Theater of Identity: (Multi-)Race and Representation of Eurasians and Afroasians." In *American Mixed Race: The Culture of Microdiversity*, edited by Naomi Zack, 79–96. Lanham, Md.: Rowman & Littlefield.

Williamson, Joel R. 1971. "Black Self-Assertion Before and After Emancipation." In *Key Issues in the Afro-American Experience*, edited by Nathan I. Huggins, M. Kilson, and D. M. Fox, 213–39. New York: Harcourt Brace Jovanovich.

———. 1980. *New People: Miscegenation and Mulattoes in the United States*. New York: Free Press.

Wilshire, Bruce. 1982. *Role Playing and Identity: The Limits of Theatre as Metaphor*. Bloomington: Indiana University Press.

Wilson, William Julius. 1987. *The Truly Disadvantaged: The Inner City, the Underclass, and Public Policy*. Chicago: University of Chicago Press.

Wiredu, Kwasi. 1993. "Africa Philosophy: Some Conceptual Issues." Presentation to Department of Philosophy, Duke University, 7 January.

Woolford, Pamela. 1994. "Filming Slavery: A Conversation with Haile Gerima." *Transition*, no. 64: 90–104.

Wolfson, Bernard J. 1995. "The Soul of Judaism." *Emerge* 6 (10): 42–46.

Wright, Lawrence. 1994. "Annals of Politics: One Drop of Blood." *New Yorker*, 25 July, 46–55.

Wyschogrod. 1964. "The Jewish Fraternity." Review of *Letter. Judaism* 13, no. 1 (winter): 107–10.

Young, Robert. 1990. *White Mythologies: Writing History and the West*. London: Routledge.

———. 1995. *Colonial Desire: Hybridity in Theory, Culture and Race*. London: Routledge.

"The Young Radicals: A Symposium." 1962. *Dissent* 9, no. 2 (spring): 120–63.

Zack, Naomi. 1993. *Race and Mixed Race*. Philadelphia: Temple University Press.

———. ed. 1995. *American Mixed Race: The Culture of Microdiversity*. Lanham, Md.: Rowman & Littlefield.

Zangwill, Israel. 1909. *The Melting Pot*. New York: Macmillan.

Zuckoff, Aviva Cantor. 1973. "The Oppression of America's Jews." In *Jewish Radicalism: A Selected Anthology*, edited by Jack Nusan Porter and Peter Drier, 29–49. New York: Grove.

INDEX

Katya Gibel Azoulay

is Chair of the Africana Studies Concentration

and Assistant Professor of Anthropology and

American Studies at Grinnell College.

Library of Congress Cataloging-in-Publication Data

Azoulay, Katya Gibel.

Black, Jewish, and interracial : it's not the color of your skin, but the race of your kin,
and other myths of identity / Katya Gibel Azoulay.

p.   cm.   Includes bibliographical references and index.

ISBN 0-8223-1975-6 (cloth : acid-free paper).

ISBN 0-8223-1971-3 (paper : acid-free paper)

1. Afro-Americans — Relations with Jews.   2. Afro-Americans — Race identity.

3. Jews — Identity.   4. Racially mixed people — United States   I. Title.

E185.615.A9   1997

305.896'073 — dc21   97-6297